DARLEY DALE REMEMBERED

Cutting the grass at the Whitworth Institute.
Left to right: George Woodhouse, X, Thomas Boam.

DARLEY DALE REMEMBERED

THROUGH 50 YEARS OF WAR AND PEACE

Keith Taylor

COUNTRY BOOKS

Published by:
Country Books
Courtyard Cottage, Little Longstone, Bakewell, Derbyshire DE45 1NN

ISBN 1 898941 79 3

© 2002 Keith Taylor

By the same author in conjunction with Trevor Brown:

A DERBYSHIRE PARISH AT WAR: SOUTH DARLEY AND THE GREAT WAR
1914-1919

A DERBYSHIRE PARISH AT PEACE AND WAR:
SOUTH DARLEY 1925-1955

CONTENTS

*Darley Dale Cricket Club team members in front of the pavilion, in 1906,
two years after it was built.*

ACKNOWLEDGEMENTS AND THANKS

A special thanks to Dick Richardson at Country Books for all his help in getting the manuscript and photographs into book form.
Frank Dickens – for computer work.
Staff of the Local Studies Library, Matlock.
Curators of Regimental Museums, with special thanks to Cliff Housley at the Sherwood Foresters' Museum.
Drummond Print and Design Limited, Bakewell Road, Matlock.
David Millar and Tony Holmes for some photographic work.
Trevor Brown for proof reading.
Reverend Stuart Radford and Dale Road Methodist Chapel.

Special thanks for their time, information, memories, advice and loan of photographs to: Mrs. B. Marsden, Mrs. Bennett, Mrs. A. Brown, J. Pope, Mrs. N. Quigley, F. Waller, Harold Pearson, Harry Pearson, Mrs. J. Mills, Mrs. E. Smith, Mrs. L. Lang, C. Beresford, Mrs. Niven, Mrs. D. Boden, Mrs. R. Wagstaffe, Mrs. T. Boden, Mrs. H. Shore, J. and B. Smith, D. Smith, Mrs. S. Wolper, Mrs. Boam, R. Conquest, K. Sheldon, K. Esplin, Mrs. W. Holmes, Mrs. J. Fletcher, Mr. and Mrs. R. Wagstaff, A. Ambery, Mr. and Mrs. Batterley, P. Soppitt, Mrs. P. Taylor, L. Jackson, R. Parks, Mrs. Convery, Mrs. G. Coleman, Mrs. H. Mellor, A. Charlesworth, Dyson Charlesworth, Mrs. E. Boyce, Mrs. Goodman, A. Derbyshire, A and C. Bennett, Mrs. B. Siddall, B. Wood, S. Slack, R. Watts, D. Goodall, Mrs. L. Monkhouse, Mrs. L. Whibberley and D. Whibberley, Mrs. J. Blair, Mrs. K. Blair, Mrs. J. Waterfall, Mrs. D. Marsden, Mrs. F. Davies, Miss V. Wardman, Mrs. E. Asbury, E. Mayall, D. Sandars, Mrs.B. Calladine, Miss D. Briddon and Miss M. Briddon, Mrs. D. McGrath, Mrs. N. Dodds, Mrs. L. Kirkland, H. Hardy, D. Lane, Mrs. J. Smith, V. Raynes, J. Travis, Mr. and Mrs. C. Hadfield, F. Morten, Mrs. A. Salt, H. and M. Wagstaffe, Bill Stringer, Mrs. S. Davison, Mrs. B. Bunting, Mrs. B. Bailey, C. Lomas, Mrs. I. Toft, Miss M. Hawley, J. and L. Slack, Mrs. C. Constable, Mrs. N. Taylor, Mrs. C. Knowles, Mrs. J. Thurman, Mrs. J. Evans, Mrs. J. Kuszynski, Mrs. S. Warner, Mrs. M. Mills, R. Carter, Mr. and Mrs. A. Straw, J. Drury, R. Broome, J. and J. Cooke, B. Clarke, Mrs. S. Clarke, Mrs. A. Andrews, E. Bartram, L. Cantrill, Mrs. B. Fish, D. Holmes, Mrs. B. Cooper, T. Salsbury, Mrs. E. Hendry, Mrs. A. Saunders, Mrs. N. Simpson, M. Johnson, M. and R. Taylor, Mrs. M. Rhodes, Mrs. L. Draper, Mrs L. Hodgson, Mrs F. Coldrick, Mrs. C. Dale Leech, Mrs. N. Briddon, J. Bannister, Mrs. I. Wagstaffe, Mrs. R. Atkin, Mrs. P. Mackay, Mrs. L. Slater, Mrs. J. Knifton, J. Plant, Mr. and Mrs. Glossop, Mrs. P. Derbyshire, P. Atkinson, Mrs. U. Payne, D. Grimshaw, Mrs. C. Bradbrook. Mrs. E. Stone, D. Marsden, Mrs. M. Wright, Mrs. S. Clarke, Mrs. J. Crossland, Mrs. A. Porter, Mrs.S. Woolley, Mrs. S. Thompson, Mrs. Cantrill, Mrs. M. Cornish, Mrs. S. Wood, Mrs. J. Fearn, S. Woodhouse, A. Smith, D. and M. Jaina, K. and J. Knowles, R. Briddon, Mrs. J. Twomey, Mrs. Cole, Mrs. P. Nutt, Mrs. Winthrope, A. Bowler, Mrs. Burton and M. Burton, B. Boam, Mrs S. Goodall, Mrs. E. Dawson, D. Ayre, Mrs. A. Greatorex, Mrs. Y. Greatorex, R. And D. Burton, T. Boam, S. Lloyd, Mrs. Lloyd, A. Gilbert, Mrs. B. Smith, M. Fentem, Mrs. E. Dawson, Mrs. D. Garrett, Mrs. B. Marsden, Mrs. M. Charlesworth, Mr. and Mrs. R. Clarke.
I apologise if any person's name has been omitted from the list.

Grateful thanks to former co-author Trevor Brown for his help and encouragement.

BIBLIOGRAPHY AND SOURCES

First World War – Martin Gilbert, Harper Collins
History of the First World War – Liddell Hart, Pan
Gallipoli – Robert Rhodes James, Pen & Sword
History of the First World War – Ed. Barry Pitt, Purnell
The Twelve Days – George Malcolm Thompson,
    Secker & Warburg Limited
Encyclopedia of Military History – R.E. Dupuy & T.N. Dupuy,
    Jane's Publishing Company
War Diaries and Regimental/Battalion Histories
Second World War – Winston S. Churchill
World War Two – Ivor Matanle, Colour Library Books
History of the 20th Century – Purnell
The War in the Air – Gavin Lyall, Book Club Associates
An Illustrated History of the R.A.F. – Roy Conyers Nesbit,
    Colour Library Books
High Peak News – 1900 to 1950 (on micro film)
    Matlock Local Studies Library
Derbyshire Times – 1900 to 1950 (on micro film)
    Matlock Local Studies Library
Derbyshire Directories – Matlock Local Studies Library
Darley Dale County Primary School Log Book – Records Office
Darley Churchtown Primary School Log Books –
    in the possession of the school
Army Records Unit – Hayes, Middlesex
R.A.F. Records – R.A.F. Innsworth, Gloucester
British National Newspaper Library – London
Commonwealth War Graves Commission Web site/Internet
CD Rom of the war dead – Local Studies Library
Mill Close, The Mine That Drowned – Willies/Gregory/Parker,
    Scarthin Books
Through Limestone Hills – Bill Hudson, Oxford Publishing Company

The most valuable sources of information and many accompanying photographs have been provided generously by past and present parishioners of Darley Dale.

INTRODUCTION

Throughout the glorious sunny weekend of 27th/28th June 1914, the Sunday School parties, Band of Hope contingents and family holiday makers continued to disembark from the Manchester and Derby trains onto Darley Dale station platform, ready to enjoy the carefree delights provided by the Trustees of the Whitworth Institute and Park. Matlock Station was also busy as visitors arrived, to be transported across the river to the hillside setting of numerous hydropathic establishments, or to indulge in the more common pleasures of the Hall Leys Park and nearby Matlock Bath.

However, these reassuring scenes of Edwardian holiday pastimes in the idyllic setting of the Derwent Valley were to be irretrievably affected by the consequences from two pistol shots ringing out in the far-away Bosnian town of Sarajevo. They came from the gun of a Serbian student nationalist, Gabriel Princip. His assassination of the heir to the Austro-Hungarian Empire, Archduke Franz Ferdinand and his wife, the Duchess of Hohenberg, on the same gloriously sunny morning of Sunday 28th June would result in Darley Dale inhabitants finding their lives changed dramatically as Britain and the European Powers became enmeshed on the road to violent conflict, during the long, hot days of July.

War was declared by Britain on Germany at 11-00p.m. on Tuesday August 4th and it would result in the deaths of 63 Darley Dale parishioners throughout the course of its five years of conflict. Many others would be injured, maimed or suffer psychological harm from the excesses of battle and very few families were to escape the awful consequences of the Great War of 1914-1919.

Yet, with the Allied victory achieved on November 11th 1918, at tremendous cost to human life, the parishioners of Darley Dale must have looked with hope to peaceful times ahead, for had they not been told so many times that this was "the war to end all wars"? Just 21 years later those hopes were to be cruelly dashed as they listened to the broadcast by Prime Minister Neville Chamberlain, on Sunday 3rd September 1939, as he declared that Britain was once again at war with Germany and was involved in a life or death struggle for survival. 30 more Darley names were to be added to the war memorial, situated inside the grounds of the Whitworth Institute.

Above all, in writing the book, I would like to celebrate the lives of these servicemen and honour their names. Their story is part of a wider shared sense of history that has shaped our age and merits the respect of Darley folk in the 21st century.

At the same time I have attempted to place those who fell during the two bloody conflicts back into the world they inhabited and knew so well before being asked to pay the supreme sacrifice. Through words and photographs I hope that a picture emerges of life in the parish in 1913/1914 and in the period before the start of the Second World War. Fascinating images emerge of parochial life in a rural setting – the tranquillity, the harshness of working conditions, the feeling of community, everyday aspects of village life and yet also the changes taking place in their world in this relative backwater of the British Isles.

In 1914 and again in 1939, the problems and disputes welling up in the wider world context intruded dramatically into all aspects of this life. My hope is that the book has provided a glimpse behind the scenes of that way of life and honoured those who fell, whilst protecting it.

Keith Taylor   July 2002

CHAPTER ONE

DARLEY DALE 1913 —
A GLIMPSE BEHIND THE SCENES

Most of the men who were to die between 1914 and 1918 had lived and been brought up in Darley during the first decade and a half of the 20th century. What was their experience of life within the parish?

In 1913, Darley Dale consisted of a number of individual settlements running between Matlock and Rowsley, mainly on the eastern side of the valley. Of these, Two Dales was by far the largest but other hamlets were Farley, Hackney, Darley Churchtown, Hillside, Northwood and Tinkersley and Little Rowsley. The 1911 census reports that 3317 individuals resided in the parish, whereas in 1881 the population was only 1848, showing a very significant increase over the intervening years.

The Midland Railway Company had constructed housing for their workers at Little Rowsley, (part of Darley parish), between 1887 and 1898, with houses also built alongside the A6 at Northwood, whilst Ryecroft, Park Lane and Chesterfield Road housing, (Hazel View and Holmes Terrace), had developed at Two Dales. Sir Joseph Whitworth constructed housing for his Stancliffe Estate workers in the 1870's on the south side of Green Lane/Church Road, whilst around 1906/1910, housing on the north side of the Green Lane/Church Road triangle was built to accommodate the rapidly expanding Stancliffe Quarries work force, with six shops built to provide for their needs. Meanwhile, in the years immediately prior to the start of the First World War, Robert Lehane began the construction of houses on Station Road. In 30 years a substantial amount of new housing had been developed in the parish.

However, for those about to be faced with the prospects of wartime conflicts, the dale between the Matlock boundary and Rowsley was still a green and pleasant land. Hooley's Estate, Stanton View, Darley House Estate, the Park Way complex, Morten's Estate (Broadwalk), The New Estate and Northwood Lane housing were absent from the landscape and the fragmented nature of small, separate pockets of habitation within the parish resulted in a much different scene to the one we view today.

1913 was a momentous year in the history of the parish, due to the establishment of a new school on May 19th. **Darley Dale Permanent County Council School** on Greenaway Lane opened under the capable leadership of Arthur "Gaffer" Child. Between 1871 and 1912, Two Dales parents and some Hackney residents had sent their young to be educated at the Church of England School and Sunday School on Chesterfield Road, in what is now Hayes Bakery. Built in 1871 by public subscription and in 1904 under the supervision of their mistress, Miss Cecily Cockeram, it was known as the Darley Dale Tempory Council School. Already it was having difficulty in catering for the number of pupils and for a number of years, since 1904, the infants had been located in rented

C.1910 showing Two Dales Anglican Church School and Sunday School (now Hayes Bakery) built 1871. The coach taking Mr. Barrow from Sydnope Hall to Darley Station may have belonged to James Watts II, who ran a cab business and was a funeral undertaker.

premises in the old Methodist Chapel nearby, under the care of Miss C.J. Ault (the building is now used as a store room by Lewis Jackson, builder).

The infants transferred to the Anglican school (Hayes Bakery today) at 7 years of age and at 10 they went on to complete their education at Darley Churchtown School, under the firm and watchful eye of Charles Scott Anthony and his assistant, Robert Alston. The Churchtown school buildings had been erected in 1847 to cater for 118 boys and girls and 32 infants.

At the Two Dales schools, the log books provide an insight into the school life of some of those who would be participating in the early stages of the coming war. On Thursday March 4th 1909 the subject of the morning's Observation lesson was 'The Cat'. Owing to the fact that the cat required to illustrate this lesson was late in arriving, the reading lesson was taken first. On March 24th Mr Anthony arrived to give the pupils an exam, whilst two days later he was asking for a list of names of boys and girls to be transferred to Churchtown.

The small playgrounds for both the Two Dales schools were bordered by Warney Brook and, children being children, on numerous occasions pupils would receive a soaking. On January 7th 1910, for example, Herbert Smith fell in the brook just before morning school. He was sent home to change his clothes and did not return till afternoon, as they had to be dried.

October 21st 1909 was Trafalgar Day and the schools were decorated with oak. On December 1st, during the dinner hour, Grace Froggatt burnt her wrist warming her hands at the stove. January 24th 1910 saw much snow during the day, with attendance poor. Many of the children arrived with wet boots and stockings. These were dried around the stove before lessons were commenced and the drying took up the time for religious instructions.

Six children were sent to Mr. Adolphus Augustus Lowe's cobblers shop on February 16th 1910 to watch the mending of a pair of shoes so that they might write composition about it. They went at playtime in the afternoon but returned late. Teachers being teachers, the composition lesson was lengthened and Brush drawing was omitted in consequence.

Ringworm was a common ailment amongst the children and on

The old Two Dales Temporary Council School c.1894 (now Hayes Bakery).
William Perry Wagstaffe (who was killed in the Great War) is holding the slate.
His brother, Ernest Stanley Wagstaffe, is to his right.

The old Two Dales School c.1911. Teacher Miss Wagstaffe is taking a nature lesson on
'The Wild Rose', Second from left on the back row is Harry Pearson.

Teacher Miss Wagstaffe takes a nature lesson on 'The Buttercup'
at Two Dales School, c.1911.

Darley Dale Temporary Council School on 20th July 1910 with Miss Cockeram.
Back row, 3rd from left is Sam Wardman and the 4th from left is Ernest Bland.

March 5th Wilfred Squires, son of the local baker, was found to be suffering and was therefore excluded from school. As Wilfred had not been examined in arithmetic he was allowed to attend school on this one day. Every precaution was taken. He sat by himself, was sent for a walk at playtime and kept his cap buttoned up in his jacket.

Jack Allen, whilst crossing Chesterfield Road at playtime on the afternoon of May 9th 1910, was knocked down by a bicycle. The cyclist, a telegraph boy from Two Dales Post Office (run by Frederick Dobson in what is now Roger Coates, the butchers), rang his bell before the accident but was coming rather fast. The History lesson was omitted in consequence.

On July 20th 1910 the children were taken in the afternoon to the brook to see a toy water wheel turned in it and then went along Oddford Lane and collected specimens of simple and compound leaves. Another ramble in Oddford Lane was taken on September 21st to distinguish different kinds of trees by their shape.

By March 31st 1911 Miss Cockeram had sent word that she wished to send up 43 children, with 34 older children to be sent on to Darley Churchtown School. Already there was an obvious concern about overcrowding and the need for another assistant teacher.

June 14th 1911 saw a talk given on the Royal family and on June 20th the singing lesson was extended in order that the children might have time to practice 'God Save the King', whilst on the 21st, singing of the same anthem took up Arithmetic and Composition time. The following day was the Coronation of King George V and in consequence of this, a weeks holiday had been granted. On July 6th a talk on 'Patriotism' was given instead of Nature Study and 14 children were allowed to go home at 2-30p.m.to be in time for a Coronation Tea.

November 10th 1911 saw a census being taken in the school to find out how many children wished to go to Churchtown School and how many to the proposed new Temporary School to be established at the Whitworth Institute, whilst a new Council School was constructed on a site at Greenaway Lane.

The opening of the new term on January 8th 1912 saw certain pupils settling into their temporary quarters in the Institute buildings under Arthur H. Child, the new head teacher, and Misses Cecily Cockeram,

A group of children from Darley Dale Temporary Council School, housed in the Whitworth Institute during 1912, whilst the new school was being constructed in Greenaway Lane.

Ethel Wagstaffe and May Gill. A total of 170 children would be eventually enrolled when the newly built school was opened.

By April 15th 1912 the First and Third Classes were accommodated in the Museum Room of the Institute, the Second Class in Mr. Evans's Evening Class school room and the Infants in the Art Room. On Empire Day, May 24th, lessons on the Empire and Patriotism were taken till 10-30a.m. At 10-45a.m. the children met on the Terrace, sang songs and hymns, saluted the flag and received brief addresses from a number of the Managers on the meaning behind the day. School was dismissed for the Whitsuntide vacation at 11-30a.m.

One year later, on May 19th 1913, a proud event in the parish occurred

Darley Churchtown School 1911. Barbell drill by the children in the 'Volunteers'.
The Vounteers were a type of Cadet force, based on military lines, established in many schools to enable those keen enough to go further in drill
and set a standard for the other children.
Teacher Billy Alston is on the left and head teacher Mr. Anthony on the right.

Darley Churchtown School 1911, Billy Alston, teacher, on the left, Mr. Anthony, head teacher on the right. Members of the 'Volunteers' are wearing their sashes.

Darley Churchtown School c.1910 with Mr. Billy Alston, Mr. Scott Anthony and lady members of staff.

when the school was re-opened after the Whitsuntide Holidays in the newly built Permanent Council School on Greenaway Lane. The perennial problem of poor attendance in rural schools still existed, however, when we hear that attendance was poor in the First and Second Classes, on the morning of August 1st 1913, owing to the large number of boys commencing work in the Nurseries of James Smiths. Mr. Child arranged for the Attendance Officer, Mr. Vallance, to take the matter in hand. In the meantime the young could look forward to the prospects of an improved education, little realising that within a few years brothers and fathers might be off to fight in the bloodiest conflict in the history of the British Empire and that a number of the eldest pupils on roll in 1913 might participate by the war's close.

Mention has already been made of the **Whitworth Institute**. It was opened in October 1890, three years after the death of the Victorian inventor and engineer, Sir Joseph Whitworth. He had purchased Stancliffe Hall in 1856 and so began his involvement with Darley Dale. Many gifts were made by him towards improving education in his lifetime and Darley benefited by provision of the Whitworth Institute and grounds. Little of Sir Joseph's overall conception saw the light of day for he had planned the Institute to be the focal point of a model village.

Primary and Secondary schools, a library, gymnasium, swimming pool, recreation room, craft apprentice workshops, a museum, lecture hall and staff housing had all been planned. His Trustees were able to provide the Whitworth Hospital in 1889 and the Whitworth Institute by 1890.

A Library of 2131 volumes (in 1911), a Reading Room for newspapers (now the Enthoven Room), a Natural History Museum at the rear of the building (containing stuffed animals and a geological collection), a Swimming Pool Room, Games Room and large Assembly Hall for 250 people, were provided. Two houses for teaching staff were built alongside the Institute and later used as a bank and for meetings of the Urban District Council (now occupied by the Whitworth Hotel).

Before the Great War, Darley Dale used to provide one of the truly big occasions in the Derbyshire social calendar when it hosted the best one day Flower Show in the county (known as the Cottage Gardens

Society Show), held at the Whitworth Institute on the Monday after the Belle Vue September Band Concert. Lady Whitworth was a keen supporter of brass bands and paid to ensure that the winning band played at the flower show. Derbyshire Cricket Club entertained 16 Darley Dale Cricket Club members on the bottom cricket field on the day of the show.

At weekends and bank holidays, park attendants wore their distinctive top hats displaying red bands with white lettering spelling out Whitworth Institute round the rim. During the

Cutting the grass at the Whitworth Institute. Left to right: George Woodhouse, X, Thomas Boam.

remainder of the week they mowed and weeded the grounds, whilst in hard winters they prepared the frozen lake for ice skating by sweeping the surface. Thirty or forty skaters used the lake and lamps were positioned around the perimeter during the evenings.

In summer months, large parties of school children and adults would arrive by horse and wagon, or by train, on excursions, and be catered for in the 500 seat Pavilion next to the bottom football pitch, with food provided by Moores of Matlock. Coach proprietors such as Allens of Belper would deposit the children at the Park and stable the horses at the Blacksmith's Arms, Two Dales. When the horses were hitched up to the wagon in late afternoon, the local "Toad Hole" children would ask landlady Mrs. Davenport if they could clean out the stables for a penny each.

By 1910-1911, evening classes, employing six teachers, were held at the Institute every weeknight from September to May, under the overall supervision of head teacher Evan Evans, with 85 students registered. Book-keeping, Commercial Geography, Physiography,

Whitworth House (now the hotel) and the Institute c.1892. Note the lamp post in the middle of the road. The remains of this are now at the top of Station Road.

View of the Whitworth Institute c.1892 taken from the fields.

The newly laid out grounds of the Whitworth Park including the boating lake, c.1899.

Whitworth Institute grounds c.1899.

Whitworth Park boating lake c.1910.

Laying the water main on A6 road near the Whitworth Institute c.1906.

WHITWORTH INSTITUTE

DARLEY DALE

In affiliation with the County Education Committee and the East Midland Educational Union.

WINTER SESSION : : 1914 - 1915

The Trustees have arranged for the following

COURSES of INSTRUCTION to commence

ON MONDAY, SEPTEMBER 28TH :

COURSES.	SUBJECTS.
Commercial	English, Arithmetic, Book-keeping, Shorthand, Type-writing.
Art	English, Arithmetic, Drawing.
Domestic	English, Arithmetic, Cookery and Home Management
Junior	English, Arithmetic, Geography, Writing, Drawing.

TIME TABLE OF CLASSES.

ENGLISH, Monday evenings 7 to 8 o'clock; teacher, E. Evans, B.A.
ARITHMETIC, Monday evenings 8 to 9 : teacher, E. Evans, B.A.
BOOK-KEEPING, Tuesday evenings, 7 to 8 : teacher, E. Evans, B.A.
COOKERY and HOME MANAGEMENT, Tuesday evenings, 6-30 to 8-30:
    teacher, Miss Howe.
DRAWING, Wednesday evenings 6-30 to 8-30 : teacher, W.N. Statham.
JUNIOR CLASSES, Wednesday evenings 6 to 8-30 : teacher, E. Evans.
SHORTHAND and TYPEWRITING, Friday evenings 6-55 to 8-25 ; teacher,
    E.W. Barnes.
RED CROSS SOCIETY WORK, Thursday evenings, 7 to 9.

FEES : 2/- FOR EACH COURSE.

Institute Ticket, admitting to all courses 3/-
Student's Ticket for all classes and Reading Room 5/-

PRIZES AND CERTIFICATES OF PROFICIENCY will be awarded for good
work and attendance.
Prospectus may be had on application.

                                  E. EVANS, B.A.

September, 1914   **SECRETARY AND DIRECTOR OF EDUCATION**

Arithmetic, Shorthand and Typing and Drawing Classes were attended. Junior classes met every Wednesday to prepare them for the more advanced lessons.

In 1911, 225 members joined the Reading Room, with 2131 volumes available in the Library. The Billiards and games section had been extremely busy with 10,298 games played. However, the receipts from visitors to the Park were the lowest on record in 1911 and the ground staff had been reduced as a result, with the House let on a private tenancy, to be conducted as a private boarding establishment.

The Savings Bank continued to be steadily popular, with deposits received every Tuesday evening from 6 to 8 o'clock. The Museum was opened every week day throughout the year, claiming more attention when wet weather spoiled outdoor recreation.

The Trustees allowed a large number of applications from Sunday Schools, Temperance, and Social and Political parties to visit the Institute, though the total number in 1910-1911 was less than in any of the previous 22 years, 7800 only being catered for. During Whit-week the grounds were closed as usual, and the Pavilion was engaged by a section of the Derbyshire Territorials, under Captain Christie Clay, for their encampment during the Whit-tide manoeuvres. Three years later they would be " fighting for real".

The annual Hospital Demonstration was held in the grounds in July, when over £50 was collected for the hospital, whilst the Work-house inmates were also entertained at their annual treat during the summer.

The grounds were open on Sundays from noon and on weekdays from 10a.m. until the bell was rung. Skating on the frozen lake cost 6d for non members between 10a.m. and 3p.m., and 2d after 3p.m.

In 1903, a decade before the opening of the previously mentioned Greenaway Lane School, foundation stones were laid on land by the A6, for another new building, **Dale Road Wesleyan Church**, replacing the former chapel in Two Dales, which was now rented out as part of Two Dales Temporary Council School.

In the late 1700's the first meetings of "folk called Methodists" were in a cottage on Brook Bottom, Ladygrove Road. As their numbers grew, it was decided a church was needed. They had enthusiasm, but little cash, and the first church was built largely by volunteer labour. It is thought that the stone was given free out of Knabb Quarry, Sydnope, and the cartage likewise was free. The date stone for this building is 1827 and provided a home for Methodism until 1904.

During the late 1800's plans were made for an extension of the Two Dales Chapel but difficulties arose over the purchase of more land and therefore arrangements were made in the early 1900's to purchase land alongside the A6 and close to the Institute, from the Whitworth and Stancliffe Estates. In June 1903 the tender of Mr. Thomas Bowler of Hackney was accepted, with the cost being £1800, but it was decided that for £60 extra, Stancliffe stone should be used rather than any other. A silver trowel costing £5 was purchased and the stone laying fixed for July 15th 1903.

Flowers and garlands decorated the scaffolding, and into a hole specially prepared in each foundation stone were sealed, in glass containers, sets of current coins and copies of local and church newspapers. The opening services finally took place on Thursday June 2nd 1904.

Dale Road Methodist Chapel. The photograph was taken after the laying of the Foundation Stone Ceremony, July 15th, 1903, showing the decorated scaffolding poles.

Interior of the newly constructed Dale Road Wesleyan Chapel 1904.

Harvest Festival at Dale Road Methodist Chapel 1921.

Two Dales Chapel Whit walks outside the Blacksmith's Arms c.1905.

Scholars gathering for the Two Dales Whit walk c.1903, outside the Church of England Schoolroom (now Hayes Bakery).

Two Dales Wesleyan Sunday School Whit walk outside the Red House c.1905.

Preparing for the Whit walk in Two Dales c.1905. The Co-op shop is on the left and the building on the right is the old Two Dales Chapel, used as the infants school.

Two Dales Wesleyan Sunday School fife and drum band c.1905, outside the new chapel.

Sunday School scholars from the old Two Dales Chapel, in their Sunday best, c.1910.

Darley Hillside Chapel at their first anniversary 1912/1913.

Darley Hillside Chapel first anniversary 1912/1913.
Front row: Nellie Needham, Jessie Wilson, Mrs. White, X, Mrs. Fearn, Mary Needham.
Ida Wardman, Mr. Wardman, X, X, X.

The former chapel in Two Dales now became part of Two Dales Temporary Council School, but also continued as Two Dales Sunday School and was well attended, as can be seen from the photographs showing the parading of the Sunday School banner on the annual Whit walks. Meanwhile, the Church Anniversary found Hackney joining Two Dales, and, starting from near the Blacksmith's Arms, they marched with a brass band playing to the bottom of Sydnope Hill, round Sally's Corner to rejoin Chesterfield Road, en route to St. Helen's Church.

The Band of Hope also met at the old chapel, with the aim of persuading people to "sign the pledge". Concerts were held to encourage new members and Eliza Domoney from the cottage "up the fields" from the Blacksmith's Arms could always be encouraged to get up and sing. She had a poor voice, sang out of tune, but performed with gusto. However, her reciting of a monologue was the highlight of the evening and these kinds of events provided welcome entertainment within the community.

At the nearby Church of England School and Sunday School building (now Hayes Bakery), entertainment was also provided by means of lantern slide shows, provided at different times by Mr. Felthouse, Mr. Fentham and Mr. Helliwell. The favourite viewing point was from the gallery and the greatest amusement was actually provided by the shaky hand of the projectionist causing the image to disappear out of the window and up the fields at times.

Another significant marching event that formed part of the social calendar was the parade of the **Odd Fellows** organisations on **Hospital Sunday**, or Demonstration Sunday, in order to collect money for the upkeep of the Whitworth Hospital and to allow free treatment for those taken ill, before the establishment of the National Health Service. The Odd Fellows Clubs raised enough money on the day, and by subscription, for members to receive two recommendations from their doctor to attend outpatients and three to stay in hospital. The Royal Harmonicum Lodge met in their Club Room at the Nag's Head Pub, Two Dales, whilst the Hearts of Oak Branch met nearby, at the Blacksmith's Arms. At its most popular, in the years prior to the Great War, the clubs marched from the Institute grounds with banners unfurled, accompanied by a number of brass bands and eventually arrived at St. Helen's Church for a short service.

Whitworth Hospital c.1895

Whitworth Hospital c.1895

Committee members at the opening of the Whitworth Hospital in 1889. The sashes belong to one of the Odd Fellows clubs. George Charlesworth stands in the doorway, on the right. Sat on the ground to the extreme right is Billy Ashton, with next to him Tom Handley and Mr Tom Wright in the centre. Wensley newsagent, blind George Knowles, sits on the second row back, on the extreme left.

Whitworth Institute Park c.1912. Members of the Royal Harmonican Lodge and Darley Band gather for Hospital (Demonstration) Sunday.

Darley Rum-Tum Band, outside the Plough Inn, Two Dales c.1910.
Tommy Norton with the donkey and trap.

Darley Rum-Tum Band, Plough Inn, Two Dales c.1910.
Front row: 4th from left is Cliff Barker. Behind him is ? Bentley and 2nd from right on front row is Bill Allwood.

Music always played an important part in pre-war parish social events, and a popular band that performed at village wakes and provided impromptu village entertainment was **Two Dales Rum-Tum-Band**. Dressed in outlandish and weird costumes and playing miscellaneous instruments, the band members produced a more discordant sound than their brass band rivals. Tommy Norton provided a donkey and flat trap and with cheap beer, they all enjoyed a rousing sing-song.

The Dale Road Wesleyan Chapel played a major part in catering for the leisure time activities of the older lads in the parish through the formation of the Darley Dale Wesleyan Bible Class Football Team, run by Ernest F. Lowe. Darley Harriers, meanwhile, upheld the footballing honour of Darley Dale's men folk. Their base was the Whitworth Institute, but before the Great War they played their matches on part of the huge field known as the Cartledge, behind the Square and Compass Inn at Darley Bridge.

Football was held in high esteem and matches between local rivals and Darley attracted large crowds, drawn by the prospects of keenly fought encounters, and of course, the occasional "punch up", both on the field and off. On cup days against Bakewell, extra carriages were attached to the local train and crowds of up to 2000 are known to have attended these matches. In the season 1908-1909 Darley Harriers earned the distinction of becoming winners of the Derbyshire Challenge Cup. It is a sad fact that five years later a number of these men would be involved in the Great War and at least one would fall on the battlefield.

Formed in 1863, **Darley Dale Cricket Club** also provided an outlet for leisure time activities within the parish. The riverside ground had been levelled and prepared by James Smiths (Nurseries) at a cost of £6-12-0d and in 1904 a splendid pavilion replaced the original corrugated iron structure, at a cost of £254. A substantial amount of this expenditure was met out of the pocket of local coal merchant and business man, Tom Wright.

By 1913 the club was still actively performing throughout the Derwent Valley, often reaching the venues by using the local train service on the London Midland Line and maintaining the high level of achievement produced when the club had become winners of the Derbyshire Challenge Cricket Cup during the 1895 Season.

The final, between Darley Dale and Codnor United, took place at the Derbyshire County Cricket ground. Darley piled up huge scores, whilst giving precious little away. After playing three days, and the game still unfinished, the conclusion of the match had to be postponed for a time. On the date arranged, however, Codnor United, in a very unsportsmanlike way, failed to "show up", with the result that Darley Dale were awarded the cup.

The cup was presented in the Whitworth Park, in the presence of 8000 people, at the September Flower Show. A dinner and presentation evening was later held at the Square and Compass Inn, on Saturday November 23rd 1895.

By the middle years of the Great War, we find that 40 members of the cricket club had joined the Colours. One member would receive the Military Cross for his bravery, whilst another paid the supreme sacrifice. It is interesting to note that during the years of conflict, the ground was closed. Where once there had been the sight and sound of leather hitting willow, sheep grazed instead, in quiet contentment.

Darley Dale Wesleyan Bible Class Team 1910/1911.
Back row: R. Wildgoose, S. Bagshaw, S. A. Wagstaffe, W. Barker, E. Milner.
Centre: A. Milner, T. Watts, A. Smedley, W. Smith, S. Frost, W. Wall, F. Barker, B. Lowe,
J. Millward, E. F. Lowe.
Seated: J. W. Walker, C. Petts, A. Travis, L. Lowe, S. Smith.

Darley Dale Wesleyan Methodist Chapel Team playing Chaddeston Athletic c.1914.
Back row: Joe Allwood, Reg Wagstaffe, X Jimmy Slack.
Front row: Joe Hanson, Rumsey Wagstaffe, Stan (Spoffy) Taylor, X X Charlie Wall, X,
Everard Waterfall.

Darley Harriers in front of the Grouse Inn, Darley Dale, pre-1914.
Standing, back: Frank Fentham, George Wall, A. Milner
Standing, centre: George Charlesworth (trainer), X, X, Jim Wilson, Bill Fawley, X, X,
George Wall, Ted Lane, Mr. Gould (landlord), Joe Hanson, Harry Hickman.
Seated: X Tommy Boam, Joe Charlesworth, X Dick Lane.

Hackney Foresters Football Team 1912/1913 season.
Sam Frost is 3rd from the left on the back row.

St. Helen's Church Football Team, 1910/1911 season, in front of the Grouse Inn.
John Potter Marsden from Wensley, who was killed in the Great War,
is second from the left on the middle row.

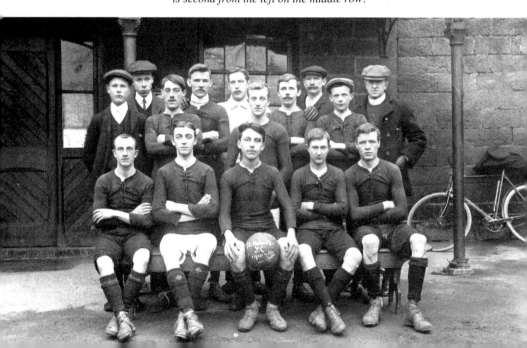

Darley Harriers Football Club – Winners of the Derbyshire Challenge Cup, 1908-1909.
Back row: H. Walker, J. Wilson, B. Gregory, Reg Wright, W. T. Webster.
Centre row: W. Pashley, E. Knowles, W. Fawley, W. Wright, W. Taylor, W. Gregory,
H. Walker.
Seated: H. Gregory, A. Boam, J. Webster, H. Wilson, H. Flint, P. Wright.

Darley Dale Cricket Team, Winners of the Derbyshire County Challenge Cup, 1895.
Back row: Ben Gregory, Tom Wright, F. Evans, B. C. Gregory (captain),
Alfred Smith (vice-captain), J. Siddall, W. M. Holness, J. Wright.
Seated: J. Gregory (umpire), Charles Pashley, R. B. Wright, Hugh Gregory,
J. J. Wildgoose, W. Gregory.

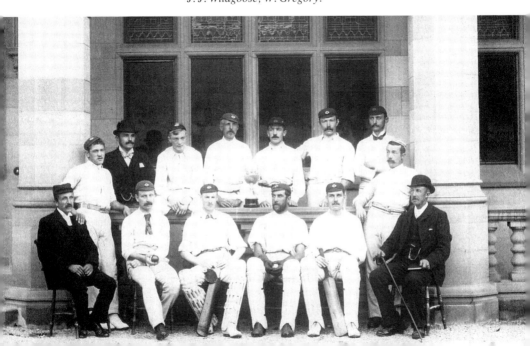

Using the roller on the wicket (1912 style) at Darley Dale Cricket Club's ground, Darley Bridge.

Darley Dale Cricket Club team members in front of the pavilion, in 1906, two years after it was built.

However, time for leisure pursuits was at a premium for the men who would soon be facing danger in the years 1914-1918. It was something to be valued highly, for most of their daily lives were spent in hard, back breaking toil as they tried to earn a living for themselves and their families.

Work of a manual nature was to be found in various Darley nurseries, on the Railway at Darley Station Yard and especially Rowsley Marshalling Yard, at Mill Close Lead Mine, John Gregory's Victoria Mill Timber Yard and in the various limestone and grit stone quarries, especially those of Stancliffe Estates Company.

The North-Eastern side of the valley from Hackney to Northwood, including moorland areas, gave rise to numerous nurseries. Gervase Smith, James Charlesworth, Matthew Smith, Henry Derbyshire and Hugh Gregory all made use of its acid based soils and protection from the cold winds, whilst the spring line provided an adequate water supply. All of these nurseries specialised in growing hardy trees and shrubs, conifers, rhododendrons, whilst some cultivated species of heather.

The largest of these nurseries, however, was **James Smith and Sons', Darley Dale Nurseries**. By 1906, the Nursery had been in difficulties, but a Company was formed, with the directors meeting every month, the meeting being called "Holy Thursday" by the workers. The Company now prospered and employed 150 men and boys at its height of prosperity in 1913. Covering 250 acres of ground, it was notable for the altitude of some of its nursery beds, which in parts of "Siberia" Nursery were 1100 feet above sea level and produced extremely hardy plants.

The "Home Nursery", off Park Lane, Two Dales, was just one of 14 branches and contained the offices and packing sheds, where all trees and shrubs were unloaded and packed under cover, thereby protecting them from drying winds. One thousand tons of trees and shrubs left Darley Station each year, with their roots wrapped in sacking and protected by a wicker work cage, made from pollarded willow branches grown in separate nurseries close to St. Helen's Church and within the 100 acre site of "Siberia" Nursery. One such consignment left the Station bound for the Potsdam Palace of Emperor Wilhelm of Germany. A few years later, both countries would be at war and a large number of the nursery men and boys in the accompanying photograph would be fighting for their country, with some losing their lives.

It was in 1827 that the firm was founded at Darley Dale, after previously conducting business as nurserymen at Matlock Moor and Ashover. The Nurseries, in 1913, were specially famed for the cultivation of hardy heathers, including the lucky white Scotch heather. Many boxes were sent to Scotland each year. Heathers were grown specifically for use in the packing of iron tubes and pipes for safe transit and large amounts arrived in horse and dray at Darley Station, to be sent in rail wagons to Stanton Iron Works, and wagon loads of spent hops

James Smith and Sons (Darley Dale Nurseries) c.1910.
Top picture: The packing sheds in Home Nursery.
Bottom picture: The staff at Home Nursery.

came into Darley Sidings from various breweries, ready for compositing and being used as a fertiliser in the nurseries.

The nursery had its own smithy, carpenters and wheelwrights' shops. Men were employed for the horses which were kept on farmland belonging to the nursery and stabled under the offices.

June to September was a very busy period as the skilled men had to bud all roses and fruit trees. Each man specialised in either budding, hip grafting, splitting, layering or enarching the various plants.

On Hallmoor Nursery, 100,000 roses would be in full bloom. The roses were packed in wild moss which was collected and brought down in carts from Beeley Moor, before being sent away in large boxes made in the carpenters' shop.

Another source of work was provided on the railway at **Darley Dale Station and Goods Yard**. The present station building was completed in 1874. During the early 1880's Sir Joseph Whitworth had Station Road built and in 1882 the installation of a level crossing gate, operated from a signal box, took place. The despatch of stone and timber became important at Darley Dale and in 1894 additional sidings were built in the goods yard. Other sidings were put in for receiving stone from Joseph Hodson's Farley Quarry.

Close to Churchtown Crossings a sidings was constructed for Stancliffe Estates Company Ltd. to enable stone from Stancliffe Quarry to be brought to the main line and loaded into L.M.R. rail wagons. From the sidings a private standard gauge track went across the fields and passed underneath the A6 road into Stancliffe Stone Yard, beyond which, it crossed Whitworth Road and ran into Stancliffe Quarry. A second section of the standard gauge line cut across the eastern slope of the valley to Hall Dale Quarry. Two saddle tank engines, named Sir Joseph Whitworth and Henry Dawson, were used on the line.

In 1911 the footbridges at Darley Dale Station and Churchtown Crossing were constructed and at the same time the footpath between Church Road, Station Road and on to Old Road, was completed.

Darley Station was relatively small but freight traffic was heavy and varied, dominated by coal and minerals. The coal trade at Darley Dale was in the hands of two dealers, Tom Wright and Thomas Smith and Sons. As Tom Wright's trade expanded, so did his rail wagon fleet, which eventually grew to 20 vehicles. He delivered coal to near and distant settlements, as well as supplying Stancliffe Quarries and Mill Close Lead Mine for powering machinery.

However, it was **Rowsley Sidings and Marshalling Yard** that provided Darley men with greater prospects of employment. The opening of the line through to Manchester resulted in an increase in traffic and the need for assisting engines as far as Peak Forest. The depot had been considerably enlarged in 1878 by the addition of a new engine shed. Freight traffic increased in the early 1870's and needed to be sorted out before climbing over the Peak. Rowsley was the most suitable site for such sidings and in 1877 the sidings were opened for traffic.

There was a marked increase in the number of men employed there and work was begun on the blocks of cottages at Little Rowsley and by 1898 the housing stock in Rowsley had increased by a half in 12 years (most of these houses on Chatsworth Road were officially in Darley Parish). A new signal-box, the busiest on the Derby – Manchester line, was opened in June 1915. Rowsley was certainly a major contributor in providing work opportunities for the local work force and many names on Darley's war memorial were railway men. By November 1914, 25 men working at Rowsley Sidings had already volunteered for action.

Staff employed at Darley Dale Station c. 1910. Third from the right is Billy Needham, a clerk in Tom Wright's coalmerchant's office, who was blinded in an accident at the Station Yard and later became a Darley Bridge shopkeeper.

*Stancliffe Stone Quarry Yard c. 1900, showing Saddle tank engine
'Sir Joseph Whitworth', used on the standard gauge railway.*

*A Johnson 060 Freight Class 2 engine at the original engine shed at Rowsley c.1905.
Second from the left on the bottom row is driver Jack Atkinson,*

(Fred Morton via Rowsley Association Collection.)

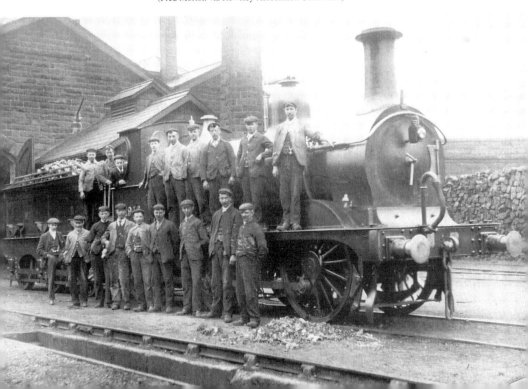

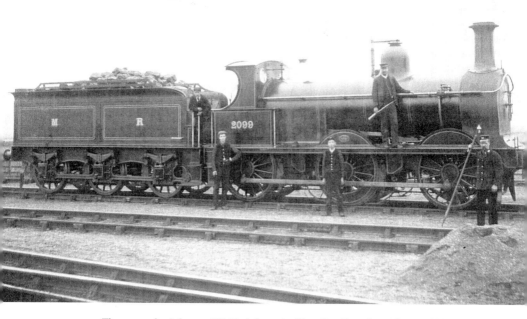

The crew of a Johnson 060 Freight train Class 2 at Rowsley sidings c.1900.
The driver carries a feeder (oil can), the shunter carries a pole and the fireman and
two sidings staff complete the group. This engine was used to pull freight to London,
Birmingham and Liverpool.

(Fred Morton via Rowsley Associ:ltion Collection.)

It was in Darley's neighbouring parish of South Darley, however, that the largest employer of men was to be found. Over 600 employees, from many different parishes, worked at **Mill Close Lead Mine**, the richest and most productive producer of lead in the country. From Roman times and before, lead had been mined in the limestone areas of Winster and Wensley and certain families could trace their lead mining pedigree from those distant times to the early years of the 20th century.

My forebears, for example, can be traced to Hackney and Northwood in the early 16th century and by 1715 John Taylor from Northwood, working at smelting lead ore on the heights above Little Rowsley, travelled across the valley to live and work at Wensley.

At this time, in 1720, the London Lead Company, often referred to as "The Quaker Company", heard of the lead mines in the Wensley district and took over these earlier workings to form the "old" Mill Close Lead Mine, on land just behind the Red Lion Inn, Wensley. John Taylor and his sons worked for the Company, but eventually the London Lead Company abandoned the workings in the latter part of the 18th century.

In 1795, John's grandchildren, James (my g—g—g—grandfather),

DARLEY DALE 1913 – A GLIMPSE BEHIND THE SCENES

George and Joseph Taylor, formed a company and began working the old spoil heaps for traces of lead. They carted vast loads of this material to the banks of the River Derwent at Darley Bridge to use its waters to "buddle" (separate) the lead. The River Derwent and adjacent land was contaminated as far down stream as Matlock Bridge. Due to this thoughtless action they spent some time in Derby Jail and received a fine of £100.

Between 1820 and 1870 their children, including my great-great grandfather, Francis Taylor, worked underground in the old mine workings behind the Red Lion Inn and under Cambridge Wood. Nowadays, deep in this mine are relics of the old miners. Clay pipes can be seen, shovels, picks and other tools lie abandoned, disintegrated wooden barrows and old rails from a small wagon way still exist, whilst many clogs and boots lie discarded, and near to "Forge Shaft" there are the remains of a bellows and a forge, where a blacksmith worked on the mining tools.

In 1859, however, Edward Miller Wass, a Lea and Holloway lead smelter, drove Watts Shaft in Clough Wood, which was to begin the story of the modern Mill Close Mine. Francis Taylor and his son Job abandoned their work in the old Mill Close Mine, and like so many other miners, became employees of the new Mill Close Lead Mine. A Cornish steam engine was erected in 1860 (the splendid remains of the old engine house can still be seen in Clough Wood).

In 1874, an inrush of water caused Watts Shaft to be abandoned for some years and a shaft at Warren Carr (close to the site of present day Enthovens lead smelter) became the main focus of activity. On this shaft a new engine, "Jumbo", was erected, to be joined later by "Alice" and "Baby".

By 1912, Millclose was the best equipped metal mine in the country and had entered a period of prosperity, resulting in large numbers of employees from Darley, Darley Bridge, Wensley, Winster and further afield working the mine 24 hours a day on a three shift system. Within two years the country was at war and those workers given exemption from the armed services would be helping to provide vital minerals for the war industry.

Victoria Mill Timber Yard and bone grinding mill had been

Mill Close Lead Mine, Darley Dale.

The miners' track leading from Clough Wood to Mill Close Lead Mine c.1914.

Mill Close Lead Mine c.1914, looking down from the Stanton Moor area.

*Group of miners at Mill Close
Lead Mine c.1900.*

*Watts Shap at Mill Close Lead
Mine (in Clough Wood) and the
Engine House, in the early
1870's. Substantial ruins of the
engine house still remain.*

Watts Shaft and engine house, Mill Close; in Clough Wood, in the early 1870's.

*Leadminer Francis Taylor
and his wife Sarah c.1867, Wensley.*

*Job Taylor, Wensley,
former lead miner, c.1918.*

Down in the Old Mill Close Lead Mine ('The Quaker Mine'), showing present day remains of the blacksmith's bellows in 'Forge Shaft'.

The Old Mill Close Lead Mine ('The Quaker Mine'), showing present day remains of lead miners' tools.

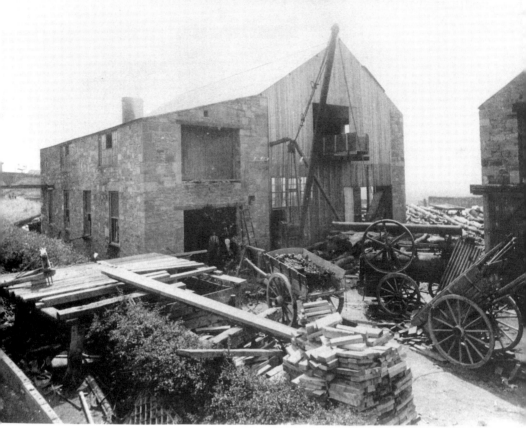

John Gregory's Victoria Saw Mills c.1910. The railway bridge on Old Road in the distance. These buildings were destroyed by fire in 1938.

Gregory's Victoria Mill Timber Yard c.1910. The buildings were destroyed by fire in 1938.

Gregory's Victoria Saw Mill, on Old Road, Darley Dale, c.1910.
These buildings were destroyed by fire in 1938.
Joe Senior, S. Middleton, J. Burnett, X, J. Bueontex, J. Jenkins,
J. W. Gregory (son of the owner).

established in the 1890's on Old Road, Darley, after the owner, John Gregory, left the family business in Tansley to set up on his own. As can be seen from the photographs, the saw mill buildings bear no relation to those of today, for they were destroyed by fire in 1938.

A significant work force was employed, for besides those working in the saw mill, travelling gangs of men would be used to fell timber over a wide area of the North and West Midlands, especially in the Ashbourne, Hardwick Woods and Hardwick areas. A caravan would provide some accommodation, whilst most workers were billeted in nearby farm buildings, together with their horses and drays. Steam and traction engines helped with some of the heavier haulage work, whilst felled timber was transported by drays to the nearest railway sidings and sent by bolster wagons to Darley Dale for seasoning and cutting.

The other significant employer of men in the parish was the grit stone quarrying industry, with Fallinge, Stancliffe, Hall Dale, Knabb, Ladygrove, Sydnope and Farley quarries stretching along the north-eastern slopes of the parish between Rowsley and Matlock.

Before the Great War, Farley and Sydnope employed 20 men each, whilst at Knabb an even larger number were employed by Mr. Palmer, who rented the quarry from the Dakeyne Estates. Majuba Quarry in Ladygrove was also rented from the Estate and made pulp stones. **Knabb Quarry** was substantial in size, with tramway rails laid down that came out onto and across the Sydnope road, at which point pulp stones and needle stones (grind stones) could be loaded onto local farmers' horses and drugs to be taken to Darley Dale Station. In 1914, whilst putting in a shot, there came a bad fall, with rocks crashing down onto the steam crane. The boiler was burst and steam escaped, with the horrendous sound being heard in Two Dales and across the valley. It was in Knabb Quarry that Tommy Norton was noted for producing an accordion during slack periods and impromptu dancing sessions took place on the quarry bottom, with the women from nearby Loscoe Row joining in.

The largest and oldest quarry, employing over 250 men, was **Stancliffe Estates Quarries** and as we have seen, they contained their own railway line and engines. Stancliffe stone had been used locally from early times, with Darley Dale's St Helen's Church constructed from it in the 10th century and the tower added in 1301. Its fame spread and in the Victorian period of urban development the proud city fathers of Manchester, Liverpool, Birmingham and London used Stancliffe stone in many of their fine public buildings and squares.

Quarrying was labour intensive and supplied a regular trickle of jobs for those seeking employment. However, the large work force would find itself depleted during 1914-1918, as the quarrymen were called up into the armed services, and some would forfeit their lives. An article in the January 12th 1918 edition of the High Peak News stated: "What England or her Allies would have done but for the ladies of the Great War, one can hardly contemplate. The women have taken many of the men's places while the men have gone to fight for England, Home and Beauty.

"The very latest development in female labour is at Stancliffe Estates Company's Quarries. Some time ago the Directors introduced a crusher

Knabb Quarry, Sydnope, in the 1880's. Harry Pearson is fifth from the left.
The rail lines went out onto Sydnope Hill.

Knabb House, Ladygrove, 14th May 1904, showing the spoil heap from Knabb Quarry.

Stancliffe Stone saw cutters c.1912.
George Derbyshire (killed in the Great War) stands on the extreme right.

Stancliffe Quarry c.1898.

Stancliffe Stone masons yard c.1912.

A section of Stancliffe Stoneyard c.l910.

A view in the Stancliffe Quarry c.1910.

One of the steam operated cranes in Stanciiffe Quarry c.1910.

Transporting stone to the railway sidings from Stancliffe Quarry,
along Green Lane and Church Road, Churchtown. c.1910.

to pulverise waste pieces of grit stone, to be used in the manufacture of cement. But when the plant had been erected, there arose the question of labour. Here the ladies come in. They chiefly load the grit stone rubble for the crusher, and also into the trucks for government work. They in fact do everything except drive the engines. Brave ladies! These ladies are keeping the home fires burning, quite truly!"

By 1913 **Ladygrove Mill** (today, **Johnson's Mill**) was empty, except for a section occupied by Mr. John Eaton and his son, from Denacre House, who were furriers and fibre cloth manufacturers. With the declaration of war in 1914, the main building complex was taken over by the army and was used as a training centre for The Leeds Rifles.

Between 1780 and the late 1870's the mill, built by the Dakeyne brothers, had operated as a flax spinning mill, employing well over 100 workers at its most productive. Flax was grown in the Scarsdale area, near Chesterfield, and brought by wagon to be made into linen or string.

At great cost, four dams were built in Sydnope Dale (Ladygrove) to provide power to drive the machinery, giving a 96 feet level of water. Instead of using one enormous wheel, the brothers made three smaller ones, each at successive levels, so that the same water was used three times.

The far end dam was called "Blue Shuttle", then came "Potter Dam" (40 feet deep), then "Fancy Dam" and nearest to the mill was "Regulator", which could regulate entry of the water into the mill. The overflow ran down into the basin hole, just before the stream goes underneath the road.

The large flue chimney for the mill was some way away in the Knabb Quarry grounds. An underground pipe led through the fields to the chimney and both pipe and chimney had to be cleaned. In the later stages, John Wildgoose, a chimney sweep from Matlock Bank performed the task.

For a while the mill became a glove factory and received notoriety locally for the stink of curing skins. In the early 1880's the buildings were empty, but between 1887 and 1901 the mill was leased by J.T. Hope Brothers to produce string and twine.

Between the mill and the dams, **Loscoe (Losker) Row**, a terrace of 14 cottages, had been built to house some of the mill workers. Large families often crammed into these small properties, which contained one room downstairs, plus a tiny back kitchen, with open stairs leading up to a landing and one bedroom. Only two of the cottages had a back door and none had an inside toilet. They used outside earth closets and the "night soil" was collected once a week, at night. Drinking water came from a well in nearby Bleach Croft, whilst water for other uses came from the dam. In the early years of the 20th century, Council roadsweeper Vincent Wildgoose, his sister Mary and half sister Sarah Dunne lived in Number 12 A, the next to the end cottage, with Sarah using the smaller premises next door (Number 14) as a shop, selling sweets, balm, studs and buttons.

The large house, known as Mill House, opposite the mill, was used by Mr. Felthouse for bottling pop and ginger beer for the **Darley Dale Mineral Water Company**, in the early years of the century. The pop was made in outhouses behind the present day Coates Butchers, Two Dales.

Early photograph of Ladygrove Mills.

View of mill workers terraced cottages, called Loscoe Row, near Ladygrove Mill. Demolished between 1959 and 1961.

Losker (Loscoe) Row c.1900. Sarah Dunne's small shop can be seen at the extreme right of the row. Earth closets are to the side of the shop. The left side of the nursery at the back of the Row was 'Bleach Croft', containing a well.
Knabb Quarry is in the background.

Mill House, the old pop factory, near Ladygrove Mill, in ruins c.1914.
It had been operated by Mr. Felthouse.

Brook Bottom, Ladygrove Road (Mill Lane) c.1910, with Ladygrove Mill in the background Thomas Barker, the tailor, lived in the end terraced house on the left.

This was the same Mr. Felthouse who provided entertainment as projectionist at the Church of England Schoolroom. Different owners have discovered old pop bottles with glass marble stoppers whilst digging in the garden.

The bottles of pop were sold locally in shops throughout the Matlock district. At the time of writing, Two Dales possesses very few shops, but in the period before the Great War it was well endowed with **shopping facilities**. On Brook Bottom, Ladygrove Road, were three cottages next to Spa Cottage. Old Mrs. Maddocks and Jack Maddocks, the chimney sweep, lived in one and Thomas Barker the tailor, in another. His tailor's shop was in the tiny cottage attached to the end cottage and he walked many miles around the district in pursuance of his trade and customers.

From a strong Methodist background, Mrs Barker looked like a Dickensian figure in her black bonnet as she went off to chapel, whilst Thomas often made his way there on his tricycle. Moores the baker from Matlock brought bread by horse and cart and left it for the locals to collect from the tailor's shop. Thomas's wife would come out of the cottage and blow a whistle to let her husband, working in his shop, know that it was time for dinner. Mr. McFadden also came round the district on his horse and cart, measuring people up for clothes.

At the turn of the century, William Wagstaffe ran a butcher's business from a hut in the corner of the field opposite Ladygrove House, at the turning from Chesterfield Road for Ladygrove. Meat was sold over the half open style stable door and horse harnesses and other items could be bought. William's sons, William Perry Wagstaffe and Ernest Stanley, came into the business with their father before the Great War began, and their butcher's shop was now on Chesterfield Road, between Brook Side and the bottom of Sydnope Hill. The slaughter house was next to Fir Tree Cottage, near to the bottom bend of the hill.

The photographs indicate that the family were also cab proprietors and William Perry drove both the butcher's van and the cabs and wagonettes for hire. It was to be a tremendous loss to the family when William Perry Wagstaffe was killed in the Great War.

Another well known Two Dales butcher was Fred Waterfall, who ran his business from No. 1 Brook Side. One can still see the iron rail outside from which they hung the meat. Fred had lived at the farm opposite "Top of the Hill", Sydnope, with his slaughter house on the opposite side of the road. The meat was then brought down to be sold at his shop.

Up until 1906, George Wall, a farmer from Tinkersley, Northwood, had a butcher's shop where Coates's butchers is now, but at that point the shop was taken over by Frederick Dobson, a

The Wagstaffe's first butchers shop (now in Holt House grounds.)

joiner from Mill Close Lead Mine, and his school teacher wife Rosamond, who ran it as the village post-office. Prior to this the post-office had been in the hands of shoemaker Adolphus Augustus Lowe, his wife Catherine and his mother Sally, at the "Corner House" at the bottom

Williarn Perry Wagstaffe, Two Dales, driving butcher's van outside his father's shop c.1913. He was killed in action during the Great War.

Butcher's shop of Fred and Agnes Waterfall, Brookside, c.1910. Their son Eric stands by the door. Harry Barker's fish and chip shop is to the right.

Corner House (Sally's Corner), Two Dales, c.1900. It was the old post office run by Sally Lowe, and her son Adolphus Augustus Lowe was the postmaster and cobbler. In the late 1920's and 1930's, Mr. Blythe the dentist hired a room here on a Wednesday, and often 'pulled ' teeth without the use of anaesthetic.

of Sydnope Hill ("Sally's Corner").

George Derbyshire, a postman, would serve the moor land district above Sydnope, whilst Tommy Boam used his push bike. Tommy Atkin from Matlock used to blow his whistle when coming down from Hall Dale to let everyone know that he was coming so they would have their letters and post

Postman Tommy Boam, delivering mail at Stancliffe View on the A6. Between 1913 and 1926 he was also the caretaker at Darley Council School, Greenaway Lane.

cards ready. With their regular rounds that were trod year after year they knew everybody on their "patch" and certainly knew their business, for most people sent local messages by post card in those days.

Two doors away from Mr. Dobson's post-office, on Holmes Terrace, Chesterfield Road, Mary Ann Knifton, wife of railway wagon repairer, Thomas Knifton, helped in funding the family finances as a dealer in toys and sweets from the front room of her house. At the time of the Great War in 1914 Thomas had died and Mary was helped occasionally by her daughter, 22 year old Agnes. For some reason the front door was closed to the public during these war years and people would have to enter through the back entrance from off Ryecroft and go through the house. Daughter Agnes was kept busy during the war in her duties as a Red Cross nurse at the Whitworth Institute Red Cross Hospital.

Across from the Blacksmith's Arms on Chesterfield Road was possibly the oldest shop in Two Dales, Cedar House, for in 1841 Margaret Dakeyne was a draper and had her shop there. Now, in 1913, Cedar House contained one of the largest and best stocked shops in Two Dales, The Co-op, run by Fred Toplis and his wife, whilst in contrast, at No. 4 Brook Side, opposite the open brook, was the small shop run by Charlotte Charlesworth (nee Holland).

Her husband George was a foreman in Stancliffe Quarries, and from their front room she sold sweets, tobacco, shoes and clothes. During the Great War her younger brother, George Holland, whom she had brought up, was killed in action in 1916. This shattered her world, and, with her heart no longer in the business, it was gradually run down in the years after the war ended.

Next door, between the Charlesworth's and the Nag's Head Pub, was the home of George and Polly Norman, and in a separate part of the house alongside the pub, Polly ran a shop selling general provisions and collected and delivered goods in her pony and trap.

At No. 2 Brook Side, Harry Barker and his wife ran a fish and chip shop in their spare time. Housed in a lean-to extension to their cottage (see photographs elsewhere), it contained three tables and chairs for people to sit down at. They fried the fish and chips on the small range in their kitchen and people had to be rather patient, for the whole process could be dreadfully slow. The business closed down during the war, after

Shopkeeper George Norman's wife Polly (nee Waterfall) in front of the shop at Brookside, Two Dales, next to the Nag's Head c.1927.
George and his son Eddie are in the doorway.

Brook Side, Two Dales, on the 17th October 1907. Hall Dale Brook is in flood. The lady to the left is shopkeeper Lottie Charlesworth (nee Holland). The 'lean-to' building was used by Harry Barker to sell fish and chips.

Brook Side and the Plough Inn, Two Dales c.1910. In the centre ground is the landlord of the Nag's Head Inn, Thomas Holmes, and his three daughters, Emma, Charlotte and Annie. Harry Barker's fish and chip shop is to the left.

his brother William was killed in action.

The bakery and shop belonging to "Tony" Walton, the corn miller, and managed by well known baker James Squires, was to be found at the junction of Park Lane with Chesterfield Road. Jimmy "Dry Bun" had been born in Nottinghamshire and at 17 years was apprentice shopkeeper to his uncle at Wash Green, Wirksworth.

In 1900 he married his wife Elizabeth and moved to Two Dales as the local baker. His wife ran the shop, selling groceries and sweets, whilst Jimmy worked in the bake house, across the back yard. Eventually his son Wilfred began to help in the business.

Deliveries were made in a basket, on foot, but a horse and trap was provided by Mr. Walton and used for deliveries as far afield as Baslow. One important daily delivery was to the St. Elphin's School for girls, along the A6. Two Dales folk could also take along their own dough, and, for a small charge, make use of the heated ovens during less busy times of the day.

Old "Tony" Walton, living at Warney House (now part of the DFS Furniture store complex) owned Warney flour and corn mill and flour was delivered on two horses and carts as far as Ashover, Parwich and Monyash. At 8-30 each morning he could be seen hurrying up Warney Road (completely devoid of houses in those days), with shoe laces undone and coat and shirt flying open, as he went to tell Jimmy Squires what was happening for the day. (As a child in the 1950's, I certainly remember with fondness the old mill race that in much earlier times had been diverted

James Squires, baker and shop manager for Mr. Tony Walton, corn mill owner, Two Dales.

Mr. Jimmy Squires outside his shop and bakehouse c.1908, at the junction of Park Lane with Chesterfield Road, Two Dales.

from Warney Brook. Operated by sluice gates, it ran underneath both Oddford Lane and the A6 and flowed into the reed fringed Warney mill pond, where nowadays the tarmac covered expanse of the D.F.S. Furniture Store overflow car park has taken its place. Each Spring and Summer Term the mill race and dam became a favourite place for we school children, as Darley Primary School teachers Harold Lomas and Mrs. Beebe led us there on nature rambles. Sadly, the tarmac and a dried up water course is all that remains nowadays).

For two years at the end of the Great War, James Squires began a job as manager of a supplies depot for the YMCA at Cologne, looking after the well being of British soldiers who were helping to monitor the de-militarised zone in the Rhineland, after Germany's defeat. When he returned to Two Dales and his family, he was to look elsewhere in Darley for a baker's job.

Park Lane, Two Dales, contained three other commercial premises, once again to be found within the front rooms of family homes and mainly run by the women of the household. At No. 18, Harry and Minnie Charlesworth ran a pot shop selling pots and pans, plates and dishes, whilst two tea rooms competed within a few yards of each other, especially in the summer months when visitors attended the Whitworth Institute.

Wood's Tearoom, in the home of George and Jack Wood, provided refreshments but also sold general provisions under the supervision of Rosa Wood. She was also in charge of the National Telephone Company Ltd's Two Dales branch, its headquarters being in her home. At No. 22 Park Lane, Offilers Tea House was smaller and on sunny days would provide extra seating by erecting a tent in the garden.

Along the A6, in the shops erected on behalf of Stancliffe Estates Company Ltd., near Green Lane, Mr. Fearn the draper did business in the shop nearest the Grouse Inn, next door to Henry Fielding the cobbler and shoemaker, with post master and grocer John Siddall next to Green Lane. Lionel Fairclough ran the newsagent's shop on the other side of Green Lane, with greengrocer James Henry Woolliscroft and his wife next door, whilst further along the block, the sixth shop was occupied until 1912 by grocer Ernest Bremner Morten (and recently occupied by shopkeepers Mr. and Mrs. Goodman).

Darley Dale grocer, E. B. Morten, in front of his shop on Stancliffe View, c.1907.

The Rectory Farm, Churchtown, when it was also Darley Dale Post Office, c.1896. It was run by Wlliam Fearn. He began to branch out as a cycle agent during the early 1900's, the small business operating from these premises. His son, Stanley Fearn, continued the business and by 1926 it was operating from the present site on Bakewell Road, Matlock. Mr. and Mrs. Wllliam Fearn are shown standing with their son, Stanley.

Besides the resident shopkeepers, travelling salesmen came round the parish. One such trader was Gervase Smith from Hackney, selling paraffin from a big drum on his cart as well as pegs, hardware and rubbing stones. Selling produce from their Hackney nurseries on Chesterfield Market, the family also ran Hackney post-office from their premises.

During this period before the Great War and well into the 1920's and early 1930's, a gypsy encampment of over twelve Romany caravans, with attendant horses, would make their home at certain times of the year on the Farley – Flash Dam road, near Sydnope Stand. They made pegs and other household items and the womenfolk travelled the district selling these wares during the following weeks.

At Two Dales, James Arthur Watts was in business as a **blacksmith** at the **smithy**, close by the Blacksmith's Arms (now converted into a house called "The Old Smithy"). His father, "Daddy" Watts, sold sweets and balm from his shop, attached to the pub. When younger, he had been known to deliver milk from their farm on his three wheeler bicycle. At the smithy, on occasions, the local children would be allowed to use the bellows to stoke the forge fire, when Arthur was making shoes for the horses.

Arthur Watts owned a flat dray cart with sides, and before the Great War he would sometimes use it as a charabanc for locals, by placing seats inside. At times, the village children collected blackberries to sell, to raise a few pennies to allow them to travel on the cart to Matlock Wakes. The Watts family also possessed a carriage and pony and trap, using them to transport parties of visitors around the district, or a local cricket team to an away venue.

George Redfern's smithy was in Ryecroft, just behind James Squires's bake house and, at the time of writing, the building contains garages. George, living at No. 2 Park Lane, shoed the horses of local farmers but also had the contract for dealing with horses from James Smith's Nurseries. As winter approached, business gathered pace and the line of steaming horses would stretch along Chesterfield Road, as they waited for frost nails to be hammered into place. The sounds from the smithy echoed throughout the neighbourhood, including a wide choice of "words" uttered by George when the horses "acted up".

The work of shoeing took precedent. The farmers' intermittent visits during the year resolved into a steady flow as July approached and horses which had wintered required shoeing for work in the hayfield. The tang of the stable, mingled with that of burnt horn, lingered perpetually in the air whilst they were being shod.A stock of iron was stored and horseshoes of all shapes and sizes were on show, whilst the forge displayed its enormous bellows, the anvil and all the fascinating clutter of the smithy.

Local workmen went to Arthur or George for gate fasteners, hinges and snecks, ordering what they wanted as they were on the point of needing it and often expected the finished article to be ready in an hour or two, which it usually was. Both blacksmiths could make a new gate for the garden or grate for the fire, do an intricate welding job on a farm implement, or repair a household pail.

The former blacksmiths forge of Arthur Watts, Two Dales, taken in 1978.

*c.1908. Arthur Watts, blacksmith, third from the left,
taking a party out along Chesterfield Road.*

On the road below Hall Dale Wood, near Painter's Nook, between Two Dales and Darley Hillside, stood "**The Laundry**". Close by, the Stancliffe Quarry saddle tank railway engines would shuttle across the road as they plied between Hall Dale Quarry and Stancliffe Stone Quarry Yard.

"The Laundry" had been built originally on to the cottage to deal with the washday needs of Stancliffe Hall during Sir Joseph's

*Believed to be George Redfern, Two Dales
blacksmith, at his forge in Ryecroft,
c.1912.*

77

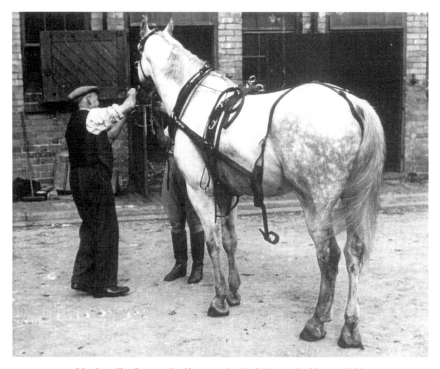

Blacksmith, George Redfern, at the Red House Stables, c.1955.

time and the water for that purpose came from a spring fed underground reservoir in front of the property.

Before the Great War, the Charlesworths lived at "The Laundry", with mother Mary in charge and her four daughters helping with the washday chores. Large coppers that could be fired up stood in a corner downstairs, while irons were heated around the sides of a large coal fired, black leaded range in the ironing room upstairs. There was no proper drying room, although clothes could be hung up, using a pulley mechanism. Four large wooden tubs, with rubbing boards inside, were used to wash the clothes and the water escaped through a drain to the outside.

Dirty linen would arrive from Stancliffe Hall, surplices from St. Helen's Church and "white" butchers coats from the Wagstaffes and Waterfalls. Eventually, a married daughter, Nelly Morten, went to live down Green Lane and had a Nissen type hut built down the yard, in which she took people's washing, especially from the "gentry", such as the Marsden Smedleys from "Rotherwood". At times, people from London would send their finery, in the form of silk dresses, by rail to Darley Station, from where the Charlesworths collected it in baskets. Sadly, one of the Charlesworth sons, Fred, was to be another Darley fatality during the course of the 1914-1918 war.

Around 1906, construction of the Darley Dale section of the **Derwent Valley Water Board's aqueduct** from the Derwent Dams took place, resulting in an influx of navvies to the district. At Tinkersley it passed through a 6 feet 3 inch diameter brick culvert, before entering a brick tunnel 200 feet (61 metres) deep under Darley Hillside, near Burley Field Farm.

The one mile long tunnel emerged under the Hall Dale Lane and at this point the water entered twin four feet diameter steel pipes. This siphon pipe passed under Hall Dale brook on its way under the bad bends in the Sydnope Hill road, and Ladygrove road and brook, near to the drive of Holt House.

Another brick tunnel then carried the water from Holt Lane, under Farley Farm, towards Matlock and the Crich Reservoir, which served Derby, Nottingham and Leicester.

The navvies were housed in two camps, consisting of corrugated iron buildings, one at Lumb Lane, Northwood, and the other at Farley. Many years ago, I remember Brook Bottom resident Goe Turner recalling how her mother mentioned the navvies arriving to construct the aqueduct through Two Dales. Those based at the Farley camp frequented the public houses and she told how on some occasions they would not be able to see the brook bottom for blood, resulting from the drunken brawls between themselves and with the local men. By the end of 1907 the work was accomplished and most of the men moved on with the work, towards Ambergate.

The foreman of one of these groups of workmen was James Watkins (see photograph), who met Sarah Bentley, the landlord's daughter from the Plough Inn. They married and he settled down in Two Dales, becoming landlord of the Plough Inn for a while.

In 1901 **David Allsop, a besom maker** (broom maker), lived at Rose Cottage at the bottom of Sydnope Hill with his wife Sarah, and next door was his 74 year old father George, also a maker of besoms. When David

Laying the water aquaduct from the Bamford area to Ambergate, through Darley Dale, c.1907. The gang, led by foreman James Watkins, second from the left, are standing in the Holt Farm field, below Ladygrove.

died in 1951 he had been the last besom maker in Darley Dale.

The besoms were made from well grown heather on Darley and Beeley Moors. A relation, George Butler from Brook Bottom, cut the heather for them on the moors, using a short bladed scythe. David travelled up Sydnope Hill on his cart, pulled by a white horse, to fetch the heather, with local children often hitching a "secret" lift by hanging on to the back.

The heather was brought back to his shed. On the edge of his work bench was a peculiar vice with a round grip in which the correct quantity of straight heather was held. The vice was worked by a foot stirrup, while with his strong hands he rapidly bound the heather at the top. Local grown withies were used. The finished product were not just for local sale. Considerable quantities would be sent out of the area by rail from Darley Station.

The bearded besom maker, David Allsop, was a true countryman, who was respected as a weather prophet. Whenever a thunderstorm broke, he had already collected his horse from off the hillside at the top of Sydnope and stabled it safely near his house.

Darley had its fair share of characters like David Allsop and two more examples were Urban District Council road length men, Sammy

Cardin and Miles Fox, both from Hackney.

Sam was a good local preacher, though noted for his long sermons. He had an artificial leg made of cork and on occasions would rest it on the wooden lectern, whilst preaching.

One Sunday, a trainee preacher and local farmer, Freddy Wildgoose, was attached to the experienced Sammy and Freddy provided him with a lift to Ashover Chapel on his horse and cart. Sammy never knew when to stop preaching and when Freddy began to fidget, Sam embarrassed him by announcing that he had better stop because his fellow preacher had obviously had enough and wished to start himself. Freddy forgot his planned text in his embarrassment. When Sammy went outside to ride back with the farmer he found that the disgruntled Freddy had galloped off into the distance and the peg-legged road man was left to walk home to Hackney.

Miles Fox was a broad, burley fellow, wearing baggy trousers tied

below the knee and was well known for his poaching activities. Both Sam and Miles were constantly plagued by the local children, who would often take and hide their barrows when they were working, or distracted. In later years, when working on his length near Flash Dam, Miles would go behind a large stone and sit there for hours at a time, hidden from view. After the years of gentle "torment", it must have seemed like heaven.

Throughout this glimpse behind the scenes in Darley Dale we have seen how the parish provided work for its residents and sustained them through its wide variety of shops, businesses and travelling traders. Entertainment

The Nag's Head Inn at Brook Side, Two Dales, c.1912. Landlord Thomas Holmes stands in the middle, with sons Thomas on the left (he was killed in the Great War) and William on the right, both members of Darley Band.

Wedding of George Gregory (Tansley) and Beatrice Davenport 1913
at the Blacksmith 's Arms, Two Dales.
They emigrated to Canada after the wedding.
Back row: X, X.
Third row: Florence Gregory, X, X, Florence Gregory, X, X.
Second row: Alan Gregory, X, Stephen Gregory, Mrs. Davenport, Mr. Davenport,
George Gregory, Beatrice Davenport, X, X X, X, X, X, Edith Hawley (nee Davenport),
X, X Charlie Gregory, X.
Front row: Doris Gregory, Charlie Gregory, Beatrice Gregory, Mary Bridden.

The Grouse Inn, Darley Dale, c.1905, landlord Mr. Gould.

The Church Inn, Church Road, c.1910. Landlord Mr. Alston.

The Reeves family of Chesterfield Road, Two Dales, c.1910. Wagstaffe's butcher's shop is shown on the left, under the stone canopy.

Brook Side, Two Dales, showing open culvert, George Norrnan's shop and Nag's Head Inn to the left and the Plough Inn to the right.

The bridge at Brook Side, Two Dales, c.1912.
On the bridge are: Harry Barker, Annie Norrnan, Mrs. Barker, Dyson Charlesworth, Mrs Tunnycliffe, Olive Bunting, X, X, X.

Gathering of children near Mrs. Reeves cottage, Chesterfield Road, Two Dales, c.1910.

Chesterfield Road, Two Dales, on Twyford 's Hill, c.1910.
The horse and cart on the right is coming out of Twyford's builders yard.

*Gathering of Two Dales folk on 'Peters Bridge' (Two Dales Bridge),
next to the Blacksmith's Arms, c.1910.*

*The Travis brothers in front of their
'artistic' work on their cottage, 'Thimble
Hall', in 1900. Joe Travis is standing next
to his brother Harry.*

*The photograph shows 'Thimble Hall', Two Dales, in 1900. The thatched cottages, now
known as Yew Tree Cottage, stood at the bottom of Sydnope Hill, on the narrow side
road thal leads towards the Plough Inn. This was 'Thimble Hall ' and the two elderly
Travis brothers who lived there painted crude pictures of the Boer leaders and soldiers,
Krueger, Cronje and Botha, during the Boer War of 1899-1902, on the walls of the
cottage. People would come from miles around to look at their work.*

Laburnam Inn, Hackney, c.1880. The second person from the right is landlord, John Taylor. It was also a farm and the barn is now where the 'gents' toilets are situated.

*Farm workers and nurserymen at Burley Fields Farrn, Darley Dale, c.1913.
Charlie Wildgoose is in the centre on the back row.*

The hay stacks at harvest time on Burley Fields Farm, 1911.

Lunch being served at harvest time on the Wildgoose farm at Burley Fields, 1911.
Back row: Charlie Wildgoose, X, Percy Wagstaffe, Annie Crowder, X, Fred Devereux, X, X.
Front row: Sidney Wildgoose, X, X, Maud Ford, X, X.

Harvest time at Charles Frederick Wildgoose's farm, at Burley Fields, in 1911.
Back row: Sam Wagstaffe, Percy Wagstaffe, X, Samuel Wagstaffe, X X, Fred Devereux.
Middle row: Charlie Wildgoose, Maud Ford, Annie Crowder.
Lying down: Sidney Wildgoose, X, X, X, X, X.
The corn was gathered in stooks and made into stacks, which were thatched. Charlie
Wildgoose was an expert thatcher. Later, in October, the threshing machine arrived and
the corn was taken from the small stacks to he threshed

could also be found "on the doorstep", within the numerous sporting and leisure time groups that catered for their needs. For many residents of Darley Dale, the parish boundary encircled their world for most of their day to day lives.

However, for shopping and entertainment requirements that could not be met in Darley, the "mecca" of Matlock attracted folk

Harvest time at Burley Fields Farm, 1911.
Maud Ford and Annie Crowder.

to its greater range of shops, its market and the new moving picture shows at "The Picture Palace" on Dale Road. The appeal of the hydros over the years had attracted a large number of visitors "in the season" and their demands for a higher quality of shops had resulted in an improvement in shopping facilities, whether in Dale Road or around Crown Square.

To the Darley Dale men about to be plucked from their rural backwater and thrust into the maelstrom of a bloody world conflict, the Matlock of 1913 seemed a bustling, thriving town. The most obvious sign of this to any visitor was the busy use of the Bank Road cable tramway system from Crown Square to its terminus above Smedley Street. For a small English town, Matlock's tramway system certainly gave it a mid-European feel and appearance.

Ceremony in Crown Square marking the opening of the Matlock tramway and its presentation to the town by Sir George Newnes in 1898. It ran until 1927.

*Crown Square and tramway shelter c.1905. The shops on the immediate right
(barber's pole) were demolished in the 1920's to make way for the Park Head.*

Crown Square, tram and tram shelter, c.1920.

CROWN SQUARE & CABLE TRAM, MATLOCK.

Tram cars at Bank Road, Smedley Street junction, Matlock, c.1910.

Checking the track and mechanism of Matlock cable tramway in Crown Square, c.1910.

Crown Square, Matlock, c.1910.

Matlock, the English Switzerland Bank Road and cable railway.
This tramway is unique in being the steepest tramway in the world on a public
thoroughfare. The length is 880 yards and the steepest gradient 1 in 4. Built by Sir
George Newnes 1893, presented to the town 1898.

It was, however, with the sound of two gunshots ringing out in just such a provincial mid-European town that the fates of 63 Darley men were to be sealed and the lives of many others affected by hardship and sadness. The onset of the Great War on August 4th 1914 resulted in many young men from the parish being despatched far afield to France, Belgium, Gallipoli, Egypt and the Pacific Ocean. Sadly 63 of Darley Dale's men would eventually be listed on the war memorial in the Whitworth Institute grounds.

CHAPTER TWO

1914 – INTO THE MAELSTROM

The two shots fired by Gabriel Princip, from a distance of two feet, had found their targets. Blood was gushing from the Archduke's mouth over his green uniform. His wife was leaning on him, unconscious but with no visible wound. They were carried to a room in the nearby Government building in Sarajevo, next to the one in which the champagne was cooling for their lunch. A quarter of an hour later both were dead.

Their deaths triggered the march towards hostilities and it is true to say that enthusiasm for war was high amongst the populations of the belligerent countries. Throughout the European capitals, vast crowds swept into the streets, each voicing support for their country's hostile stance. The belief in a successful, brief but bloody war was held by all armies.

The assassinations had resulted in Austria presenting Serbia with impossible conditions to avoid annexation; Russia immediately mobilised in support of her fellow Slavs, Germany responded at once and France followed suit.

On Tuesday, 4th August, 4300 trains, decorated with flowers and tricolour flags, overflowed with a noisy, enthusiastic mass of young men in old-fashioned uniforms and resounded with an endless chanting of the "Marseillaise". The trains were carrying the French army towards the German army, which was moving to meet it in 11000 trains.

Hopes that Great Britain could somehow stay out of the conflict were dashed when, following the long prepared Schlieffen Plan, German forces entered neutral Belgium en route to northern France.

"There they are! Yes, there they are!" exclaimed the Belgian lieutenant. From the wooded height he had been able to make out the details of the grey uniforms of the lancers on the sunlit road to the east.

Tearing a page from his pocket book, he wrote, "Saw a troop of uhlans in direction of Remouchamps, 4th August, 2 o'clock."

"Pass me a pigeon," he ordered. The troopers watched the bird for a moment as it flew off.

From the slopes of the hill where they had halted, the Belgian army scouts had a daunting spectacle under their eyes; a nightmare-like swarming of men. Here and there, camp fires reddened. They counted six cavalry regiments, two infantry regiments, one infantry battalion, one cyclist battalion and some artillery. Before them was the 9th German Cavalry Division.

The days before war was declared by Britain had been the Bank Holiday weekend and Monday 3rd August was the day for a trip out. The weather was beautiful, with brilliant blue skies and a warm temperature, ideal for a visit to the seaside. Thousands flocked to the railway stations to catch special trains bound for the coast. However, Winston Churchill had mobilised the fleet and all excursion trains were taken over by naval reservists. London attractions, such as the Zoo, did a roaring trade, whilst in Darley Dale and the Matlocks the tourists flocked in their hundreds, but, for all, Armageddon was looming.

At 4p.m. the British Army was mobilised. Britain demanded that the German army be withdrawn from Belgium by midnight 5th August or a state of war would exist between the British Empire and Germany. The ultimatum was ignored and war was declared at 11p.m. The Great War had begun.

In British cities everywhere, excitement reigned. On 5th August 1914 the pride of London's famous streets poured into the recruiting offices at Great Scotland Yard and elsewhere. They had come from watching Surrey play Notts at the Oval. They were sunburnt from a weekend at Brighton. They had been learning to dance the tango. Some still carried the memories of the scene outside Buckingham Palace the previous night when they had sung "God Save the King". The prospects were dangerous but romantic ; the mood was confident.

In 1914, Britain was essentially a maritime power with only a small, if highly trained and professional army. Only 120,000 would initially make up the British Expeditionary Force that embarked for France, compared with some 4,000,000 Frenchmen and 4,500,000 Germans.

Lord Kitchener shocked a meeting of the War Council on August 6th by predicting a long war ; countering the popular cry of " It will be all over by Christmas". On August 7th Kitchener publicly called for 100,000 volunteers. By September 12th an amazing total of 480,000 men had enlisted as volunteers.

The majority were from urban areas where large numbers of workmates and neighbours joined together into the famous "Pals Battalions". In more scattered rural districts such as Darley Dale and South Darley, the rush to enlist was not quite so pronounced, but at various recruitment meetings the local dignitaries soon did their best to alter this situation.

In Buxton, on 4th August, the King's proclamation was posted and the town was alive with excitement on Wednesday. By 10a.m. many Territorials were at the Drill Hall, the building being lined with rifles and kit. The Yeomanry became more numerous around the Midland Station and baggage and saddles were piled on the platform. The Reserves departed, destined for the Front, and many an eye was dimmed as the 10-45a.m. train moved slowly away. At 11-25a.m. the Yeomanry departed by train with the strains of Rule Britannia ringing out, travelling to Bakewell, from which district they were to draw their supply of horses. The Territorials marched by road and camped at Ashford-in-the-Water before moving off to Chesterfield on Thursday.

Matlock and Wirksworth Territorials were suddenly ordered home on Monday 3rd August, when half way through their training at Hunmanby, on the Yorkshire coast, near Scarborough.

Monday 10th August saw 70 members of the High Peak Squadron of the Derbyshire Imperial Yeomanry leaving Bakewell at 9-30a.m. by road. Twenty others, without horses, left by train.

The previous Thursday had found the local Territorials (6th Battalion, Sherwood Foresters) leaving Bakewell in good order. The Foresters and Derbyshire Yeomanry had arrived in the town from the various districts and the town presented quite a military appearance. An open air service in Rutland Square at 8-30a.m. was held to send them off.

In front of a large crowd, a horseless landau had been drawn up facing Rutland Square and from here the Bishop of Derby conducted a stirring service. Bakewell Brass Band paraded the streets, together with

100 Territorials and some Boy Scouts. The troops filed up and headed by the brass band and scouts with drum and bugle band, set off on their long march to Chesterfield. The band dropped out at Castle Hill, but the scouts proceeded all the way.

Horses had been commandeered for the service of the Yeomanry. Many farmers brought in horses and these were chosen in the Rutland Hotel stable yard. On occasions the authorities commandeered horses attached to vehicles and the owners had to get home the best way they could. By the end of August Bakewell had received over 200 horses.

A meeting was held in Matlock Town Hall on Monday 24th August in an effort to provide its quota to Lord Kitchener's Army of 100,000, the main speaker being Mr. F.C. Arkwright. He made an urgent appeal for the young men to show their patriotism and come forward like men to serve their country and back up their cause. He asked for Matlock not to disgrace itself.

The Chairman then appealed for recruits. Immediately a young man from the rear of the hall walked to the front and signed on amidst a scene of great cheering. In a moment or two a score were at the enlistment table. Another batch of young men went to the roll, and before the meeting had concluded the number had reached nearly fifty. These were placed two deep on the platform and accorded ringing cheers from the audience. Arrangements were then made for the whole of the enlisted men to join the 9-30a.m. train from Matlock and Mr. Arkwright volunteered to go with them to Derby barracks and to pay all expenses.

Monday 31st August 1914 saw a meeting being held at the Whitworth Institute, addressed again by F.C. Arkwright, when 34 volunteered as recruits and 30 of these passed the medical examination the following day. Five men had enlisted in the Hussars and all went from Darley Station on the 2nd September. At the last moment, as the train began to pull away from the platform, they were joined by young Sam Riley, the Darley Bridge fishmonger's son, who had dashed across the Cartledge and had to be pulled through the open carriage window.

By September 12th 1914 a Rifle Club had been formed at Darley Dale. Dr. Cecil Sharpe was President, Dr. Wills Captain and Charles Dawson, managing director Stancliffe Estates Company Limited, volunteered to be their instructor. The Trustees of the Whitworth Institute had generously granted the use of the Pavilion (the Tea Room) in the grounds for an indoor rifle range and an age limit of 16 years was imposed. By November, three guns had arrived for use, and, with a membership of 40, a miniature range was set up.

However, it was still believed in October 1914 that not enough volunteers had come forward in Darley, for a recruitment meeting was held at the Whitworth Institute on Friday 23rd October, before a large and enthusiastic audience. Mr. F.B. Wildgoose presided, with Mr. F.C. Arkwright, Colonel H. Brooke-Taylor and Mr. Charles White being prominent amongst the speakers.

Mr. Arkwright was reported to have given another stirring speech, making a "splendid appeal" for patriotism amongst the young men of the district. "The sons would be able to point the finger of pride at their father, if his name was on the Roll of Honour for taking part in so great a

Band of Volunteers leaving Darley Station to enlist at Derby on 2nd September 1914, after the August recruitment meeting.
X, Jack Allwood, X George Carter, X John Wilson, Jack Siddall, X X X, X, X.
Fred Pearson, X X X X X George Cook Alf Holland.
X, X X X Joe Derbyshire, Reg Wagstaffe.

Matlock 'Patriots' leaving Matlock Station, September 1914.
C, Crowder, H. Holmes and Stanley Cocking, off to join the Colours.

Matlock Rifle Club out practising October 1914.

crisis such as they were now engaged in". By November 1914 Darley had responded well to the plea for volunteers, with men such as Fred Pearson, John Wilson, Jack Allsop, Horace Lowe, John Siddall, George Holland and many others joining the Colours.

Meanwhile, the British Expeditionary Force had promptly crossed the Channel and moved into Belgium. Near Mons the British were struck by the full weight of the aggressive First German Army Group. Outnumbered, the British fought back stoutly, their fire discipline taking heavy toll of the close German formations, but they were forced back onto a long retreat during August.

At the Battle of the Marne, September 5th to the 10th, the German advance was brought to a halt, and then turned back, with the B.E.F., severely mauled but showing great powers of recuperation, playing a vital role. Now came the "Race to the sea", between September 15th and November 24th, as each side tried to outflank the other in a bid to take the Channel ports.

The final action of the "Race to the sea" was the bloody First Battle of Ypres, October 30th to November 24th (there would be three further battles here), in which the B.E.F. was nearly wiped out in a successful, gallant defence against a heavily reinforced German drive that was expected by them to capture the Channel ports.

It was early in November, in the desperate fighting S.E. of Ypres, that South Darley soldier, Grenadier Guardsman, William Allen, had been wounded and evacuated to Boulogne Hospital, where he died on 30th November, aged 18 years (see "A Derbyshire Parish at War – South Darley and the Great War 1914-1919") .

Throughout December 1914 an Allied offensive beat unsuccessfully for ten bloody days against the rapidly growing German system of field fortifications. The era of stabilised trench warfare from the North Sea to the Swiss border had begun: the spade, the machine gun, and barbed wire ringing down the curtain on manoeuvre.

However, it was during this period, in November, that Darley Dale received news of its first casualty, not on these battlefields of the Marne or Flanders Field, but far away in the vast open spaces of the Pacific Ocean:

WILLIAM WILEMAN HART, Musician (RMB/1681), Royal Marines Band on H.M.S. "Monmouth" Royal Navy.

(Died on Sunday 1st November 1914, aged 19 years.)

William was the son of William and Rebecca Hart of Meadow House, Darley Dale, although he had been born and lived for a number of years at Burton-on-Trent. Musically gifted, he had joined the Royal Navy before war started and found himself stationed in the Pacific Ocean when war was declared.

His ship, the armoured cruiser H.M.S. "Monmouth", was lost at the Battle of Coronel, off the coast of Chile on November 1st 1914.

This unlikely location for a sea battle between two European nations came about as a direct result of their Empire building rivalry. The Germans had built up a considerable number of possessions in the Pacific prior to 1914 and from its Chinese base at Tsingtao the East Asiatic Squadron, under the command of Admiral Von Spee, patrolled the German Pacific "Empire".

H.M.S. 'Monmouth'.

With the outbreak of war this squadron dispersed, with the light cruiser "Emden" causing chaos in the Bay of Bengal, while the other ships, "Scharnhorst", "Gneisenau", "Nurnberg" and "Leipzig", vanished into the Pacific. Eventually it became clear that the squadron was heading for the Atlantic via Cape Horn, and Britain feared supplies to Britain from Argentina could be cut off. The East Asiatic Squadron had to be stopped but the ships available to do it were not "up to the job".

The armoured cruisers "Monmouth" (with Wileman Hart and a young stoker from Matlock

Bath, Charles Gregory, on board) and "The Good Hope", together with the light cruiser H.M.S. "Glasgow" and armoured merchant cruiser "Otranto" were too lightly gunned to take on the modern German squadron. However, the Commander, Rear-Admiral Cradock, felt he had no option and attacked at 6-18p.m., to the cheers of his 2000 men.

Within an hour "The Good Hope" and "Monmouth" were mangled wrecks of metal, burning from bow to stern, and out of action. Night fall might have meant escape but the fires on "Monmouth" made her an easy target. To compound her misfortune the moon was now

Able Seaman Charles Gregory of Matlock Bath, lost on H.M.S. 'Monmouth' with R.M. William Wileman Hart, November 1914.

shining brightly and the "Nurnberg" caught her trying to limp away.

"Nurnberg's" captain, Schonberg, trained his searchlights on the defiant white ensign, hoping for surrender. None came. He had no option but to open fire on the "Monmouth". Her crew of mainly volunteer trawler men and coast guards from Scotland, young cadets fresh from Dartmouth and Royal Marines, were all lost and the Germans had suffered just two wounded.

The German triumph was short lived. Admiral Von Spee's squadron was to be destroyed a month later off the Falkland Islands by a powerful British force. Von Spee, planning to run into Port Stanley to raid the British wireless and coaling stations, discovered the British squadron there, refuelling. The surprised Germans took to their heels, and the British, in hot pursuit, destroyed the German ships at long range. Of the five German ships, only the "Dresden" escaped. 2200 German sailors and their admiral were lost. The "Monmouth" was avenged.

William Wileman Hart and Charles Gregory's names are to be found on Panel 6 of the Portsmouth Naval Memorial, on Southsea Common, commemorating Royal Naval personnel who have no known grave.

As 1914 drew to a close and Darley Dale mourned the loss of Wileman Hart, the enormity of the conflict became apparent to everyone as casualty lists were posted. By this time, operations on the Western Front had already cost the Allies nearly one million casualties, with German losses almost as great. The Germans had not won a quick victory and now the Western Front would settle down to four years of bloody attrition. Darley Dale would not be spared.

CHAPTER THREE

1915 – HOPES ARE DASHED

The realities of war in 1914 had dispelled all thoughts of an early end to the conflict. The eyes of the British public had been rudely opened by the widening of the conflict to new theatres of war and by the vast casualties resulting from the early campaigns. Nevertheless, the feeling persisted that once Kitchener's New Army was ready in 1915, the combined efforts of the Allies would then soon defeat the enemy.

In Darley, meanwhile, the reality of war was soon being absorbed when the Whitworth Institute and grounds were closed to the public and by December 1914 a Red Cross Hospital had been set up on the premises. The local paper, "Matlock Guardian and List of Visitors" of November 28th 1914 reported that "at the beginning of the war the Trustees of the Whitworth Institute decided to offer some portion of the building as a hospital for the care of wounded men from the Front".

*The swimming pool room had been converted into a ward for
the Whitworth Institute Red Cross Hospital 1914-1919.*

Doctors and nurses on the terrace, Whitworth Institute Red Cross Hospital 1914-1919.

A Voluntary Aid Detachment (VAD) of nurses under the Red Cross Society, had been established some 18 months, with well attended courses of lectures and practice demonstrations conducted by Dr. Cecil Sharpe of the Red House. A complete women's VAD unit (including Darley women Agnes Knifton, Lottie Charlesworth, Jessie Hayes and Lucy Hayes) had been enrolled, with Dr. Sharpe being the Commandant, Miss Pringle the Lady Superintendent and Miss Louise Dawson the Quartermaster. Generous local support in money and kind was freely promised. A similar VAD unit at Matlock, under the direction of Dr. Marie Orme, joined forces with Darley, so that by working together, a large number of beds could be provided at the Institute.

The Whitworth Trustees had given over the whole of the large swimming bath room and had laid a wooden floor. The whole of the interior had been thoroughly cleaned and painted, and it made a splendid hospital ward some 70 feet by 30 feet. The use of the hot baths was also given, together with a dining room and kitchen accommodation. The Museum Room also provided another ward for those soldiers who were convalescent.

20 beds were the gift of residents in Darley Dale and Matlock and by 21st November 1914 the War Office had approved of the Whitworth Institute to serve as an Auxiliary Home Hospital under the Northern Command. The first arrival of wounded soldiers was on the 10th May 1915 from Derby Infirmary, with 21 attending. Only two were serious surgical cases, with others having suffered frost bite, shots in the arms

and legs, whilst some were convalescent. During the next six months 109 patients were treated. The sight of these casualties was an ever present reminder to Darley people that war demands its victims.

A Young Mens Christian Association (YMCA) hut was erected in the corner of the field where nowadays Hibbard's chemist shop stands, at the junction of Chesterfield Road and the A6. The YMCA hut was for the use of wounded soldiers and light refreshments and games were provided.

Meanwhile, between February and June 1915 some 3000 soldiers were in the Darley district, with the vast majority being Royal Army Service Corps personnel, billeted in Bell tents on the large field that now houses Darley Telephone Exchange and villas near Broadwalk, and in fields near Darley Hall. The High Peak News of March 13th 1915 commented, "The advent of a large body of soldiers at Darley caused a pleasurable commotion. The camp of the R.A.S.C. near Darley Hall and the men billeted at the Institute numbered quite a small army. The men in camp drew most attention and the streets were mostly full of residents having a look at our brave defenders". This large influx resulted in a problem for the local councillors, for they had to lay on four water points

Royal Army Service Corps camp at Darley Dale, 1915.
During the Great War, it was located in the fields now housing the telephone exchange,
Parkway and John Turner housing development. It was particularly active
from January to June 1915.

and underground pipes. The Council was worried that the Government or War Office should be made to foot the bill.

Most of these troops were destined for service overseas and 1915 saw continued British involvement on the Western Front and in other theatres of war. Turkey's entrance into the war on Germany's side in October 1914 had changed the war's complexion. Russia, already shaken by the reverses of 1914, was now virtually cut off from Franco-British war supplies. In an attempt to help Russia, a naval expedition was mounted to clear the Dardanelles for Russian ships in the Black Sea. When this venture stalled, an attack was planned on a little known peninsula called Gallipoli.

On the Western Front during 1915 British casualties mounted as attacks were launched in France against the Germans at Neuve Chapelle (March), Festubert (May to June) and Loos (September to October) and by the Germans during the 2nd Battle of Ypres in Belgium (April to May). This latter assault saw poison gas being used by the Germans for the first time in the West.

Increase of lethal fire power had given the advantage to the defence, for a continuous battle line prevented classical offensive manoeuvres. The Germans, recognising the change long before the Allies, had adopted an elastic defence, in two or more lines, highly organised with entrenchments and barbed wire, heavy in machine guns and supported by artillery. Assaulting troops broke through the first line only to be decimated by the fire from the succeeding lines.

As a consequence of these facts we find that the number of Darley men who fell on the battlefield or died from wounds received throughout 1915, would gradually mount to a total of 13, with the first fatality being:

PRIVATE GEORGE WILLIAM SKINNER,
No. 9873, 2nd Battalion East Lancashire Regiment.
(Died Sunday 14th March 1915, aged 27 years.)

George Skinner had lived for much of his life at No. 27 Midland Cottages, Chatsworth Road, the home of his parents, William Skinner, a railway foreman, and mother Annie. At the age of 14 years George was earning a living as an errand boy at a stone yard but by 1914 he was living in Hampshire, at Hurstbourne Tarrant.

He came home to enlist at Chesterfield in 1914 and joined the East Lancashire Regiment. By February 1915, George was with his Battalion in the vicinity of Neuve Chapelle and preparing for the forthcoming British assault set for the 10th March..

The attack was both original and well thought out. After an intense bombardment of only 35 minutes duration on a 2000 yards frontage, the artillery lengthened their range and prevented German reinforcements reaching their battered trenches, which were rapidly overrun by the British infantry.

With complete surprise being attained, most of the first positions were captured. However, when the frontage was extended, the artillery support proved inadequate, whilst too long a pause occurred, giving the Germans five clear hours to organise fresh resistance. The narrowness of the attack sector made the breach more easy for the defenders to close, which they did by the 13th March. Then, too late, General Haig ordered the attack to be pressed "regardless of loss"

Heavy loss there certainly was and on the 14th March George Skinner lost his life "pressing on regardless".

He is buried in grave V11. B. 9 at Vieille-Chapelle New Military Cemetery, Lacoutive, N.E. of Bethune.

At a memorial service held on the 16th May in Rowsley Parish Church, the vicar alluded to "the noble and heroic way this son of England had laid down his life for his country's honour".

PRIVATE GEORGE HULLEY,
No. 8698, 2nd Battalion Grenadier Guards.
(Died on Saturday 10th April 1915, aged 34 years.)

George and his brother Arthur were born at Beeley, where their father Benjamin worked on the Chatsworth Estate as a carter. Benjamin had married a Whitby girl and afterwards they travelled home from the Yorkshire coast to Beeley in his horse and cart, camping by the roadside at night. By the time of George's death in 1915, his mother had already passed away.

Some years before the war began George left Beeley to live at Northwood, for he had married and settled with his wife, Mary Emily, in their new home, where they cared for their three young daughters. Unhappily, Mary died and George was left to raise the young family.

Earlier in his life, he had served in the Boer War and used to say that the most thrilling experience was the cavalry charge on the enemy. On several occasions he had his horse shot from under him. At the conclusion of the South African War the High Peak News reported that he was awarded the Victoria medal with two bars.

Private George Hulley

For the following nine years he was a Reservist and then signed on for another four years. He was summoned to join the Colours on the outbreak of the Great War and his time was spent in training recruits for Lord Kitchener's New Army. George was a born soldier and could not be satisfied till he was called to the Front.

On January 4th 1915 he crossed the English Channel with the 2nd Battalion, Grenadier Guards and by the end of the first week of the New Year was in the trenches. George had a number of hair breadth escapes including his hat strap, on the top of his head, being cut in two by a bullet, and seeing men to the left and right of him being killed whilst he remained unscathed.

Unfortunately, news came to his father Benjamin that the end came on the 10th April 1915. After having passed through untouched all the fierce fighting in March around Neuve Chapelle, he was killed in action and buried in grave I. F. 18 in the Guards Cemetery, Windy Corner, Guinchy, France, east of Bethune.

A week after his death the vicar of Beeley conducted a very impressive memorial service on Sunday evening. George had been a chorister in the parish church, where for so many years his father had been clerk and sexton.

Sadly, his death left three little girls orphaned and they were brought up by George's sister, Mrs. Wall, and her husband Tom.

Within two months of George Hulley's death, three more Darley parishioners had lost their lives fighting desperately to stem the German assault on the Ypres Salient during the 2nd Battle of Ypres.

PRIVATE SYDNEY ALFRED SMITH,
No G/6552 3rd Battalion Middlesex Regiment.
(Died on Tuesday 11th May 1915, aged 17 years.)

Sydney was one of the eight children of Councillor Joseph Smith and wife Hannah. In 1902 Hannah died, aged 35 years, and Joseph, a clerk on the railway at Derby, married Lydia Mary Taylor and they lived at The Myrtles, Hackney Road. Sydney had a number of brothers, including Fred, who arrived in England in November 1915 with a Canadian contingent, after joining up in Toronto when war broke out.

Private Sydney Smith.

Sydney had been born in July 1897 and enlisted on December 5th 1914, after lying about his age. He was sent into the trenches in France by February 25th 1915, a record achievement for a volunteer from Darley. He joined the 3rd Battalion of the Middlesex Regiment and was wounded on May 1st at 7-30p.m. at Zonnebeke, between St. Julian and Ypres, in Belgium, while delivering a counter attack on the enemy during the 2nd Battle of Ypres.

He was in the first line of trenches with his regiment, known as "The Die-Hards". The Germans got the range of their trenches and started shelling them. The first two shells went clean over their heads, but the third fell right amongst the men. There were over ten of them laid out, and Sydney got the full force of the blast. He was picked up eventually and carried to the dressing station and then removed to No. 2 Stationary

Hospital at Boulogne, from which a letter was sent to his parents saying he was lying wounded in many places.

Sydney next came home from France in the hospital ship "Valdavia" and landed at Southampton, from which place he was taken to the Bagthorpe Hospital, Nottingham. Notice came that he was dangerously ill and he died on the 11th May, ten days after receiving terrible wounds (thirteen in all down his left side).

On Thursday the body was brought by rail to Matlock Station and thence to the home of Sydney. The coffin was securely sealed in order that the family would not see his wounds. The funeral in St. Giles Church, Matlock, was at 2-30p.m. on Friday, but so great was the procession that it was some time after that hour before the cortege reached the church, after processing through Hackney, Matlock Bank, Matlock Green and Matlock Town. Business premises suspended work and at private houses the blinds were drawn. Hundreds of people lined the route.

Men and officers from the Royal Army Service Corps' tented

Funeral procession of Private Sydney Smith passes along Smedley Street on 14th May 1915, bound for St. Giles Church.

encampment at Darley Dale sent a contingent of 100 in uniform to form a guard. Policemen led the cortege, followed by the Matlock United Prize Band playing "Dead March" in Saul, with their drum covered in black. Next came the firing party of the R.A.S.C., bearing their guns reversed. The coffin followed on a gun carriage drawn by two horses and was covered in wreaths, whilst the coffin was draped in the Union Jack. Behind were Matlock Boy Scouts and the mourning coaches. The main party of the R.A.S.C. brought up the rear. At least 1000 sympathisers stood near the church at Starkholmes.

Five months later, in October 1915, Sydney's brother, Private Edward Henry Smith, of the 3rd Battalion Grenadier Guards was wounded, but thankfully he made a good recovery.

PRIVATE GEORGE THOMPSON,
No. 1514, 6th Battalion, Sherwood Foresters.
(*Died on Wednesday 12th May 1915, aged 21 years.*)

George was a single man living at his father's house at Needham Terrace, Upper Hackney, when he enlisted at Matlock in 1914. His father, George senior, had worked as an electrician at Smedley's Hydro and for William Twigg, his brother Matthew was a porter at Matlock Station, whilst George himself was an under-shunter at the Matlock Midlands Goods Yard.

Something of a dare-devil, George owned a motor bike and on one occasion crashed it whilst descending Cromford Hill. He lay underneath the wall until next

Private George Thompson.

morning but survived to tell the tale. He was not to be so fortunate when he went off to fight in the Great War.

Having volunteered for action he was posted to the Sherwood Foresters. In the Spring of 1915 George was with the 6th Battalion in the Ypres Salient, in readiness for the commencement of an offensive.

Unfortunately these preparations were spoiled by a surprise German attack on April 22nd, preceded by their use of chlorine gas for the first time in the west. The 2nd Battle of Ypres had begun.

During April and early May the Battalion spent much time in the forward trenches at Kemmel, with periods of relief. On the 9th May they returned to the trenches for four days after three days of rest. The trenches were not very good and on the 10th May one officer and other rank were killed, whilst 25 were wounded, including George.

News arrived at the family home that he had been wounded at the Front. The previous day his parents had attended the military funeral of George' friend, Sydney Alfred Smith, who had enlisted at the same time as George, and had died from wounds received whilst fighting in the same battle. They had provided a floral tribute.

Hardly had the news of George's wounding been circulated when sad tidings came from the War Office on Sunday morning to say he was dead and buried, two days after being wounded. He had received these wounds from shrapnel and was buried in a soldiers' cemetery near the trenches.

Sadly, after the deceased had been interred at the Front, a letter – a last letter – came to his parents. This was written before he was wounded and in it he stated they were suffering from the gas used by the Germans and he went on to ask his brother to put it in the papers that they could do with some respirators. George added that he was writing his letter in a dug-out with shells flying around him.

Private George Thompson is buried in grave E. 31 at Kemmel Chateau Military Cemetery, 8 kilometres south of Ypres.

PRIVATE WALTER HOUGHTON,
No. 2051, 6th Battalion, Sherwood Foresters.
(Died on Monday 7th June 1915, aged 26 years.)

Walter Houghton was born at Hognaston but came to live with his family at Hackney. His father worked for John William Wildgoose at Matlock and Walter was a plate layer on the Midland Railway.

Walter, a single man, enlisted at Matlock early in the war and two other brothers, Bert and Leonard were also serving in the forces. He saw much action, for, by April 1915, he was serving in the Ypres Salient at the time of the 2nd Battle of Ypres (April 22nd to May 25th). Walter had spent his last birthday in the trenches.

Two German corps drove through two terrorised French divisions, after the use against them of chlorine gas, and bit deeply into British lines, creating a wide gap. The Germans, however, had made no preparations to exploit such a breakthrough and had few reserves available because of their build up in the east, against Russia. Local counter-attacks by the British finally stemmed the German advance after bitter fighting. German losses were some 35,000 men; the British lost 60,000. On the last day of the battle, the Sherwood Foresters were in the trenches and lost four killed and 22 wounded.

By June, therefore, there was some respite, but there was always the ever constant danger of shelling. On the 3rd June the Battalion returned to the trenches for five days in the Kemmel sector. During this period three men were killed and one officer and eight other ranks wounded. One of those who was killed was Walter Houghton, of Hackney. One day later they were relieved by the 5th Battalion and were able to bivouac. But for Walter, it was too late.

His resting place is grave D. 28 in Kemmel Military Cemetery, south of Ypres. Sadly for his parents, brother Bertram was to be killed two years later in the same vicinity, and another brother, Leonard, also paid the supreme sacrifice. This devastating death rate within one family was unfortunately not uncommon during the Great War.

LANCE CORPORAL FREDERICK SAMUEL FENTEM, No. 10227, 1st Battalion ("A" Company) Sherwood Foresters.
(Died on Saturday 19th June 1915, in Northern France, aged 26 years.)

Fred Fentem was the youngest son of Thomas and Elizabeth Fentem, from Darley Hillside, one of ten children in the family. His father worked on the staff of Smedley's Hydro. Fred was in the regular army with the 1st Sherwood Foresters and had served for some years. Admired as a splendid soldier, he had served in India five years and two in Ireland and finished his service in October 1914.

Fred came home but was only there for four days when he was recalled and he embarked with the Battalion for France on the 4th November 1914. During March 1915 the Battalion became involved heavily in the Battle of Neuve Chapelle, receiving many casualties. By 8th May they again played their part in some very fierce and costly fighting when they went over the parapets south of Rue Petillon and came under severe machine gun fire. The wire had not been breached by the bombardment so they had to fall back. Many casualties were sustained in the German shelling.

The Battalion was relieved but in this fighting, the prelude to the Battle of Festubert, casualties had been high. June passed uneventfully but it is ironic that after such bloody action in the previous three months, through which Fred Fentem came out unscathed, he should die during the everyday shelling of opposition trenches. He was killed near La Gorgue, between Bethune and Armentieres.

A letter arrived with news of his death from one of his colleagues in France. It reads : "Dear Mrs. Fentem, I sadly write you the most grievous news, that of your son's death. He was killed outright by a shell along with two more poor souls. It happened about 5 o'clock p.m. on Saturday 19th June. The whole of the Company send you their deepest sympathy in the loss of your beloved one, for he was liked by us all. Yours sincerely, Lance Corporal Lee."

Frederick Fentem was buried in Neuve Chapelle British Military Cemetery, France, in grave E. 2

Meanwhile, by July in the Ypres Salient, Belgium, the 2nd Battle of Ypres had drawn to an end, but in the routine day to day shelling and sniping of trench warfare, casualties still mounted and another Darley soldier was to pay with his life.

PRIVATE HORACE WILMOT LOWE,
No. 3117, 6th Battalion Sherwood Foresters.
(*Died on Sunday 4th July 1915, aged 19 years.*)

Born at Chesterfield, Horace was the son of Mrs. Elizabeth A. Lowe, a widow, living at Knabb House, Ladygrove, Two Dales, from where she sold sweets and other items. Before enlisting in October 1914 he had taken a keen interest in the Boy Scout movement and was a member of the Matlock Troop. He had been encouraged to volunteer to fight when he was amongst the enthusiastic crowd at the recruitment meeting at the Whitworth Institute on Friday 23rd October.

Private Horace Lowe.

After his training in the 6th Battalion he left Luton on Thursday night, 24th June and Southampton on Saturday 26th, reaching his Battalion at Ypres on Sunday 27th. On the following Sunday, after only one week at the Front Line, he was killed.

He had missed the action during the 2nd Battle of Ypres, when we have already seen that the British lost 60,000 men. Local counter-attacks by the British 2nd Army finally stemmed the German advance after bitter fighting. It was to be a relatively quieter front line that Horace Lowe arrived at on Sunday 27th June.

Whilst settling into his positions, he wrote a last letter home to his mother, which she only received after his death was notified. It reads: "My dear mother, will you please send me a parcel of tea and sugar. We are quite all right if we had a little more. I will write you as fast as I can. We are going into the trenches shortly. God speed us. We shall be quite safe. Fear God, we shall be all right. We are in sound of the guns now. This is a nice country but I would sooner have our own. Give my love to sister Edie. I will write her soon. I will close now. God be with you till we meet again. Your loving son, Horace."

By the 28th June they were resting at a farm between Poperinghe and Westoutre, with Horace having just arrived from England with 95 other men. They had moved into forward positions at Ypres on the 4th July. On that day a working party of 200 men under Captain Heathcote was badly shelled whilst returning from their duties, with nine killed and 21 wounded. One of those killed on this day of routine maintenance on front line duty was Horace.

He is buried in grave IV. B. 64 at Bedford House Cemetery, just south of Ypres.

A similar fate was to greet a young Darley Methodist preacher whilst serving on a sector of the Western Front in France, though on this occasion it was to be a sniper's bullet that would find its target.

PRIVATE JOHN (JACK) WILLIAM ALLSOP, No. 13976, 1st Battalion Sherwood Foresters.
(*Died on Thursday 5th August 1915, aged 25 years.*)

Private John (Jack) Allsop.

Born at Ashbourne, but living at Two Dales, Jack was a local preacher on the plan of the Matlock Wesleyan Circuit and was also Assistant Superintendent of Darley Dale Wesleyan Sunday School. Before joining the army he worked for Tony Walton, the Darley miller from Warney Corn Mill, delivering flour on a horse and dray.

Jack Allsop married Charles and Fred Pearson's cousin, Beatrice Pearson of Two Dales, but she died four years before the war, after the birth of their daughter. After the death of his wife, Jack lodged with relations at Ryecroft, Two Dales.

He joined the army on the 2nd September 1914 and went to France on February 1st 1915, in "A" Company, in preparation for the Battle of Neuve Chapelle. Jack would have attended the recruitment meeting at the Whitworth Institute on Monday 31st August 1914 but for the fact that he was still working that evening, delivering corn to the distant parts of the district. However, he registered on the roll the following day and on Wednesday 2nd September he was on the platform at Darley Station with other volunteers, such as John Wilson, Fred Pearson and George Pratley, to be seen off to Derby. Jack was only home once after he enlisted, and with his death he left a young daughter to be brought up by relatives.

The 1st Battalion, with Jack Allsop to the fore, had taken part in desperate fighting at the Battle of Neuve Chapelle on 10th March 1915, resulting in heavy casualties. In early May they were called upon to play their part in some especially fierce fighting N.W. of Fromelles. Jack Allsop came out of these actions unscathed.

Between June and August the 1st Battalion was not involved in any stirring events. However, it was during this relatively quiet period of intermittent shelling and sniping by both sides that Jack was to meet his death, serving in the trenches near Rouge De Bout, north of Neuve Chapelle.

A letter from his pal, Fred Pearson, arrived at Ryecroft, saying that he was writing in his dug-out in the trenches. "Jack got killed on Thursday afternoon about 5p.m.. He was shooting at the Germans when a bullet hit him in the head. He only lived a few minutes and died on the way to hospital". Fred had been fetched to the spot when his best friend was shot.

Jack Allsop was 25 years of age and left a four year old daughter, who was living with his mother at Ashover. On Sunday 5th September a crowded memorial service in honour of the popular local preacher was held at Darley Dale Wesleyan Chapel and particular mention was made during the address to Jack Allsop's great Christian character.

He is buried in the Rue-Petillon Military Cemetery at Fleurbaix, S.W. of Armentieres, in grave I.D. 23.

PRIVATE ARTHUR ATTWOOD,
No. G/7559, 3rd Battalion Middlesex Regiment.
(*Died on Thursday 30th September 1915, aged 20 years.*)

Arthur Attwood had been born at Peak Forest but had come with his parents, James and Mary, to live at No. 3, Hazel View, Two Dales. He enlisted at Coventry and became a member of the 3rd Battalion, Middlesex Regiment, in late 1914.

In September 1915 the British planned an assault on German positions near the village of Loos, in the coal mining region between Arras and Lens. The ground was unfavourable, being bare and open, and swept by machine gun and rifle fire from the German trenches and numerous fortified villages behind them. Many of those taking part on the British side were untried members of Kitchener's New Army.

The Battle of Loos opened on 25th September with an artillery bombardment and the release of chlorine gas. Unfortunately for the British, the gas drifted back into sections of the advancing troops, killing their own men.

When gaps did appear in the German defences, the British reserves were held too far back and could not exploit the opportunity. By the 26th September the Middlesex Regiment was marching across country in the dark and rain. They were launched to attack against a strong second line of defence, covered by a thick wire entanglement. The attack broke down and survivors turned and flowed back.

Meantime, German counter-attacks were multiplying dangerously, especially on the flanks, and during one such attack, on the 30th September, Arthur Attwood was killed. 60,000 casualties were sustained by the British, whereas the German loss was barely 20,000, despite their costly counter-attacks.

Arthur's body was never recovered and he is commemorated on Panel 99 to 101, the Loos Memorial, just N.W. of Lens.

Up to this stage of the fighting during 1915 all of Darley's casualties had resulted from actions taking place on the Western Front. It was now to be on a more distant battlefield, at Gallipoli, in fighting against the Turkish forces, that the remaining four fatalities of 1915 were to occur.

LANCE CORPORAL JOSEPH BARBER,
No. 12793, 9th Battalion Sherwood Foresters.
(Died on Monday 9th August 1915, aged 22 years.)

Joseph's father, Joseph senior, a signal man at Rowsley Station, his mother Sarah and the family, eventually lived at the old station master's house at the start of Chatsworth Road. Joseph junior had been born in Marple, Cheshire, before his father took up his position at Rowsley.

After leaving school he became a book stall clerk at Rowsley Station and afterwards transferred to Messrs Smith's book stall at Derby Station. He took a keen interest and pride in the formation of the Rowsley Troop of Boy Scouts and was one of the first to join. When war broke out he promptly offered his services, enlisting at Derby.

PRIVATE GEORGE DERBYSHIRE,
No. 23663, 9th Battalion Sherwood Foresters.
(Died on Monday 18th October 1915, aged 21 years.)

Private George Derbyshire, 9th Battalion, Sherwood Foresters.

George was the son of Frederick and Ellen Derbyshire, of Cross Green, and worked locally in the stone yard of Messrs. Hodson at Darley Dale Station, as well as Stancliffe Stone Yard. A keen footballer and member of the Wensley Wuffits when they won the Fengle Cup in 1914, George Derbyshire responded to Kitchener's call for volunteers in 1914, and he enlisted at Buxton into the 9th Battalion, a battalion raised specifically for service overseas. He was joined by Joseph Barber and Godfrey (Goff) Taylor, from Darley and South Darley respectively. Of these three, only Goff Taylor was to survive.

By April 1915 the Foresters were part of the 11th Division of Kitchener's New Army. They were now ready to take their place in the eight month campaign in Gallipoli. The deadlock on the Western Front had prompted attempts to attack Germany and her allies in other theatres of war. An assault on the Gallipoli peninsula was now attempted by landing a large force of troops, in order to force Turkey out of the war and open the supply route to Russia through the Dardanelles and Black Sea.

The landings on the 25th April had not gone very well and progress was limited. Demands were made in Britain for some of Kitchener's New Army to be sent to Gallipoli, and so it was that Lance Corporal

Barber and Private Derbyshire sailed from Bristol on the "Empress of Britain" on July 1st.

Stopping en route at Malta and Alexandria, there followed a pleasant crossing of the Aegean Sea to Mudros Bay on Lemnos, a Greek island off the Gallipoli peninsula, which was the Allied base for the whole operation.

On the 20th July Joseph and George landed at Cape Helles, to find the British Army in a state of complete exhaustion and they were withdrawn to Lemnos to prepare for a new attack on the peninsula.

The landings took place north of Suvla Bay on August 6th but little headway was made in the scorching heat and against fierce resistance by the Turkish soldiers. The vegetation was tinder dry and when, on August 9th the Royal Navy shelled the intervening ground, a series of fires were started.

At dawn on August 9th, orders were received to move forward. After advancing about 1000 yards the Battalion encountered heavy fire and suffered many casualties. Eventually the advance was held up on the right and in the centre near the orchard at Hetman Char. The majority of officers had been casualties by 7a.m. However, the Battalion held on to the line until 6p.m., when it withdrew 100 yards to the rear. At the end of the day there had been 19 officer casualties and about 300 men

It was during this bloody day of battle that Joseph Barber was killed, whilst attacking "Chocolate Hill". His body was never recovered and his name is now commemorated on the Helles Memorial, on panel 150 to 152. The memorial stands on the tip of the Gallipoli peninsula, taking the form of an obelisk 30 metres high that can be seen by ships passing through the Dardanelles.

On the 22nd August the remains of the Battalion, including George Derbyshire, were relieved and returned to the beach. At some point George was evacuated to Lemnos suffering from dysentery. He would have found a base camp overwhelmed by ill and injured men, with pitifully inadequate facilities. In August some 44,000 had been evacuated, of whom 13,000 were suffering from dysentery. Sadly, on the 18th October 1915, George succumbed to his illness and died. He was buried at Portianos Military Cemetery, Mudros Bay, Lemnos.

LANCE CORPORAL CLARENCE HUGH COATES,
No. 16694, 10th Battalion Hampshire Regiment,.
(*Died on Monday 4th October 1915, aged 20 years.*)

In October 1915 Tom Coates of "Riversdale", Matlock Bath received news that his younger son Clarence of the 10th Hampshire Regiment had died on the 4th October. He had been a clerk in the office of E.H. Bailey, miller, of Matlock, and for some years resided with his uncle and aunt, Mr. and Mrs. George Walker of Farley Hill (part of Darley parish). In Matlock, where he was perhaps better known than in Matlock Bath, he was a popular vocalist and assisted at many entertainments on behalf of charitable bodies.

Just before war broke out he was in the Derbyshire Yeomanry and the 6th Battalion Sherwood Foresters, and was very keen to participate in the action. As there appeared to be no sign of this, and with a desire to join the cavalry, he transferred to the 18th

*Lance Corporal
Clarence H. Coates*

Hussars. As it became rumoured, however, that cavalry would not be required for some time, he and two comrades transferred to the 10th Battalion, Hampshire Regiment.

It was not until August that his regiment were sent out to the Dardanelles, to take part in the action against the Turks at Gallipoli. The landings at Cape Helles on the 25th April had not gone well, especially for the raw volunteers from Australia and New Zealand. Progress was very limited in difficult terrain and against a determined foe. Demands were made in Britain for some of Kitchener's New Army to be sent to Gallipoli and so L/C Clarence Coates, like so many others, arrived at Mudros Bay. The whole operation was to be launched against a new target, just north of Suvla Bay, where the Anzac troops were pinned down. The raw troops lacked leadership and direction. The attacking force could not reach the high ground and fell back to the coast, with heavy casualties sustained. On August 21st another attack took place to attempt to gain the hilly ground inland but no real progress was made, with the British receiving 5000 casualties. The heat was terrific, water scarce and the sanitary conditions appalling. The area was described as a midden and smelt like an opened cemetery.

At some point in September, Clarence was evacuated to Lemnos suffering from dysentery and transported by ship to Alexandria in Egypt, where he was to succumb to his illness in the Hospital on Monday 4th October. Clarence Coates was buried in Alexandria (Chatby) Military and War Memorial Cemetery, in Egypt, in grave D. 79.

His brother, Richard Frederick Coates, also volunteered and entered the 9th Battalion Sherwood Foresters. He too was sent to the Dardanelles, where he survived the fighting and disease and served throughout the rest of the war in France and Belgium.

Clarence had been involved in the Scout movement before the war and after news of his death was received, there was a large scouts' memorial service held for Clarence at the parish church, Matlock Bath. His name is commemorated on both Matlock Bath and Darley war memorials.

PRIVATE ERNEST ARTHUR BODEN,
No. 19094, 1st Battalion King's Own Scottish Borderers.
(*Died on Monday 8th November 1915, aged 23 years.*)

Ernest was the son of Mr. and Mrs. Arthur Boden of Ivy Cottage, Darley Dale. Except for a short session as under-gardener at Ringwood Hall, Chesterfield, he had been employed for many years at Smart's Quarries, Matlock, where his father also worked. He was married and had a young son, Lewis, the family residing at Bonsall.

He had enlisted in April 1915 and had only been in the Dardanelles a fortnight when he was killed in action on the 8th November, fighting in "A" Company of the 87th Brigade and 29th Division at Gallipoli.

In his last letter home he writes,

"Dear mother, I write these few lines to let you know I am still "in the pink" and I hope you are all right. It is still very hot in the daytime but cold at night. Will you send me some writing paper and envelopes? It is not at all a bad place here, only you can't buy anything. Please send me a letter. I am still in good health and I hope you are all the same. Remember me to all at home. You will send me your photo as promised? From your loving son, Ernest."

It is sad to report that five letters had been sent to him, as well as a photograph but he had obviously not received them. It is poignant to know that only that week, last Tuesday, his parents and sister had also sent Ernest their Christmas parcel.

Private Ernest Boden.

The following Sunday, memorial services were held at St. Helen's, Darley Dale, and Bonsall Parish Church, for Ernest was well known and highly respected in both parishes. Shortly before the war broke out he had married Eva Sudbury of Bonsall and now she was left a widow with a young son.

Three-year-old Lewis Boden and mother, Eva Boden (nee Sudbury) at Puddle Lane, Bonsall, c.1917. He was the son of Private Ernest Boden.

125

At the service in Bonsall, the pulpit and reading desk were draped with Union Jacks and the flags of the Allies. A large Union Jack was suspended between the chancel arches.

Ernest is buried in grave II. A. 4 at Skew Bridge Cemetery, Turkey, N.E. of Seddulbahir.

Lewis was about three years of age when his father was killed and not too long afterwards his mother, Eva, remarried and left the village, with Lewis remaining to be brought up by his strict Sudbury grandparents in a farm cottage on Puddle Hill, Bonsall.

Gallipoli was finally evacuated on January 19th 1916, with the eight and a half month campaign costing the Allies some 215,000 men, of whom 145,000 were due to sickness, 50,000 from dysentery.

Meanwhile, appalling losses had been suffered on the Western Front during 1915 on both sides. 612,000 German, 1,292,000 French and 279,000 British lives were lost. The year ended with no appreciable shift in the hostile battle lines scarring the land from the North Sea to the Swiss Alps.

Both French and British had gained in experience, if not in wisdom, from the 1915 battles, but they had afforded the Germans still better experiences in the way to frustrate such attacks. In 1916 it was the Germans who profited heavily both by the offensive and the defensive lesson.

CHAPTER FOUR

1916 – A SAD AWAKENING

The year 1916 will always be remembered by the British and the French for its association with the names SOMME and VERDUN. The Battle of the Somme (July to November) and the Siege of Verdun (February to December) cost the British and French upwards of one million casualties and ground gained was minimal.

By the end of 1915 most people shared an optimistic view of how the war would progress, but this was shattered by the unfolding events of 1916. Ten Darley men were to die in battle during that year and eight of these lost their lives during the Battle of the Somme (five men fell within the first ten days of battle and three others in the later stages of the fighting).

Voluntary enlistment was no longer an option for Britain and even before the Somme, casualties on the Western Front demanded replacements that could only be filled by conscription. In January 1916, by the Military Service Act, the voluntary system was abandoned and compulsory enlistment came into being.

As a result of these actions, all families were now deeply affected by the Great War. In addition, casualties were increasing from bombing raids from Zeppelins, food stuffs were not so readily available and a movement of labour from the land and in service to munitions was mounting.

The Battle of the Somme was launched on June 24th by a stupendous 7-day artillery bombardment. On July 1st, 120,000 British infantry, following a rolling artillery barrage, dashed themselves against highly organised German defensive positions on a sixteen mile front. On that first day casualties were 50%, with 19,240 killed, 2152 missing presumed killed, 35,493 wounded and 585 taken prisoner. These were the worst casualties in the history of the British Army. Losses on that one day easily exceeded the battle casualties sustained in the Crimean, Boer and Korean Wars combined.

Despite the appalling losses of the first day, the British continued to forge ahead in a series of small, limited attacks. A British night attack on July 13th cracked the German second line. Cavalry rode into the gap but other reserves were slow to arrive and the horsemen were soon mowed down by machine guns, then engulfed by a German counter-attack. The Allied offensive deteriorated into a succession of minor but costly small actions.

General Haig launched another major offensive on September 15th, S.W. of Bapaume. Tanks had been secretly shipped to the front, and spearheaded the attack, but were too unreliable and few in numbers to gain a decisive victory. Substantial gains were made but a breakthrough eluded them. Nevertheless the British and French continued attacking, gaining small areas of ground through mid-November.

British losses in this campaign were 420,000; French, 195,000. German casualties, including many pre-war officers and N.C.O.'s, came to a shocking 650,000.

Of the five Darley Dale men who took part in the initial assault in July 1916, three were members of the same unit, the 6th Battalion, Sherwood Foresters.

PRIVATE WILLIAM CARTER,
No. 4465, 6th Battalion Sherwood Foresters.
(Died on Saturday 1st July 1916, aged 21 years.)

William Carter and his brother George lived with their parents, John Carter, a stone cutter, and Georgina Carter, at a cottage next to the Plough Inn, Two Dales. William also worked in the quarries, but by the start of the Great War, their father had died and the two sons were the "breadwinners".

Despite this, both enlisted early and George was wounded on March 10th 1915 during the 2nd Battle of Ypres and was in hospital for awhile. After recovering he went with his battalion to the Dardanelles and was again wounded, on the 10th October 1915, this time in the jaw.

Meanwhile, William Carter was serving with the 6th Battalion Sherwood Foresters, together with Darley colleagues George Pratley and William Barker. By the middle of June 1916 the Battalion was on the Somme sector of the front line, in France, and preparing for the forthcoming Allied offensive. Back in January, the brothers had received bad news when they learned that their 60 year old mother, Georgina, had died and been buried at St. Helens Church on 1st January 1916.

Private William Carter.

PRIVATE WILLIAM LEOPOLD BARKER, No. 2183, 6th Battalion Sherwood Foresters.
(Died from wounds on 10th July 1916, received on 1st July, aged 30 years.)

William was the son of William and Salome Eliza Barker, of 7 Hazel View, Two Dales. His father worked as a labourer in James Smith's nurseries and William, one of seven brothers, eventually became a

William Leopold Barker.

Arthur Barker.

nurseryman labourer for the same firm. His brother Harry and wife had run the fish and chip shop at Brook Side before the war, whilst another brother, Arthur, served in the army and was blown up several times, as well as being gassed. Though Arthur survived the war he suffered with his nerves for the rest of his life.

PRIVATE GEORGE RAYMOND PRATLEY,
No. 1713, 6th Battalion Sherwood Foresters.
(*Died on Saturday 1st July 1916, aged 23 years.*)

Born at Witney, Oxfordshire, George had arrived in Darley Dale with his parents Mark and Elisha Pratley, but by 1901, his mother had died and seven year old George was living with his widower father, a grit stone quarryman, and sisters Annie and Emily in lodgings with the Thraves family at the top of Northwood. George eventually began work on the railway and at the time of his enlistment he was living at Midland Cottages, Chatsworth Road.

All three men had enlisted at Matlock and were drafted into the 6th Battalion Sherwood Foresters. In June 1916 they found themselves preparing for the Battle of the Somme.

On 23rd/24th June they were at Foncquevillers, digging advanced trenches and providing covering parties and reserve diggers. Rather heavy machine gun fire and shelling interrupted them. Heavy rain fell, and when the Battalion marched to their billets, every man was wet through and covered with mud. Meanwhile, on the 30th, the Battalion were relieved in the fire trenches and drew stores in preparation for the attack on the German trenches.

At 7-30a.m. on July 1st 1916, the 139th Brigade, made up of the 5th, 6th, 7th and 8th Battalions of the Sherwood Foresters, attacked on a front in the vicinity of Gommecourt Wood. The Brigade was positioned at the northernmost point of the July 1st offensive and the Gommecourt attack was essentially a diversion to draw fire and men away from the main thrust further south, but if successful would have eliminated the Gommecourt salient. This sector had the worst of the wet weather and German shelling had caused heavy casualties prior to the attack.

The 5th, 6th and 7th Battalions assaulted in four waves of three companies, with the remaining companies of each Battalion carrying bombs and material.

The first three waves of assault carried the first, and to some extent, the second and third German trenches, under the partial cover of smoke. However, part of the fourth wave and most of the 5th and 7th Battalion companies could not get away before the smoke lifted, due to the very muddy state of the trenches, and their advance was checked severely by the German heavy artillery and machine gun fire. The attack therefore failed, with assaulting Battalions receiving heavy losses, but the main object of containing the enemy forces near Gommecourt, was achieved.

At about 8p.m. the 6th Battalion was relieved in the trenches by the 8th Battalion Sherwood Foresters and rested near Battalion headquarters at Foncquevillers. Total casualties for the day were 170. The following day the remains of the Battalion marched into huts at Warlincourt.

Private Jack Wilson, standing.

Private George Pratley was killed in action by shell fire during the attack on Gommecourt. There is no known grave and he is commemorated on the Thiepval Memorial (Pier and face 10c 10D and 11A).

The news of William Carter's death on the 1st July came to his sister, Mrs. Andrew Holmes, by letter from his Company Commander. He is buried in grave I.L.33 in Foncquevillers Military Cemetery, the burials in July being especially numerous.

Their Battalion colleague, Private William Barker, was severely wounded on the same day and eventually found himself at No. 1 General

Private Jack Wilson sitting second from right on front row at the convalescent hospital.

Hospital at Etretat, a small seaside town 26 kilometres north of Le Havre. There he died on July 10th from wounds received on the battlefield and lies buried in grave II. D. 11A, in Etretat Churchyard, France.

In the same advance on the Somme in July, it was reported that Darley soldiers Lance Corporal John Siddall (the Darley post-master's son) and Private John Wilson had been injured, with John Wilson confined to a Birmingham hospital.

PRIVATE HAROLD SMITH,
No. 13963, 11th Battalion Sherwood Foresters.
(Died on Saturday 1st July 1916, aged 28 years.)

Harold was the son of Mr. and Mrs. William Smith, living at Underwood Terrace, Smedley Street West (part of Darley parish in those days).

Harold was 28 years of age, single, and had joined the forces near the beginning of the war, having enlisted at Derby.

Joining the 11th Battalion Sherwood Foresters, he found himself stationed in Picardy in June 1916, in training for the planned Battle of the Somme.

The battle in Picardy was to be the main offensive campaign of the Franco-British armies in 1916. Into it was thrown the entire British effort of the year on the Western Front. As historian Liddall Hart writes in his "History of the First World War": "It proved both the glory and the graveyard of

Private H. Smith.

"Kitchener's Army" – those citizen volunteers, who, instantly answering the call in 1914, had formed the first national army of Britain".

The 11th Battalion waited in the front trench at Ovillers, between Albert and Thiepval. Hart writes: "Ahead, across the Somme landscape lay a range of hills and this ridge gave the enemy command and observation over the Allied lines. The German defences had been considerably strengthened and in most parts of this front our men had to go uphill to attack. The question was whether the British infantry could cross no-mans land before the barrage lifted. These waves of soldiers were to advance at a steady pace, symmetrically aligned like rows of nine-pins ready to be knocked over. The infantryman was so heavily laden that he could not move faster than a walk. The 'race' was lost before it started, and the battle soon after.

"July 1st dawned a swelteringly hot day. At 7-30a.m. the infantry, including Harold Smith, advanced from their trenches, and thousands fell, littering no-mans land with their bodies, before the German front trench was even reached. While the shells flattened their trenches, the Germans sheltered in dug-outs or shell holes, and as the barrage lifted, dragged out their machine-guns, to pour a deadly hail of lead into the unduly dense wave of the attackers.

"It is hardly remarkable that by nightfall many battalions were barely a hundred strong. The attack in the north around Orvillers was a failure.

Against Ovillers the waves of the 8th Division, including the 11th Battalion, beat practically in vain. Some hardly left our trenches, many never crossed the open space, many died in the enemy wire and many had to fall back".

On that fateful day of July 1st 1916, 28 year old Harold Smith was killed in action when in the attack on Ovillers. He has no known grave and is commemorated on the Thiepval Memorial (Pier and face 10C 10D and 11A). His parents were told that he was missing, but it was only months later that they received news that he had been confirmed as killed in action. Even greater tragedy came to haunt the family, when, a little later in the war, news arrived to say that two of their other sons, Jack and Sydney, had also fallen in battle. 19 year old Sydney, of the Sherwood Foresters, died of wounds received in France on April 19th 1917, without ever recovering consciousness, whilst John, serving in the South Staffordshires, died later in the war.

PRIVATE WILLIAM CROSSLAND,
No. 19724, 10th Battalion Sherwood Foresters.
(*Died on Sunday 9th July 1916, aged 22 years.*)

William Crossland had been born at Coweaddens in Lanarkshire, Scotland, but by 1914 he was living with his parents, Samuel and Sarah, in Ryecroft, Two Dales. Sam had arrived with his family in Darley Dale when he acted as a foreman during the construction of the aqueduct through the parish, and stayed when the job was completed. His son, William, worked as a gardener for Mr. Clay at Darley Hall. He enlisted at Buxton, joining the 10th Battalion Sherwood Foresters (known as "The Bantams" because of their lack of height).

By January/February 1916 they were fighting on the Ypres Ramparts and on the

William Crossland.

banks of the Ypres Canal, where they sustained heavy casualties during two days of attack and counter-attack. Between 18th May and 11th June, time was spent near Armentieres, in intensive training, and on the 12th June they moved by train to a camp in the Amiens area on the Somme. By the 1st July they were in billets near Albert but William was not involved in the first day of battle, when 20,000 British soldiers died.

Orders were received on the 2nd July to support an attack on Fricourt village, just east of Albert, which had resisted all efforts to capture it on the first day of battle. They discovered that the 50th Brigade had suffered dreadful losses and were unable to make progress, but when the Germans decided to retire from the village, orders came to press on to take Fricourt Wood.

The advance began at 12 noon on July 2nd. Bombing parties cleared the trenches and the Battalion pushed on to the northern boundary of the wood. They continued probing through the night of 2nd/3rd July, whilst on the morning of the 3rd William's Battalion attacked Railway Alley Trench and gained it, taking 800 prisoners. The Battalion was relieved on the night of the 4th July and in the rest camp, close behind the lines, they enjoyed the spoils of war.

By the 7th July William returned to front line duty and at 11-20a.m. the Battalion moved to take over Quadrangle Trench, north of Fricourt Wood. At 3p.m. heavy shelling came in from 15 cm. Howitzers. Casualties were extremely heavy due to unabated shelling and the men were moved into shell holes in an attempt to reduce the risk..

In continuously falling rain, an attack on nearby Contalmaison suffered from the heavy machine gun fire, and over the heavy ground they were withdrawn. During this unsuccessful attack, William Crossland was seriously wounded and two days later he died, close behind the lines. He was buried in grave I. B. 36 at Dartmoor Cemetery, near Becordel, S.E. of Albert. Strangely, his name is not commemorated on the Darley war memorial but is to be found on the wall plaque inside St. Helen's Church.

Three more Darley Dale men were yet to die on the "killing fields" of Picardy but their deaths came in the later stages of the Battle of the Somme.

PRIVATE JOHN SLANEY,
No. 70688, 'D' Company 2nd Battalion Sherwood Foresters.
(*Died on Monday 16th October 1916, aged 30 years.*)

John was born in October 1885 at Deeley's Row (now demolished), near Northwood on the A6, the son of William Samuel Slaney and Emily. His father was a plate-layer on the Midland Railway, based at Rowsley, and the family eventually moved to Green Lane. William died at a relatively early age and this left the newly widowed Emily to support a family of eight young children. She began work at Smedley's Hydro laundry in Matlock and would walk there and back each day.

John was one of the eldest of the three girls and five boys and he volunteered to join the Colours in late October 1914, after attending the recruitment meeting at the Whitworth Institute on Friday 23rd October. In the High Peak News it mentions that he was living at Meadow Cottages and it is believed that he had been employed in James Smith's nurseries, Two Dales.

His younger brothers, Harry and Charles, eventually enlisted and young Charles had the distinction of serving in the forces in both the Great War and the Second World War. During his service in the Great War, Charles was seriously wounded when he was shot in the jaw, the bullet entering one side and leaving through the other.

Although the Battle of the Somme began in July, the 2nd Battalion was only involved in its third stage, from September 9th till its end on 18th November. On August 29th they route marched for seven days, reaching Meaulte on 7th September and after dark on the 11th they took over the trenches S.W. of Guillemont by 11-10p.m. The Battalion attacked at 6a.m. on the 12th in the vicinity of the shattered village of Ginchy, advancing 700 yards but suffering heavy casualties from enemy shells and machine guns and finding the enemy wire still intact. Three tanks were used ineffectively for the first time by the British Army. Casualties had been terrible between the 12th and the 19th (17 officers and 421 other ranks were killed, wounded or missing) and the Battalion was rested behind the lines and joined by 320 fresh arrivals.

By the 25th September they were back at the front, N.W. of the Ginchy – Les Boeufs road, east of Albert, and remained there during the rest of the month. On October 14th the Battalion was occupying a section north of Les Boeufs when they were ordered to attack certain gun pits and new German trenches at 5-30a.m. on the 15th.

After an intense bombardment, the gun pits were captured and held, but the rest of the attack made little ground. The Battalion maintained its position during the 16th/17th October, under great pressure from the enemy, but on the 19th October they were relieved. Unfortunately, John Slaney had been hit during the action on the 16th October and was killed when the Germans shelled "Cloudy" Trench.

He is buried in grave XXII. A. 10 at Cabaret-Rouge British Cemetery, Souchez, France, 3 kilometres north of Arras. Later, Emily and the family went to live at 9 South Park Avenue.

PRIVATE JOHN (JACK) WILLIAM WILKINSON, No. 29166, 1st Battalion East Lancashire Regiment.
(*Died on Wednesday 18th October 1916, aged 33 years.*)

Jack Wilkinson was a single man of 33 years of age, living at home with his elderly parents, William and Elizabeth, at Glen View, Two Dales. In his earlier days he had been a scholar at the Methodist chapel, worked in Stancliffe Quarry as a quarry picker and later helped the local blacksmith.

In late 1915 Jack enlisted with the South Staffordshire Regiment, before transferring to the East Lancashires, and by the latter part of August 1916 was to be found in Picardy, ready to take part in the later stages of the main Allied offensive of that year, the Battle of the Somme.

Private J. Wilkinson.

In the weeks following the 1st July, huge resources of manpower and equipment were deployed in an attempt to exploit the modest successes of the first day. However, the German Army resisted tenaciously and repeated attacks and counter-attacks

137

meant a major battle for every village, copse and farmhouse gained. At the end of September, the key village of Thiepval was finally captured. The village had been an original objective on the first day of the battle.

Attacks north and east continued throughout October and into November in increasingly difficult weather conditions. The Battle of the Somme finally ended on 18th November with the onset of winter. In those grim, rainy days of October, Jack Wilkinson was killed by an exploding shell as the East Lancashire Regiment pushed slowly, oh so slowly, forward. His body was never recovered. He was reported missing and it was not until the following year that his death was confirmed to his distraught parents.

During those same three months of the battle,

PRIVATE JOHN WILLIAM BODEN,
No. 37041, 1st Battalion Lancashire Fusiliers,

another Derbyshire man, was to fight alongside Jack Wilkinson, and he too died in the final stages of the battle, on October 23rd, five days after his colleague. He was 22 years of age and, like his colleague, his body was never recovered.

John Boden was the son of Ada Boden, of Stanton-in-the-Peak and the late John James Boden, and the family had connections with Darley Dale.

Both soldiers are commemorated on the Thiepval Memorial, on the Somme, Jack Wilkinson on Pier and face 6C and John Boden on Pier and face 3C and 3D.

Although the attention of Darley Dale residents would be focused on events in Picardy between July and November, with particular concentration on the fatalities of early July, it has to be remembered that local men were serving in other sectors of the Western Front and facing danger every day.

Away from the Battle of the Somme, two other men were killed during 1916:

PRIVATE GEORGE FREDERICK HOLLAND,
No. 17048, "C" Company 7th Battalion
Northamptonshire Regiment.
(*Died on Thursday 13th July 1916, aged 27 years.*)

George was the youngest son of William and Hannah Holland of No. 3 Brook Side, Two Dales. His father, William, was a carter in James Smith's nurseries but he left the family home to go and live in Sheffield, whilst George's mother, Hannah, died relatively young. This left his sister, Charlotte (Lottie) to raise George and the rest of the family. When she married George Charlesworth, she helped with family finances by running a shop in the front room of her cottage.

Private George Holland.

By the start of the Great War her brother George had left Darley Dale and was working in Peterborough as a carter. It was there that he enlisted and joined the 7th Battalion, Northamptonshire Regiment.

As the great offensive battle on the Somme began, the 7th Battalion were serving well to the north of those battle lines. They were holding the front line in the vicinity of Wulverghem, a few kilometres south of Ypres, Belgium.

His name had gone on the muster roll of the 7th Battalion whilst at Woking on the 17th August. This was just prior to the Battalion's embarkation to France on the 1st September 1915.

On the 11th July, 1916, the Battalion once again went into the front line trenches, knowing that on the night of 17th July they were to take part in a relatively minor attack on the enemy lines. Gas was to be used in the attack and over the next few days, batches of gas cannisters were carefully brought up in readiness.

Although the general situation on the 12th July was generally quiet, a few High Explosive shells came over the Battery positions at about 9p.m. One soldier was seriously wounded in this commonplace, routine

George Holland at work c.1913 almost certainly in Peterborough.

duel of the artillery.

That soldier was Darley Dale man, George Holland, and he was quickly taken to the Casualty Clearing Station, a short distance behind the lines. The next day, July 13th, was again quiet, although German machine guns were active after dark.

However, it was on this day that George Holland died from his wounds and was buried in grave I. A. 9 at St Quentin Cabaret Military Cemetery, south of Ypres, close to the village of Wulverghem. As we have already seen in Chapter One, the news of his death came as a shattering blow to his family, especially sister Lottie.

The final account for 1916 deals with William Slack and here I am not completely sure that I have the right man. Examining all the evidence I believe it may have been:

PRIVATE WILLIAM SLACK,
No. 3835, 6th Battalion Sherwood Foresters.
(Died on Thursday 13th April 1916, aged 27 years.)

He was the son of Mrs. E. Slack of 2, Castle Yard, Chesterfield. William was born in London and enlisted at Chesterfield, but may have had connections with the Darley area through work.

He joined the 6th Battalion and by the end of March 1916 he was in the trenches at Capelle Fermont, on the River Scarpe, a few kilometres N.W. of Arras. During the tour of duty two soldiers had been killed, and six men wounded, mainly from the day to day shelling that resulted in an ever present danger.

One of those wounded was William Slack, but after two weeks medical attention he died and is buried in grave I. A. 36 at Aubigny Communal Cemetery Extension,N.W. of Arras.

By the end of 1916 ten men from Darley Dale had perished on the Western Front. Although this total was less than in 1915, the sadness was no less for the families concerned. The black month of July 1916, alone, resulted in six lives lost, and for so little gain.

The British armies could not stand up to machine-gun fire interlacing a defensive zone, stretching in depth for miles. In four and a half months of almost continuous attack, they were able to advance only a little more than eight miles.

The German defensive role was magnificent, but repeated German counter-attacks proved even more costly than Allied assaults. That army would never be the same again.

CHAPTER FIVE

1917 – ON FLANDERS FIELDS.

1917 witnessed the gloomiest drama in British military history, the Third Battle of Ypres, more commonly spoken of by the title "Passchendaele" (July 31st to November 10th). It achieved little except loss and was so depressing in its direction that its name became associated with military failure. The seemingly inexhaustible powers of endurance and sacrifice shown by the soldiers was amazing and made even more poignant by the futility of the purpose and result.

Twenty men from Darley Dale were killed during 1917 and twelve of these met their deaths during a three month period, in the hellish quagmire that was Passchendaele.

Earlier in the year the German general, Von Ludendorff, had prepared a much shorter, highly organised defensive zone – the Hindenburg Line, some 20 miles behind the over extended line from Arras to Soissons, to which they would withdraw.

Behind a lightly held outpost line, heavily sown with machine guns, lay two successive defensive positions, highly fortified. Behind these again lay the German reserves, concentrated and prepared for counter-attack.

Between the original line and the new zone, the countryside had been devastated; towns and villages were razed, forests levelled, water sources contaminated and roads destroyed. The actual withdrawal, conducted in great secrecy, began on February 23rd and was completed by April 5th.

By the late Spring of 1917 the Allies were in disarray. The Hindenburg Line had proved too great a defensive line to break through and, more significantly, the French offensive directed by the hero of Verdun, Nivelle, had proved an expensive disaster. Elements of the French Army mutinied and large numbers of soldiers stated that, although willing to defend their positions, they would refuse any order to attack. Great pressure was therefore placed upon the British to take up a greater proportion of the front and to take the fight to the enemy.

General Haig became encouraged to pursue his long-held aim – to break out of the Ypres Salient on to the Flanders Plain, and on to take the Channel ports used by the German U-boats. Sanctions for a limited offensive were given by the British Government.

The first part of the operation was a complete success. Nineteen huge mines were exploded under German positions in the southern end of the Salient, and the British 2nd Army swept the enemy off the Messines – Wijtschate Ridge between 7th and 14th June.

Instead of an immediate follow up in the dry summer weather, six weeks passed before the main assault on the Gheluvelt –Passchendaele Ridge took place. This infamous battle began on the 31st July and the rains began immediately. Empire troops were expected to advance through swamp-like terrain in full view of the defending Germans on the higher ground. Around 80,000 Empire troops were killed and twice that number wounded before Passchendaele was taken and the battle halted on 10th November, 1917.

Twelve Darley Dale men would be among the fatalities, victims of one of the most awful battles in the annals of war. As General Kiggell, Haig's Chief of Staff, is purported to have stated after he visited the front, "Good God, did we really send men to fight in that?"

The first of these fatalities was:

LANCE CORPORAL FREDERICK PEARSON,
No. 13962, 1st Battalion Sherwood Foresters.
(Died on Tuesday 31st July 1917, aged 23 years.)

Fred Pearson was born on July 8th 1891 at Brook Bottom, Ladygrove Road, Two Dales, the son of Henry and Ellen Pearson. The family of four brothers and three sisters later moved to Ryecroft, Two Dales.

Together with brothers Joseph and Isaiah, Fred was a respected local lay preacher for the Methodist church. Another brother, Jim, was an excellent wicket-keeper for Darley Dale Cricket Club. A stonemason, Jim unfortunately died from silicosis in 1916, at the age of 32.

At the August recruitment meeting at the Institute in August 1914, Fred was one of those who jumped up onto the stage to volunteer to fight for "King and Country", declaring aloud to his mother that he would soon be back. His friend and fellow local lay preacher Jack Allsop volunteered the next day and on the 2nd September they found themselves on Darley Station,

Lance Corporal Fred Pearson and his fiance from Sunderland.

on their way to enlist at Derby. Both men were posted to the 1st Battalion, Sherwood Foresters, on the 10th March 1915, serving with "A"

The Pearson family c.1918. Harold, Benn, Ada and Harry.

144

Company. Meanwhile, his brother Benjamin, a quarryman, volunteered five months later and joined the Royal Engineers. Serving in France and Belgium, Ben was fortunate to survive throughout four and a half years of war.

On 29th March 1917 Fred was in hospital after being wounded and returned to duty on the 5th July, joining "B" Company. By July 1917 the Battalion was stationed at Ypres, Belgium, but on July 9th they left the Salient to train at Beaumetz-les-Aires, where they practised the coming attack over similar ground. Fred joined them at this stage. Whilst in training they were inspected by Commander-in-Chief, Sir Douglas Haig, and caused quite a stir when they borrowed all the washing tubs from the nearby village, making open air baths for the Battalion in a field.

On the 21st July they returned to the Ypres front by rail, bus and route march. On July 31st 1917, at 3-50a.m., the Foresters moved to the attack in artillery formation. The front of the attack, which was to open the 3rd Battle of Ypres, was 15 miles in length and the main British effort was directed against the seven miles between Boesinghe and the Zillebeke-Zardvoorde road.

There was a thick mist, the sky was overcast, and the ground was saturated. All through the 30th and the night of the 30th/31st July the Allied bombardment was sustained and then at 3-50a.m. the whole Allied front burst into flame and the infantry went "over the top".

The attack was through Hooge, by the large sheet of water known as Bellewaarde Lake and the surrounding marshy ground. The first serious resistance for the Sherwood Foresters was in the chain of isolated strong points to the east of the lake and the trenches over Bellewaarde Ridge. The Sherwoods cleared Chateau Wood, swept over the southern slopes of the Ridge and were in the enemy support trenches. An especially strong fortified position lay at the cross roads, consisting of the ruins of an old inn, converted by the enemy into a nest of concrete machine gun posts. It was stalked and attacked by the bombing party and taken. The enemy barrage increased during the day, and in the early afternoon, counter-attacks began and the heaviest fell on the Sherwood Foresters at 3-30p.m. The Foresters held their own and drove the enemy back to Zonnebecke and Polygon Wood.

It was during this sustained bombardment and counter-attacks that

Fred Pearson was killed by a shell. His body was never recovered and he is commemorated on Panel 39 and 41 of the Ypres (Menin Gate) Memorial at Ypres. A comrade, however, found Fred's small bible that he always kept in his breast pocket, lying on the ground. It had a photograph of Fred's six year old nephew, Harold Pearson, inside. The soldier brought it home to the Pearson family and at the time of writing, 92 year old Harold still has the bible in his possession.

During his service in the army, Fred saw many of his colleagues killed, including his best pal, Jack Allsop, in 1915. Whilst in training in 1914/1915 in the Sunderland area he had met a girl and became engaged. Most of his few leaves were spent with her. They had decided to get married when he returned on his next leave, but sadly Fred died on the battlefield.

PRIVATE ABRAHAM H. DOXEY,
No. 42378, 13th Battalion Sherwood Foresters,
transferred to 195th Company Labour Corps (No. 116494).
(*Died on Tuesday 7th August 1917.*)

The Doxey family lived at Hackney and sent three brothers, Philip, John and Abraham, to fight for King and Country. They also had two half brothers, Harry and James, with James seeing war time service, both at the Dardanelles, and in France. Born at Hackney, but enlisting at Hathersage, Abraham joined the 13th Battalion, Foresters, but at a later stage of the war was transferred to the 195th Company of the Labour Corps.

In 1917 the British Army's Labour Corps was formed, manned by men who were either ex-front line soldiers who had been wounded or taken ill or men who on enlistment were found to be unfit for front line service because of ill-health or because they were too old. By the end of the war the Labour Corps was some 400,000 strong and 9,000 men in the Corps were to die serving their King and Country.

By July 1917 Abraham found himself in the Ypres Salient and taking part in the preparations for 3rd Ypres. It was the job of the Labour Corps to provide and maintain the trench system in good working order, to provide communications with the front line and to allow for the transport of men, animals and war provisions between the front line fighting men and base. Construction of tramways, railways, concrete bases for gun platforms and provision of duck board walkways were vital in all sectors, but especially in the swamp-like conditions found in the Ypres Salient between July and November 1917.

It was also an extremely dangerous job, for Abraham was often working close behind the front line trenches, within easy shelling range of the enemy, who commanded the high ground on the ridge above Ypres.

After the initial attack began on the 31st July, the advance was held up by the early days of August. Whilst waiting for the second blow to be unleashed on the 16th August, in the vicinity of Langemarck, preparations were made by the Labour Corps to enable reinforcements and guns to be brought through the quagmire, ready for the fresh assault. It was during this period that Abraham Doxey was killed by shellfire whilst in a working party, on August 7th.

He is buried at Ypres Reservoir Cemetery in grave I. D. 56.

PRIVATE FRANCIS W. REED,
No 19235, 12th Battalion Sherwood Foresters.
(Died on Friday 10th August 1917, aged 32 years)

Frank Reed was born at Yate, near Bristol, Gloucestershire, and came to Darley when, as a railway man, he was posted to Darley Station as a porter.

In late 1912 he married Mabel Crowder, daughter of South Darley Urban District Council's roads

Left: Private Frank Reed.
Right: Mabel Reed with daughter Daisy and son Frankie.

147

surveyor, Harry Crowder, and sister of Lance Corporal Louis Crowder, who was to die at Ypres a month after Frank's death.

Frank and Mabel's first child, Daisy, was born in October 1913 at Glen View Cottages, Two Dales, but eventually the family moved to No. 4 Ryecroft. Late in 1914 a son, Frankie, was born.

Joining the Colours in November 1914, soon after the October recruitment rally at the Whitworth Institute, Frank was certainly in France by February 1916 but was invalided home in August of the same year. Remaining in hospital until Christmas, he returned to France shortly after Easter.

When Frank went back to the Front Line for the final time, Mabel was expecting their third child. Three months after Frank's death, Edith Elizabeth was born. Whilst in Belgium during this last period he met his brother-in-law, Louis Crowder, just before both were killed.

PRIVATE ERNEST JOHN WILLIAMS,
No. 18242, "C" Company 12th Battalion Sherwood Foresters.
(*Died on Saturday 11th August 1917, aged 23 years.*)

A single man, Ernest had been born at Carmarthen, Wales, and had arrived in Darley Dale to live with his sister, Mrs. Turberville of Oaker View, Farley Hill. He was an employee of the Smedley Hydropathic Company, working in the Hydro in winter and on the farm in summer.

Ernest joined the army in October 1914 and had seen two years service at the front by the time he died.

Both Frank Reed and Ernest found themselves joining the 12th Battalion Sherwood Foresters, which was the Pioneer Battalion of the Regiment. As with the

Private Ernest Williams.

Labour Corps, its primary role was to dig and repair trench lines, lay barbed wire and enable men, supplies and artillery to reach the front line.

It was a difficult and dangerous job, performed under shellfire from the enemy positions.

They found themselves performing these duties in the Ypres Salient in July and August 1917 as the 3rd Battle of Ypres started on the 31st July. The second blow of the offensive was to begin on the 16th August, in the vicinity of Langemarck, and in the lull, they were involved in the preparations for this second phase of the battle.

On the 4th August they extended the light railway to Armagh Wood and Valley Cottages, draining tracks and laying duck boards. For five days the work continued to allow supplies to move through the quagmire conditions into forward positions, in readiness for the attack on 16th August.

On the 9th August six soldiers were killed and eight wounded by shellfire as they worked. The day of the 10th dawned bright and warm. Tramway extensions continued and the railway was repaired. The shelling was even more intense, resulting in another six men of the working parties being killed, eight wounded and one posted missing. Sadly, one of those who was killed by shell fire was Frank Reed.

His Platoon Officer, 2nd Lieutenant H. Suringler, wrote to his wife, "Private Reed was a gallant soldier and will be greatly missed by all who knew him. I personally regarded him as one of the most reliable and steadfast men in my platoon. He was buried close by where he fell."

The following day, 11th August, the weather was cooler, with some rain. "C" Company and Ernest Williams continued work on Voormezeele light railway, under shell fire, with one man killed by the end of the day. That soldier was Ernest Williams.

His Platoon Officer, 2nd Lieutenant A. Langsdale, wrote to his sister, Mrs. Turberville, "I regret to inform you of the sad death of your brother, who was killed in the early morning of August 11th while nobly doing his duty in the front line. He was of a cheerful and willing disposition and was highly thought of by his comrades. His death was instantaneous and he was carefully buried by his comrades."

The officer was obviously attempting to ease her pain, for in the swampland conditions, his body was never recovered and both Frank Reed and Ernest Williams' names are commemorated on the Ypres (Menin Gate) Memorial. During the 1920's, when the Menin Gate was officially unveiled and dedicated, Fred Reed's brothers and sisters from Gloucestershire travelled to Ypres and attended the ceremony.

PRIVATE LESLIE DRURY,
No. 43013, 11th Battalion Royal Inniskilling Fusiliers.
(Died on Thursday 16th August 1917, aged 23 years.)

Leslie, born in August 1894, lived with his brother Edgar at No. 3 Oakwell Terrace, Matlock, together with their parents, James and Annie Jane Drury. James worked as a cashier at Smedleys Hydro. It is believed that James and Annie eventually split up, with Edgar being brought up by his grandfather in Matlock and Leslie living with his mother at Darley Dale. By the start of the Great War Leslie was living and working in London. However, he returned to Derbyshire and enlisted at Buxton, before joining the Royal Inniskilling Fusiliers.

On August 16th 1917 the Fusiliers took part in Haig's second blow against the German lines in the Ypres Salient. The left wing advanced across the shallow depression formed by the little valley of the Steenbeek and past the ruins of what had been Langemarck Village.

But on the right

Edgar Drury, brother of Leslie, with family and friends at Birchover, whilst home on leave. Edgar is second from left on the back row, next to his pal, Ted Dakin, third from the left.

150

a heavy price was paid for nothing gained. The enemy's skilful resistance and above all the mud, contributed to the failure and the fruitless sacrifice. All hopes of success were submerged in the swamps beyond Ypres.

Leslie Drury was killed on this first day of action, 16th August, and in the hellish quagmire ground conditions his body was never recovered. He is commemorated on Panels 70 to 72 of the Tyne Cot Memorial, Belgium.

His brother, Edgar, had also enlisted at Buxton and joined the 2nd /6th Battalion Sherwood Foresters, spending time in Dublin during 1916 in helping to suppress the Irish Easter Rising. He then served in France and Belgium and rose to the rank of sergeant, being mentioned in dispatches.

On March 21st 1918, on the first day of the German offensive, Edgar was wounded and taken prisoner. As a P.O.W. he was made to work underground in a German coal mine, but survived the ordeal and settled down to married life at Birchover after the war.

LANCE CORPORAL LOUIS CROWDER, No. 25801, 16th Battalion Sherwood Foresters.
(*Died on Saturday 22nd September 1917, aged 33 years.*)

Born at Upper Hackney, Louis lived with his father Harry and mother Lydia on Park Lane, Two Dales, where he was brought up with brother Ernest and sisters Annie, Mabel, Olive, Edith and Jessie. His father was the surveyor on the South Darley Urban District Council.

Left: Lance Corporal Louis Crowder.
Right: Harry Crowder, surveyor of roads for South Darley, on Park Lane.

The Lance Corporal, a single man, was a member of the Darley Dale Cricket Club and one of the principal members of the Whitworth

Institute Billiards League team, being recognised as one of the most skilful exponents of the game in the Peak District.

He was one of the first Darley men to volunteer and joined the 16th Battalion, known as the Chatsworth Rifles, when he enlisted at Buxton. At least nine men from South Darley were in the same Battalion and two of these, Arthur Boam and John Potter Marsden were also to die, the former soldier in the same battle as Louis Crowder (see "A Derbyshire Parish at War – South Darley and the Great War 1914 - 1919").

Louis was involved in many actions with the Chatsworth Rifles and took part in the Battle of the Somme between July 1st and November 1916. His father, Harry, received a letter from his son, commenting upon the actions he had taken part in :

Dated 15th October 1916 it reads, ..."I can tell you a little bit about what it is like in the big push which we have been in the thick of for almost six weeks now, so that we who are left think ourselves lucky. I have seen things that are marvellous, how a fellow can stand the sights and see his pals being killed and wounded and cut up. Well, the last battle we were in was the fall of Thiepval. The Germans said we could never take the place, but our boys showed whether they could or not, and it is in our hands completely now, but it was nothing else, only murder – but that has got to be done, and everybody does his bit without a murmer.

As soon as the hour comes they are over the parapet and at it in fine style. They stop for nothing, but there is always someone's mother and wives that have to grieve after these battles – yes, somewhere in England. They ought to make all the men that have had to be fetched up come here and go over the top with the first wave of men and then they would have something to grouse about. They don't know what hardship the boys go through out here. The Germans have about had enough of this and I don't think they will stick it very much longer, as they are giving themselves up wholesale now. They seemed pleased to be taken prisoner and right well they might, for they cannot stand these tanks of ours.

One of the tanks got stuck at the top of a German dug-out and they thought they had captured it and a great number of them gathered round and fixed bayonets. Then the men in the tank opened fire on them with their machine guns so you can bet that they went west, never to fight again.

You would be surprised to get into the German trenches and see their dug-outs. They are thirty to forty feet deep and like a palace inside, beds and blankets, electric lights and everything to make them comfortable, but they must keep their spirits up with drinking as there are hundreds of empty wine bottles left behind.

Well, I hope that what is left of us men get through. We have gone through the heaviest of the fighting that has been up to now, and we should get leave between now and Christmas. I shall be able to tell you more when we get leave. This is the first chance we have had of putting anything in a letter since the offensive began.

Well, I think it is a brighter outlook for us all now. We shall all be thankful when it is over to know that we have done our bit without being fetched, so you must buck up and wait patiently, as it cannot last forever. Buck up and keep smiling."

Towards the end of July 1917 the Battalion took part in the 3rd Battle of Ypres and after many harrowing actions came out of the front line on the 29th August. After rest and training, buses took them back to the Ypres Salient, into the Shrewsbury Forest sector, on the 12th September. The landscape afforded little or no security and they were subjected to persistent and comprehensive shelling, with officers and men killed.

Preparations were made for an advance on Bulgar Wood and they went into the line on the 19th September, as part of the overall plan to capture Passchendaele Ridge. The assembly over slippery duck boards was carried out in good order in spite of intense darkness and rain.

They fought in a thick mist and were subjected to hostile rifle and machine gun fire, but owing to the fog, suffered few casualties. Two machine gun posts were captured and they were on top of the concrete dug-outs before the enemy had chance to get out of them. The fog dispersed and they worked around a strong point and rushed it under cover of Vickers guns.

The leading waves advanced steadily through Bulgar Wood, close up to their own barrage. The Battalion's Lewis Gun teams performed splendidly, causing the enemy to retire. Seventy yards ahead was a large concrete dug-out with machine guns sited. Rifle grenades were used in knocking one gun out whereupon the enemy sought refuge in the dug-out, where they fell an easy prey to the Foresters.

Casualties were heavy in the Battalion and the enemy on four occasions tried to relieve the position but were dispersed by rifle and Lewis gun fire. The next day was spent in their new lines in Bulgar Wood, and they were under shell fire all the time, but being well dug in, suffered few casualties. The Battalion was relieved in the early morning of 22nd September, though relief was delayed by casualties among the guides and runners. In two days fighting over 200 prisoners were taken, together with nine machine guns and one trench mortar. However, three officers of the Chatsworth Rifles, plus 36 other ranks had been killed, including Louis Crowder. He survived the two days of battle but was killed in the last action of the Bulgar Wood offensive.

Lance Corporal Louis Crowder is buried at Tyne Cot Cemetery, Belgium, in grave LXIV. G. 18.

PRIVATE FREDERICK CHARLESWORTH,
No. 202253, 2nd/5th Battalion North Staffordshire Regiment.
(*Died on Saturday 29th September 1917, aged 20 years.*)

Fred Charlesworth, eldest son in the family, was born near Lumb Lane, Northwood, but the family moved shortly to "The Laundry" at Painters Nook, run by his mother Mary, whilst his father Joseph worked at Stancliffe Quarry, as did most of his sons. Joseph's job was to drive the saddle tank engines on the Stancliffe railway that ran from the main Midland line into Stancliffe Yard and quarry and

Lottie Charlesworth, a Red Cross Nurse at the Whitworth Institute and her brother Fred Charlesworth.

then by means of a loop into Hall Dale Quarry, just a short distance from his home.

Both Fred and his brother Charles went early into the army, but eventually Charles was seriously injured and remained on crutches for the rest of his life. He had served in the Royal Field Artillery as a driver for the transport, when he was wounded in both legs by a shell in January 1916. His colleague was killed and by March 1916 Charles was in a Nottingham hospital.

Fred enlisted at Matlock and joined the 2nd/5th Battalion Prince of Wales's (North Staffordshire Regiment). Meanwhile, his sister Lizzie had trained as a Red Cross Nurse and worked during the war years looking after the convalescing soldiers at the Whitworth Institute Red Cross Hospital, together with Two Dales women Lucy Hayes, Jessie Hayes and Agnes Knifton.

In September 1917, the North Staffs were involved in the second phase of the attack against the main ridge, east of Ypres. At midnight 25th/26th September the Battalion moved into position for the attack at dawn on the 26th, east of Wieltje.

At 11-30a.m. the companies moved forward, under atrocious ground conditions and hostile heavy fire from artillery and machine guns. During the day and especially about 5p.m., prior to a German counter-attack, the enemy put down very heavy artillery barrages, causing a good many casualties. Rations, water and hot tea in petrol tins surrounded with straw were brought up by pack ponies at 6pm, from where they were fetched by carrying parties.

On the 27th September attacks and counter-attacks took place throughout the day, but on the 28th orders were received that the Battalion was to be relieved.

Casualties for the 26th and 27th September were 19 men killed, 135 wounded and three missing.

Fred Charlesworth was wounded during the two day battle and taken to the Casualty Clearing Station. He died from his wounds on September 29th and was buried in grave VI. F. 23 at Mendinghem Military Cemetery, Poperinge, 17 kilometres N.W. of Ypres.

Amongst all the tragic events unfolding during the Passchendaele offensive, we now come to possibly the saddest and most poignant story, that of the Evans brothers.

PRIVATE CHARLES HENRY EVANS,
No. 29976, 2nd/5th Battalion East Lancashire Regiment.
(Died on Tuesday 9th October 1917, aged 20 years.)

PRIVATE JOHN EDWARD EVANS,
No. G/66019, 2nd Battalion Royal Fusiliers.
(Died on Tuesday 9th October, aged 27 years.)

Both they and their brother Tom were born at 9 South Park View (Meadowtown), Northwood, the sons of Thomas and Grace Evans. Their father, born at Alport, was a carter employed by Stancliffe Estates Company.

John enlisted at Derby and joined the Royal Fusiliers, whilst Charles enlisted at Bakewell before joining the Sherwood Foresters and later transferring to the East Lancashire Regiment. Their brother Tom also joined the Colours.

In 1917 John and Charles, serving in different Regiments, were unfortunate to find themselves in the Ypres Salient during the 3rd Battle of Ypres, almost fighting side by side.

By the end of September 1917 the 3rd Battle of Ypres had cost the British Army some 90,000 killed, missing and wounded for an advance of some three and a half miles, just half way to Passchendaele Ridge.

On October 4th, an heroic action by the ANZACS took the Broodseinde Ridge but conditions were appalling: torrential rain and heavy shelling had turned the ground into a vile swamp, the men were exhausted and at the limit of endurance. On the night of the 6th October Generals Gough and Plumer conferred and jointly proposed to General Haig for the campaign to be closed down for the winter. There had been rain each day since October 4th and on the afternoon of the 8th it became torrential, with no improvement expected.

Haig refused the advice. He believed Passchendaele and the open country beyond was within reach. It just needed one last push. Plans were laid for another attack on the 9th October and thus the fate of the Evans brothers was sealed.

This renewed offensive was officially known as "The Battle of Poelcappelle" and began at dawn on the 9th in pouring rain. The village of Poelcappelle fell but the advance stalled on the Passchendaele Ridge, as did the other attack on Bellevue, directly in front of Passchendaele village. The attack on an eight mile front proved a tragic fiasco, except in the low ground to the left.

Casualties were enormous on both sides. Two of those who died on that same day were brothers John and Charles. Private Morton, also from Meadowtown, Darley Dale, a pal of Charles Evans and serving in the same Battalion, went to his rescue but was himself wounded. Charles's body was never recovered from the swampy battlefield and he is commemorated on Panels 77 to 79 and 163A of the Tyne Cot Memorial. John is buried in grave I. D. 13. at Cement House Cemetery, Langemarck, north of Ypres.

As if the sadness in the Evans household was not enough to bear, news came in May 1918 that their only surviving son, Thomas, aged 24 years, was reported missing. Happily it was later reported that he was a P.O.W. of the Germans.

GUNNER GEORGE CLIFFORD POPE,
No. 122072, 'D' Battery 94th Brigade,
Royal Horse Artillery and Royal Field Artillery.
(Died on 14th October 1917, aged 28 years.)

Clifford's parents, John and Hannah Pope, lived at 11 Chatsworth Road (Midland Cottages), which in those days were part of Darley parish. John was a signal man at Rowsley Sidings, a Black country man who had lived and worked on the railway at Macclesfield, before arriving at Rowsley. Their children were Arthur, Roland, Edith, Clifford, Edgar and Alice. The two brothers, Clifford and Edgar, both worked away from home in the Co-op grocery department at Clowne, Chesterfield, before the war began.

Enlisting at Mansfield, Clifford joined the Royal Field Artillery and his younger brother Edgar also joined the army. The Great War has often been depicted as lines of infantry being swept aside by machine guns, and this certainly was a major feature of the conflict. However, the use of artillery and the terrible damage done to frail human flesh by shell fire was much more common an occurrence. No attack went in without first there being an artillery bombardment, hopefully to cut the barbed wire defences and certainly to cause the maximum casualties in front line trenches.

On July 31st "D" Battery was in the Ypres Salient and ready to support the Allied attempt to take the village of Passchendaele. The assault involved the greatest artillery attack in the history of the British Army. Three thousand guns fired over four million shells in just the first two weeks of preparatory bombardment and three days of battle

September 1917 saw Clifford Pope and the 94th Brigade fully involved in the slog towards the Passchendaele Ridge. By October the battle was reaching its most dreadful stage. The massive use of artillery had destroyed the ditches, drains and small streams which kept the water table below ground level. Combined with atrocious wet weather, this devastation left a landscape of nightmares. Shell craters now lay lip to lip, separated only by slimy mud.

Clifford's Battery moved up to cover the attack on the Abraham Heights during the first week in October. The Germans had a grandstand view from the Passchendaele Ridge of the slow advance, and rained shells down on the unfortunate troops. Many simply disappeared in the pools of slime. Guns, horses and men were drowned in hell.

Another assault was launched up Abraham Heights on October 12th. This time it was successful but during stubborn German resistance, Clifford Pope was hit by shrapnel and killed on the 14th October.

A deep gloom was cast over his family when they received news of his death. It came through a letter from his comrades, who stated that whilst in a trench, an enemy shell made a direct hit and blew it up. The sad news was made more tragic by the fact that he had sent a cheerful letter, stating that he expected to be home on leave shortly. In fact, preparations had been made for his wedding.

Some months earlier, in June 1917, whilst moving up to the forward positions, he had met his brother Edgar's Battalion of the Sherwood Foresters withdrawing from the front line. They saw each other at a distance, and although not allowed to communicate by word of mouth, were able to acknowledge each other.

On July 1st 1917, three months before Clifford's death, 22 year old Edgar Pope was reported missing but fortunately for John and Hannah they later learned that he had been taken prisoner by the Germans. As a P.O.W. Edgar was made to work in a salt mine. On the few occasions he spoke about this period, he mentioned that when he removed his clothes at night, he could stand his trousers upright on the floor, they were so ingrained with salt.

After the war, a wooden plaque was made for the inside of Beeley Chapel, where the family had always worshipped, with Clifford's name carved on it. When, many years later, the chapel was about to be demolished, the family was able to retrieve it and it is now proudly displayed in the family home.

Clifford Pope is commemorated at La Clytte Military Cemetery in grave III. D. 25.

A month later two other Darley Dale members of the Artillery died, one many miles away near the Belgian coast and the other in the same area as Clifford:

GUNNER ARTHUR FIELDING,
No. 94421, Royal Garrison Artillery.
(Died on 27th October 1917, aged 30 years.)

Arthur Fielding was born in September 1886 at Upper Hackney, where he, his older brother James and sister May were brought up by their parents James and Louisa. Their father worked in one of the local grit stone quarries. In 1901, fourteen year old Arthur was working as a nursery labourer. By the start of the Great War he had married and he and his wife Laura were living at No. 2 Westdale Cottages, Hackney.

Arthur enlisted, joining the Royal Garrison Artillery as a Gunner, and by October 1917 his Battery was positioned in the Ypres Salient, N.W. of the town. Between the 17th and 20th October a reconnaissance was made on the extreme left of the British lines, to the south of Houthulst Forest, in preparation for an attack.

The Forest, which Napolean called "the key to the Low Countries", had been occupied by the Germans since driving the Belgians out in 1914. It was now strongly fortified and perfectly positioned to shell any Allied advance towards Passchendaele.

As the offensive began on the 22nd October the weather broke. So thick was the mist that the men could see no more than a yard before them, and the mud quickly became knee deep. As dawn broke German howitzers above Houthulst and behind Passchendaele smashed into their ranks. The batteries supporting the Allied advance were not spared and when a shell exploded amongst the artillery guns of Arthur Fielding's Battery, he was one of the soldiers who was severely wounded.

Eventually, Arthur was taken to the Casualty Clearing Station at Zuydcoote, ten kilometres N.E. of Dunkirk. Despite receiving medical attention he died five days later, on the 27th October and was buried nearby, in Zuydcoote Military Cemetery.

GUNNER BERTRAM HOUGHTON,
No. 671862, 158th Brigade Royal Field Artillery.
(Died on Saturday 10th November 1917,)

He died on his 20th birthday, as the Allies at last successfully took Passchendaele Ridge and Passchendaele village.

He lived in Hackney and had been in Egypt, on his way to Gallipoli, when news reached him that his brother Walter had been killed at Ypres in June 1915. Now two years later, Bert was killed in almost the same place as his brother. The High Peak News reported that the war had removed one who was a fine soldier and much respected. Two other brothers were still serving and one of these, Leonard, was also to be killed (sadly, I have been unable to find the details of Leonard's death).

In the nightmare conditions of Passchendaele, Bert's body was never recovered and he is commemorated on the Tyne Cot Memorial, Panel 4 to 6 and 162.

3rd Ypres finally ceased in November as Passchendaele fell to the Canadians (who suffered over 15,000 casualties in a month). The whole campaign cost 80,000 British lives and upwards of 250,000 wounded. All the ground gained would be lost with hardly a fight in the German offensive of April 1918 as the British withdrew to a "better strategic position" around Ypres.

During 1916, Darley folk had focused their attention on what was happening on the Somme. In 1917 the focus was once again on the main British offensive for that year, at Ypres.

However, once again action was taking place in other sectors of the front line and death occurred daily due to sniper fire or the deadly work of High Explosive shells. Life or death was a constant lottery, even on a "quiet day".

Throughout the year, another eight Darley men were killed or died, away from the actions in the Ypres Salient. The first of these was:

PRIVATE GEORGE LINDSAY CLAY,
No. 240129, 6th Battalion Sherwood Foresters.
(Died on 29th January 1917, aged 24 years.)

Lindsay Clay was the youngest son of Joseph Francis Clay and Jane Clay. He was born in 1892 on Jackson Road, Matlock Bank, and his father Joseph was employed as a draper, before going into business as an ironmonger before the Great War. The family had strong connections with Farley Congregational Chapel. Before the war Lindsay was on the staff of Matlock Gas Company's offices and was an accomplished

George Lindsay Clay.

gas fitter. He eventually married Margaret Anne Knowles, setting up home at Elton, where his relative, Rubin Bunting was the village blacksmith and Mrs Bunting ran the Red Lion pub. At the time of Lindsay's death the couple had a two year old daughter, Winifred,

Matlock and District Gas Company, Bank Road, Matlock in the late 1920's.

George Lindsay Clay at the annual camp of the National Reserve organisation 1911/1912. He is fourth from the left on the front row.

(known as Nesta), and were now living at Spring Cottage, Hackney.

The Clay family from Matlock were closely connected with the National Reserve, an organisation aiming to recruit members from each locality to train as soldiers at annual camps and so be able to be added to the Reserve List, ready for action at times of national danger. A relative, Henry Clay, was the Honorary Secretary and Quartermaster of the Matlock branch.

In 1911, at the age of 18 years, Lindsay was persuaded by his family to join and took part in military training each year. It was no surprise therefore that on 5th August 1914 he enlisted at Matlock, as did his two older brothers, Charles and Arthur Francis. Lindsay saw service with the 6th Battalion of the Sherwood Foresters in France and Flanders, but on the 10th August 1915 he was attached to the Second Army Workshop at Hazebrouk, where his skills as a gas fitter could be utilised. It was at this time that he was listed as an acting lance corporal.

Tragically, at 4-40p.m. on the 29th January 1917, there was a series of explosions within the rod sorting shop and oxy-acetylene room at the munitions works, believed to have been started by accident when oxy-acetylene equipment exploded due to the extremely cold conditions. Three soldiers were killed, including Lindsay Clay, and many French civilian workers were injured, together with seven other British soldiers. From the Army investigation records it becomes clear that Lindsay was killed instantly, with little remaining of the body, but letters sent home to his wife attempted to ease her pain. Margaret received the following three letters:

"Dear Mrs. Clay, You will have realised that in these days our men folk are not free from danger in the sacred cause for which we are struggling. Many are called upon to make the supreme sacrifice. It is my sad and solemn duty to inform you that your husband has, in doing his part, been called upon to make the supreme sacrifice. He now wears an immortal crown of glory where cares and troubles are no more. He passed away painlessly. We shall bury him with gentle hands in the local cemetery."

From Major General F.M. Glubb:

"I was very much distressed to hear of the terrible accident yesterday and of the death of three British soldiers and four French civil employees and of the injury to so many others. Please convey the deep sympathy of the Army commander and of myself. They were serving their country as truly and really as if they had lost their lives in action against the enemy."

From Sister-in-Charge C.B. Rubb, Casualty Clearing Station:

"I have very distressing news for you. There was an accident yesterday and your husband, along with some other workers, were killed. He was brought into the hospital, but there was nothing could be done for him. I am sorry there is nothing I can tell you to make the news easier for you. I got your address from a letter that had been found on him. I am enclosing this letter as you might like to have it."

George Lindsay Clay was buried in Grave I. C.17 in Hazebrouck Communal Cemetery.

*** (Some time after the end of the war, Margaret Clay married Edward Wood and two sons and a daughter, Joseph, Edward and Pearl, were born at Elton. In 1930 they moved with their four children to live first at Spring Cottage, Hackney, and then Oaker View, Farley.

The two lads, Joe and Ted, were very close, and after leaving school they worked in the gardens of Smedley's Hydro, before

Left: Ted Wood. Right: Joe Wood.

working for themselves at timber felling in various parts of the country. In November of 1943, during the Second World War, Joe and Ted volunteered together for the Royal Navy. They trained together at Plymouth, at H.M.S. Glendower as naval gunners. Joe put in a request that they remain together and when proficient they became crew members of H.M.S. President 111, bound for the Indian Ocean. Whilst there, they were seconded to the Merchant Service as gunners to protect the merchant ships from possible enemy attacks.

On the 6th July 1944 they were in a contingent of ten naval gunners on board the Steamship S.S. "Shahzada", belonging to the Asiatic Steam Navigation Co. Limited, when it sailed from the Portuguese enclave of

Goa, on the western coast of India, bound for Aden..

Three days into the journey, on the 9th July at about 9-15p.m., when 500 miles west of Goa, the ship was torpedoed by a submarine. There was a rough sea with heavy swell and rain squalls in this part of the Arabian Sea at the time. The ship was hit on the starboard side and after remaining on a level keel for about ten minutes, listed to port and commenced to settle down by the head.

After S.O.S. messages had been sent out an order to abandon ship was given and six lifeboats were launched, of which numbers 2, 4 and 6 subsequently landed in India and the occupants of number 5 were rescued at sea. These four boats had remained anchored in the vicinity overnight but the next morning there was no sign of the steamer.

The survivors reported safe were 8 Europeans and 44 Indians and included in the missing 44 members of the crew were the Master (Captain A.S. Hamilton), 4 Engineers, 3 Radio Officers and 9 Gunners. Two of these gunners were Joe and Ted Wood.

Within 15 minutes of each other, Mr. and Mrs. Wood received two telegrams on Monday evening, 30th July, stating first that Ted was missing and minutes later the same telegraph boy returned to deliver news that Joe too was missing.

It is a sad fact, therefore, that during the first half of the 20th century Margaret Wood (Clay) had lost her first husband in the First World War and had now lost her two sons in the Second World War).

Another Darley soldier was to die, after taking part in the Battle of Arras, the British preliminary to General Nivelle's French offensive on the River Aisne:

PRIVATE HERBERT W. STONE,
No. 240353, 6th Battalion Sherwood Foresters.
(Died on Monday 23rd April 1917, aged 24 years.)

Born at Wensley, Herbert was the son of Mr. and Mrs. William Stone of 44 Midland Cottages, Chatsworth Road, and husband of Florence E. Stone of 41 Morton Road, Leicester. His father was an engine stoker and like him, Herbert was employed by the Midland Railway Company. A member of the Territorials, he was in camp near Scarborough when he had orders to mobilise.

Private Herbert Stone.

Herbert left home on 13th August 1914 for Chesterfield, where he went into training and was drafted out to France on 8th November 1915. He saw several major engagements and in the May 8th edition of the High Peak News 1916, it is reported that Herbert had been severely wounded in the foot by shrapnel from an exploding shell and had been invalided home after hospital treatment, where he stayed about a month.

Herbert had married Florence at Grantham on October 20th 1915, and they made their family home a few steps from Herbert's parents on Chatsworth Road. After convalescence in 1916 he returned to France with his draft on 6th November 1916.

Between April 9th and April 15th 1917 Herbert's Battalion took part in the Battle of Arras in Northern France. Following a heavy bombardment and gas attack, the British crashed into the positions of the German 6th Army. British air supremacy was rapidly gained and Canadian troops stormed and took Vimy Ridge on the first day. The British 5th Army, assisting in the south, made little progress, however, and the advance was finally slowed down in succeeding days of battle. There was no breakthrough.

Some days later, after the major battle had come to a halt, Herbert was killed in action by an exploding shell whilst trying to capture an enemy position and several others in the platoon were killed with him. On the day of his death, the 23rd April 1917, the Battalion attacked Lievin, on the outskirts of Lens, receiving heavy casualties. 21 other ranks were killed and 71 wounded.

Herbert's body was not found and he is commemorated on a panel in Bay 7 of the Arras Memorial, France.

We have seen that in early Spring the Germans had withdrawn to new defensive positions on and behind the Hindenburg Line. Darley soldier, Thomas Pugh, lost his life as the British Army pursued the retreating German forces:

PRIVATE THOMAS PUGH,
No. 241747, 'C' Company 2nd/6th Battalion
Sherwood Foresters.
(Died on Friday 27th April 1917, aged 21 years.)

Living at 23 Midland Cottages, Chatsworth Road, within the parish of Darley Dale, Thomas worked on the railway and lived with his father Thomas, mother Lily and a sister who became a teacher at Darley Council School, 1918-1921.

Thomas Pugh, together with a South Darley quarry worker, Thomas Walters, was posted to France in March 1917. The great battle on the Somme (1916) was over and the German Army retired methodically to the Hindenburg Line, their new line of defences between Arras and St. Quentin. This 70 mile long stronghold of bunkers, three great belts of barbed wire and cleverly hidden emplacements, was intended to block any further Allied advance.

The Allies cautiously pursued the retiring Germans over the scorched earth left behind and despite enormous logistical difficulties of moving through the devastated Somme area, made comparatively rapid progress.

Thomas Pugh's 2nd/6th Battalion's main actions were centred on the German's fighting retreat to St. Quentin. By 27th March the Battalion held Vraignes, some ten miles west of St. Quentin. At 2-30a.m. on the 31st they moved north and occupied the quarry at the village of Bernes. The momentum of attack was kept up and, despite heavy shell fire, the Battalion took the next village eastwards, Vendelles. A desperate battle now took place for the larger village of Jeancourt and, despite a determined German defence, the position was again taken.

On April 6th Thomas and his Battalion were withdrawn into nearby Hancourt for rest. By the 27th April the Foresters were again in action, this time to the east of Roisel, in an attack on the quarries and Colagne

Farm, near Hargicourt and Harcourt. Sadly, it was in this action that Thomas Pugh was to lose his life at the age of 21.

The attack was launched at 3-55a.m. and the quarries were successfully captured and a line consolidated east of the quarries, virtually reaching the Hindenburg Line. Seventeen prisoners and one machine gun were captured. The Battalion had come under severe shell fire and casualties had been heavy. Thomas Walters, his companion from South Darley, was killed on this day, though his body was never recovered. Thomas Pugh, however, is buried at Templeux-le-Guerard British Cemetery, east of Peronne, in grave I. A.35.

The next soldier from Darley died whilst in a working party carrying out routine day to day duties. He truly was in "the wrong place at the wrong time".

PRIVATE BEN HEWITSON,
No. 252028, 2nd/6th Battalion Manchester Regiment.
(*Died on Friday 4th May 1917, aged 19 years.*)

Ben was the second son of Councillor and Mrs. H. Hewitson of Farley Cottage, Hackney, and was on the staff of Messrs. Handley and Wilde, the accountants, of Bank of England Chambers, Manchester. He joined the Colours on 25th May 1916 with the 2nd/6th Manchesters and went out to the front in late April 1917, in the Lewis Gun section of the Battalion. They served in the trenches just east of Bethune. The last letter received by his parents was dated May 3rd and contains the following :

Private Ben Hewitson.

"We have been in the trenches 20 days now, and of course, that includes what they call the reserve lines. This is the longest stretch we have done. The cake you sent did not last long. It was too tempting. I have read about the potato scarcity in England.

Things must be pretty bad. The food we get here is good, and liberal, but, as I have told you, we develop such appetites that a little extra is always acceptable. Thanks very much for the High Peak News. It will be very interesting reading".

News of his death was delivered in a letter from his commanding officer as follows :

6th May 1917. "Dear Mrs. Hewitson, I am extremely sorry to have to tell you that your son was killed on Friday 4th May. A shell dropped in the middle of the party who were carrying water and he and another man were hit by fragments and killed instantly. He is a great loss to myself and the Company. He showed great aptitude as a soldier, especially with the Lewis Gun. He was always cheerful, even under difficulties, and one of the very best men of the Company. He was buried yesterday by a Church of England chaplain in the little cemetery close by. His personal belongings will be sent down to the base and you should receive them in due course. Please accept for yourself and the other members of your family the sincerest sympathy of my brother officers and myself in your bereavement. Yours faithfully, J. H. Whitworth, Captain."

Ben was buried in Cambrin Military Cemetery, 24 kilometres north of Arras and 8 kilometres east of Bethune, in grave J. 26. The village of Cambrin was only 800 metres from the front line throughout the war.

In July Darley folk were saddened to hear of the death in France of Two Dales butcher's son. William Perry Wagstaffe.

GUNNER WILLIAM PERRY WAGSTAFFE,
No. 89839, 336th Siege Battery, Royal Garrison Artillery.
(Died on Tuesday 17th July 1917, aged 28 years.)

We have already met William Perry Wagstaffe, the Two Dales butcher, in Chapter One. He enlisted at Matlock in June 1916, joining the Royal Garrison Artillery, where his pre-war work with horses proved invaluable.

By July 1917 William was with his Battery of heavy guns between Arras and Bethune, in France, when news reached his father that his son

William Perry Wagstaffe c.1913, Two Dales. He and his father were butchers but also cab operators, He died in the Great War.

had been instantaneously killed.

Gunner W. E. Powell, a friend, wrote to his parents :

"I write this letter with a heavy heart, but as your son's friend, I think it only my duty to inform you that he was killed on Tuesday evening July 17th at about 6p.m. His death was instantaneous so that he suffered very little pain. He was buried yesterday, July 18th, in the village cemetery

Gunner William Perry Wagstaffe.

by his comrades, and his funeral was attended by the Battery officers. The N.C.O.'s of the section send their deep sympathy to you in your sad bereavement".

Gunner Wagstaffe, who was 28 years of age and single, was a well known local sportsman, and at one time was captain of the Matlock Thursday Football Club. Before joining up he worked for his father, William,

William Perry Wagstaffe's sister, Norah, who was a victim of the 1918 flu epidemic.

170

who informed the High Peak News that he had to sell nine of his eleven horses, owing to lack of assistance. Not only had William junior joined the forces but another son, Ernest Stanley, was serving as a lorry driver in the Royal Flying Corps at an airfield near Thetford, East Anglia.

William Perry died during the routine artillery duels taking place each and every day. On that day the observation and targeting by the opposition German gunners had been accurate and shells had struck the Battery, with devastating effect.

William Perry Wagstaffe is buried in grave K. 35 at Cambrin Military Cemetery, close to that of his Darley colleague, Ben Hewitson.

PRIVATE FRANK TAYLOR,
No. 26991, 1st Battalion Grenadier Guards.
(Died on Sunday 21st October 1917, aged 25 years.)

Frank was born at Wensley, but by 1901, the nine year old is to be found living at Brook Side, Two Dales, with his father, farm labourer Uriah Taylor, and his mother Mary Anne. Two other brothers, Herbert and George, were born. When Frank was called up he was working in Yorkshire and he enlisted at Harrogate.

By 1917, Frank Taylor and his Guards Battalion were on the Western Front and facing the Hindenburg Line in France. Wounded during a small scale night time scurmish, he was brought to the Base Supply Depot and the 3rd Echelon of General Headquarters at Rouen, many miles behind the front line. Here there were eight General Hospitals, five Stationary and one British Red Cross Hospital. Despite medical attention Frank died on the 21st October and was taken 3 kilometres south of Rouen Cathedral to be buried in grave P. III. M. 4A. at St. Sever Cemetery Extension.

On November 20th General Haig completely surprised the Germans by launching an attack towards the French town of Cambrai and against the Hindenburg Line. A dawn attack by 381 tanks, with relatively small infantry support and no initial artillery bombardment, completely stunned the Germans. The tanks and infantry support broke through on a six mile front to a depth of five miles.

Throughout the British Isles, church bells were rung out on the 21st November for the first time since the beginning of the war. A break through at last! Or so it seemed; but the chance was thrown away. Insufficient reserves were available to exploit the breakthrough and the German defences stiffened, and then on the 30th November, a determined counter-attack by the Germans forced the British Army back. It was on the day of the German counter-attack that the next Darley soldier was killed:

2ND LIEUTENANT JAMES SALSBURY SMITH,
1st/5th Battalion, The Loyal North Lancashire Regiment.
(*Died on Friday 30th November 1917, aged 19 years.*)

Salsbury Smith lived with his younger brother Eric and parents James and Frances Ellen Smith at "The Winnatts", Two Dales. His father was head of the well known nursery firm, James Smith and Sons.

The High Peak News of December 1917 mentioned that he had passed through the High Schools with honour and was starting a useful career as an analytical chemist when he joined the Colours. Salsbury Smith had only recently crossed the Channel to France, after his training in the army and Cambrai was to be his first and only experience of battle, at 19 years of age.

After ten days of fighting, 2nd Lieutenant Salsbury Smith was suddenly caught in the German counter-attack of November 30th. Unheralded by any long artillery preparation, a short, hurricane bombardment with gas and smoke shell paved the way for the infiltrating advance of the German infantry. The Germans came through the weak points in the British line, then expanded into a broad torrent which overwhelmed the British and surged towards Gouzeaucourt. The emergency declined with the recapture of Gouzeaucourt, and with Haig ordering a partial withdrawal, the Battle of Cambrai came to a close on December 3rd.

However, on 30th November, James Salsbury Smith had been killed in the German counter-attack, another soldier whose body was never recovered. With over 7000 other soldiers killed at Cambrai whose graves are not known, James Salsbury Smith is commemorated on Panel 8 of the Cambrai Memorial, Louverval, S. W. of Cambrai.

*** It is interesting to note that Dr. Wills, the respected doctor from Darley Dale, who had volunteered his services in the Army Medical Corps, was taken prisoner by the Germans during the same action in which Salsbury Smith lost his life. It came as a great surprise to the doctor when the Germans released him in late February, 1918. Dr. Wills told the High Peak News that he was 1000 yards behind the lines when taken by the enemy. He was sent first to Karlsrhue and then to Heidleburg.

Finally, William Holden is one serviceman who I have not been able to find out about to my satisfaction. It is possible that he was:

RIFLEMAN WILLIAM JOHN HOLDEN,
No. C/7276, 18th Battalion King's Royal Rifle Corps.
(Died from wounds on the 15th March 1917.)

Born at Derby, he enlisted in the same town and was in the Ypres Salient in February/March 1917, during a relatively quiet period. However, during the day to day shelling and trench activities he was wounded and died on 15th March. William was buried in grave XI. B. 38 in Lijssenthoek Military Cemetery, Poperinge, near Ypres.

As the last Darley Dale man to be killed in 1917, Salsbury Smith's death brought the total of local servicemen to be killed during the year to twenty. The pain and heartache for their loved ones must have been virtually unbearable but there was to be no "let up" in 1918.

Even more parishioners would become eligible for service overseas in 1918 as conscription now included married men with children, exemptions became rarer than ever and still no prospect of victory was in sight.

CHAPTER SIX

1918 – TOWARDS VICTORY, BUT AT A PRICE

On April 6th 1917 America had declared war against Germany, but with her small army of 210,000 men, it would take some while before her manpower resources could become a decisive factor.

During the winter of 1917-1918 General Ludendorff realised that Germany's only hope of winning the war lay in a decisive victory in the west in 1918 before the weight of American man power began to tell. The Bolshevik Revolution of 1917 in Russia had resulted in that country being knocked out of the war.

Ludendorff shifted most German forces from the east and prepared for an all out offensive to be launched as early as possible in the spring, using "shock troops" as spearheads for the assault. He planned to smash the Allied armies in a series of hammer blows, driving a wedge between the British and French forces, and then destroy the British in subsequent assaults. Preparations were made for this massive attack in the Somme area to begin on March 21st between St. Quentin and Arras, towards the goal of capturing Amiens.

Two more Darley Dale parishioners would lose their lives on the very first day of the "Kaiser's Battle", when overwhelming German forces would roll forward and swallow them up.

The British were well aware of German intentions and made preparations for the inevitable attack. One of the most ironic re-deployments was to abandon the Passchendaele Ridge and form a tight defensive line around Ypres. All the sacrifices of the previous Autumn seemed as nought.

Liddell Hart, the military historian, wrote,

"At 4-30a.m. on March 21st, the sudden crash of some 4000 German

174

guns heralded the breaking of a storm which, in grandeur of scale, of awe and of destruction, surpassed any other in the World War. By nightfall a German flood had inundated 40 miles of the British front; a week later it had reached a depth of nearly 40 miles and was almost lapping the outskirts of Amiens, and in the ensuing weeks the Allied cause itself was almost submerged. Germany came desperately near to regaining that lost chance of victory which she had forfeited in early September 1914".

On that first day, the 21st March, the Germans were favoured by a thick fog that cloaked the infiltrating soldiers as much as it masked the defending machine guns. The specially trained German "shock troops" rolled through the fog, behind a rolling barrage and passed around the British strong points which would be later "mopped up" by reserves.

Darley's first two casualties in 1918, on this opening day of battle were :

BANDSMAN THOMAS HOLMES,
No. 36498, 7th Battalion Leicestershire Regiment.
(Died on Thursday 21st March 1918, aged 37 years.)

Thomas was the son of Thomas and Annie Holmes of Two Dales. His father was landlord of the Nags Head Inn at Brook Side, whilst his mother Annie had died in the late 1890's, leaving Thomas, senior, to bring up three daughters, Emma, Charlotte and Annie, and sons Thomas and William.

Thomas, junior, and William were musically gifted, especially Thomas, who was solo cornet player and conductor of Darley Dale Band, and the only band member to die in the war. He worked as a nurseryman labourer in James Smith and Sons Nurseries, nearby.

When called up to the Colours, Thomas enlisted at Chesterfield and joined the Sherwood Foresters, but at some point he was transferred to the 7th Battalion, Leicestershire Regiment, where his talents as a musician were put to good use. Bandsmen such as Thomas Holmes would also be called upon to act as battalion stretcher bearers during the day to day occupation of the trenches and in attacks on the enemy

175

positions. They would tend to the wounded and carry them to safety.

By the middle of March 1918, the 7th Battalion were in the front line near Epehy, between St. Quentin and Cambrai, on the old Somme battlefield. Unfortunately, they were in the direct line of the planned Ludendorff Offensive of the 21st March (Operation Michael) and were to receive horrendous casualties during the next few days as they faced overwhelming odds.

At 4-30a.m. the enemy put down a heavy barrage of phosgene and mustard gas on the Battalion area, developing gradually into High Explosive and

Brook Side, Two Dales, c.1912.
Tommy Holmes (killed in the Great War),
Annie Holmes (his sister), Hannah Charlesworth
(mother of Joby), Maria Frost and daughter.

shrapnel, until 9-30a.m. Under cover of a thick mist, combined with smoke and dust from bursting shells, the enemy crossed no-mans-land unobserved and captured the forward positions. "C" Company, with the help of two tanks cleared the nearby village, with the enemy retiring.

During the day the enemy made many attacks, using bombing parties and a flame thrower, but the cylinders caught alight and the enemy were burnt with their own weapons. By 6p.m. the enemy had again occupied the nearby village of Peiziere and the counter-attack companies were ordered to again clear the village, which they did so successfully by 8p.m.

During the bitter and ferocious fighting on this first day of battle, Bandsman Thomas Holmes was killed and his body never found as the Germans swept onwards. His name is commemorated on Panels 29 and 30 of the Pozieres Memorial, Somme, 5 miles N. E. of Albert.

In September 1916, Thomas Holmes, senior, had retired from his position as landlord of the Nags Head and now came the news of the loss of his eldest son.

PRIVATE FREDERICK TRAVIS,
No. 268180, "A" Company 2nd/7th Battalion
Sherwood Foresters.
(*Died on Thursday 21st March 1918, aged 39 years.*)

(This account comes from Dr. John Travis, grandson of Frederick Travis)

Frederick Travis was born in 1879 and was the eldest child of Adam and Eliza Ellen Travis. He grew up in the family's cottage on Darley Hillside. His father worked with horses at Stancliffe Quarry and after leaving school Frederick also found employment at the quarry as a grit stone cutter.

Frederick was a member of the local cycling club, a rifle club and a pigeon fanciers' group. It was bell ringing though that was his main interest. He was a member of the fine bell ringing team at St. Helen's Church. They practised regularly in the evenings and sometimes were invited to ring in other churches and cathedrals.

Private Frederick Travis.

In 1906 Frederick married Frances Emma Watts from Tansley and they moved into a newly erected house in Stancliffe View. They had two sons, Harold and Eric. Tragically, Frances died of cancer in January 1910, only two months after the birth of her second child. Frederick then moved back to his parents' house at Hillside, so that his mother could

177

St. Helen's bell ringers c.1912.
Back row: Alfred C. Wright, John Siddall, Harry Gregory, James Wright,
Edwin Blackwell, John W. Derbyshire.
Front row: William Taylor, George Cooke, Thomas White,
Fred Travis (killed in the Great War).

help bring up the children. Soon afterwards the family moved to live in the Lodge, a larger house at the entrance to the Stancliffe Works.

On the evening of the 4th of August 1914 there was a knock on the door of the Lodge. It was Charles Dawson, Managing Director of Stancliffe, who wanted to gain admission to his office in the Works so that he could phone the local newspaper for news (phones at that time being few and far between). A few minutes later he came back to tell Frederick that the country was at war with Germany.

At first Frederick didn't think he would be needed for service in the army as when war broke out he was 35 years old and had two young sons to care for. However, war casualties were heavy and when Kitchener made his appeal for more men he felt he had to join up. He joined the Sherwood Foresters and within six months was fighting at the Front in Belgium and France.

Back at home his parents had a large wall map showing the progress

178

of the war. Pins were placed to show where the main battles were being fought. Soldiers' letters home were censored, but the family always knew where Frederick was because when he wrote home he spelled out the nearest town by putting dots after certain letters in the words.

In January 1918 Frederick obtained leave, arriving in Matlock on the night mail train and walking to Darley. At about 5a.m. the family were wakened by an excited bark from Frederick's dog and came rushing down in their night wear. As a treat his mother produced a tin of Fray Bentos corn beef, not realising that "bully beef" and hard biscuits had been his staple food for weeks on end while in the trenches. When she realised her mistake she at once began to carve some home-cured ham to fry with some eggs. Frederick was infested with trench lice so his mother soon had water heating up in the copper for his bath. All his clothes had to be disinfected, washed and then put in a hot oven to ensure that they were deloused.

The fortnight's leave went all too quickly. Edith, one of Frederick's sisters, took Harold to see his father off on the train from Darley Station. He was not to know that he would never see him again.

On his return to France Frederick went straight back into the front line, in the Noreuil sector, N. E. of Bapaume. At 4-56a.m. on the 21st March the enemy put down a very heavy barrage of gas shells on the front line system. Trench mortars and field artillery continued the bombardment until 9-45a.m. Communication by wire was broken, with only one message being received after this, and that by pigeon.

High Explosive shells now fell on the positions. Only 14 men of the Battalion escaped unwounded from the trenches as the enemy broke through on both flanks, and coming round behind the railway line, cut off and completely surrounded the Battalion between 9-30a.m. and 10a.m.

Frederick was operating a Lewis Gun in no-mans-land near Bullecourt when he was killed by an exploding shell, but in the confusion of battle, he was first of all reported as posted "missing"

Not until Christmas, when the war had ended and former prisoners of war were returning from France, was it possible to find out for certain what had happened to Frederick. An aunt took Harold to see a Nottingham man who had been a runner with the job of keeping

Frederick supplied with ammunition and drinks. This man had actually seen the shell explode that killed Frederick. When he saw Harold he recognised him as being one of the two brothers in a photograph that Frederick had shown him. It could not have been easy for the man to have to confirm to Harold that the boy's father was dead.

The bell ringers at St. Helen's Church rang a muffled peel for Frederick. Arthur, Frederick's younger brother and a stone mason at Stancliffe, made a gravestone that still stands in the churchyard. On it is Frederick's name, together with that of his wife and also his youngest brother who had died in childhood.

Frederick's body was never recovered from the battlefield and his name is commemorated on Bay 7 of the Arras Memorial, France.

So Frederick was dead and it was left to Adam and Eliza, his grieving parents, to bring up his two young sons.

By April 5th, the German offensive came to a halt after gaining a 40 mile deep salient. They had advanced across land devastated by four years of war and could not keep up the supply of ammunition and food to their forces advancing through a quagmire. It also prevented them from providing adequate reinforcements and the infantry quickly outran their artillery support. They eventually lacked the fire power to maintain the momentum of their drive.

A few days later, on April 9th, Ludendorff launched his second offensive (the Lys Offensive) further north in Flanders, on a narrower front, threatening the Channel ports. During these bitter days of fighting throughout mid and late April, five more Darley lads would sacrifice their lives in an effort to stop the momentum of the offensive.

PRIVATE THOMAS TWYFORD,
No. 203095, 10th Battalion Lincolnshire Regiment.
(*Died on Thursday 11th April 1918, aged 34 years.*)

Thomas Twyford was a stonemason and builder who worked with his elder brother Alan for their father, building contractor Thomas Twyford, senior. They lived at Hazel Cottage, Two Dales, with parents Thomas and Ann.

Having enlisted at Derby, Thomas joined the 10th Battalion Lincolnshire Regiment. On the 1st April 1918, during the lull before the second German storm, they found themselves occupying poorly constructed trenches near Armentieres, France, and began improving them by digging during the day and wiring at night. At times they came under severe pressure from gas shells exploding and on the 8th April a captured prisoner stated that an enemy attack was imminent.

The second phase of the German offensive began at 4-00a.m. on April 9th with heavy shelling on support and reserve trenches and from 5-00p.m. to 7-00p.m. large enemy parties tried to advance but were repulsed.

At 8-00a.m. on the 10th April the enemy again attacked but were held in check, except on the right flank, where he was pushing along the river towards Armentieres and commanding the railway and bridge. At 3-15p.m. an order came for general retirement at once. A rear party of twelve soldiers covered the retirement, behaving most gallantly and killing five of the enemy in close fighting.

It was touch and go whether the Battalion got through Armentieres at all. The railway bridge was in German hands, but they crossed a river bridge that was still not demolished.

On the 11th April Thomas's Battalion retired to the Armentieres - Bailleul Railway. From 10-00a.m. to 2-00p.m. the enemy made continuous attacks down the railway and from farms on the nearby road, which were stopped by the Battalion machine and Lewis gunners.

At 5-45p.m. the enemy was seen to be forming up for a further attack but were dispersed by the British 60 pounders and machine guns. At 7-30p.m. Very lights were observed and the Battalion came under heavy machine gun fire from the railway and farm buildings, forcing them to follow the main Bailleul road to the junction of Steenwerck Station Road and the main Bailleul road.

During the desperate fighting retreat on the 11th April, Thomas Twyford was killed in action. In the confusion on the battlefield, as the Germans attacked in overwhelming numbers, his body was never recovered and he is commemorated on Panel 3 of the Ploegsteert Memorial, just across the border in Belgium.

PRIVATE JOHN (JACK) WATERFALL,
No. 301313, 2nd Battalion Royal Scots,
formerly of the Lincolnshire Regiment.
(*Died Friday 12th April 1918, aged 26 years.*)

John was a son of Charles Ormond Waterfall and Annie Maria Waterfall of Hazel Farm, Sydnope Hill, Two Dales. He worked on the farm, whilst his older brother Benjamin was a quarry worker.

He went early into the war, enlisting at Darley Dale, in 1914 and joined the Lincolnshire Regiment, before being transferred to the Royal Scots. John saw a good deal of action but was to die in the final year of the world conflict.

Private Jack Waterfall first joined the Lincolnshire Regiment before transferring to the Royal Scots Regiment.

His Regiment was in position in Flanders when the Germans mounted their huge offensive (Somme Offensive) on the 21st March 1918, along a 60 mile front. The British were taken by surprise and were swept back but the German drive, after gaining a 40 mile deep salient, lost momentum and the offensive came to an end on the 5th April.

Throughout this period, however, John Waterfall had been on leave at home in Two Dales. On his last night, a Sunday, he was drinking in the Blacksmith's Arms with his friends and by the following Friday he was back in the front line, where he was killed in action.

On reaching the Battalion's positions he had found that other reinforcements were arriving, like himself, to make up for the casualties received during the previous days of battle. However, on the following day, April 9th, Ludendorff's second offensive (Lys Offensive) struck the British Army in Flanders, threatening the Channel ports. The situation was desperate, with the British army in disarray, when on the 12th April Haig's order forbidding further retirement bolstered British resistance.

However, on that same critical day of desperate fighting, a shell burst close to John Waterfall, wounding one man and killing John outright. The family was notified that he was missing and later, the same soldier who had been wounded arrived in Two Dales to tell the family what had happened to their son.

John Waterfall's body was never recovered and his name is commemorated on Panel 1 of the Ploegsteert Memorial, Belgium.

Private Benjamin Waterfall, Leicestershire Regiment, seated on the left.

His older brother, PRIVATE BENJAMIN MARSDEN WATERFALL, No. 30770, Leicestershire Regiment, saw much service and action in France and Belgium and survived the conflict. Sadly, however, in November 1918 he became a victim of the flu endemic raging throughout the world and was buried at St. Helen's Church on November 24th, aged 34 years. He was buried with full military honours and his name was inscribed on the war memorial in 1920.

PRIVATE JOHN WILLIAM SMITH,
No. 53235, 2nd/5th Battalion Lincolnshire Regiment.
(Died on Monday 15th April 1918, aged 19 years.)

In 1901 William Smith was a two year old child living with his father, Thomas, a nursery labourer, mother Ruth Elizabeth, and brothers and sisters on Upper Hackney. At the age of 13 years, his mother died and Thomas married again, with the family moving to Ryecroft, Two Dales. William followed his father's' occupation by working in the nurseries of James Smith and Sons.

In 1917, the time came for Billy to be called up. He did not appear at his first enlistment appointment, but fortunately the understanding local policeman called round to point out that he had better be there the next day or there would be trouble.

The young lad, who had not travelled further afield than Matlock, enlisted at Darley Dale the next day and before long had joined the 5th Battalion of the Lincolnshire Regiment. Not long afterwards, his younger brother Ernest lied about his age and he too joined the Colours. At 16 years of age he was serving with the King's Own Light Infantry and eventually saw action in France.

On March 21st Ludendorff launched his massive offensive against the British on the Somme. Amongst the units facing the overwhelming might of the Germans, just north of Bapaume, was the 5th Battalion, but Billy Smith was still back in England, awaiting embarkation.

Between the 21st March and the 26th March, the Battalion and the rest of the Brigade fought hard and long but had to retire. The Brigade casualties had been heavy (1360) and the survivors were all in the last stages of weariness.

Private Ernest Smith, brother of Private John William Smith of Hackney.

However, the depleted ranks were quickly filled up with drafts from England, including Billy Smith, and the whole Division was moved northwards to "rest" in the comparative calm of Passchendaele Ridge.

During its short rest, it was also honoured by a visit from the King.

On April 9th Ludendorff launched the second stage of his offensive and the 5th Lincolns found themselves involved on the northern fringes when, on the 14th April, they were moved into the trenches at Locre, near Kemmel, south of Ypres. By 6a.m. on the 15th April they had "taken over" their sector, near Feuter Farm.

During the morning enemy patrols made repeated, but unsuccessful attempts to penetrate the forward line of posts. At noon came a heavy bombardment, followed by an intensive barrage at 2p.m., with series of attacks made by the enemy.

At this juncture the 2nd/5th Lincolns, who so far had not been so severely pressed, became involved in desperate hand to hand fighting. Eventually, at 6-15p.m., a gradual withdrawal of the whole line took place – a new line being formed along a "ditch" running behind the railway. The railway by this time was completely untenable owing to shell fire.

The enemy advanced with great rapidity in the darkness and losses in the series of attacks and counter-attacks throughout the day, had been heavy.

Numbers of the rank and file, including Billy Smith, were young soldiers fresh from England – lacking nothing in courage, but inexperienced – and so ill-fitted to cope with the complexities of a big battle. The casualties sustained by these forward troops in the day's fighting totalled some 2,300 and one who died in the shell fire directed onto the railway line was John William Smith.

His body was never recovered and he is commemorated on Panel 3 of the Ploegsteert Memorial in Belgium.

PRIVATE HERBERT WAIN,
No. 43078, 14th Battalion Durham Light Infantry, attached to the 11th Battalion Lancashire Fusiliers.
(Died on Saturday 20th April 1918, aged 25 years.)

Herbert, a single man of 25 years, lived with his father, John, a railway goods guard, and his mother Charlotte at 22 Midland Cottages,

Chatsworth Road. Before enlisting at Derby, he was in the employ of Bakewell butcher, T. Thacker. Herbert was a very popular young man, who, in his early years, had won the respect of local Rowsley and Darley people when he rescued two young girls from drowning in the River Wye.

Private Herbert Wain.

On the afternoon of Saturday 24th August 1901, Dorothy Ashbury, aged four, and Mildred Tindal, aged three, of Midland Cottages, were playing on the banks of the Derwent when a basket they had, rolled into the river. In attempting to recover it, they fell in and eight year old Herbert Wain heard their screams.

He quickly managed to pull Dorothy to safety but only saved Mildred after some difficulty. It was thought at first that she was dead, but she recovered from her ordeal. Some time later, in the village schoolroom, Herbert was presented with the Royal Humane Society's certificate by Lady Granby of Haddon Hall.

During the war, Herbert served first of all in the Derbyshire Yeomanry before joining the 14th Battalion Durham Light Infantry. By March 21st 1918 he was attached to the 11th Battalion Lancashire Fusiliers and stationed at Lebucquiere, just east of Bapaume, on the Somme, where the Battalion was severely mauled in the tremendous German offensive of 21st March. They received nearly 300 casualties before the offensive was halted.

The Battalion withdrew by train to rest behind the lines, before going back into the front line at Steenwerck on the 9th April, close to the French and Belgian border, west of Armentieres. Unfortunately, the Battalion was once again to feel the full weight of Ludendorff's second stage of the German offensive across the River Lys, starting on the day the Fusiliers entered the trenches.

The Fusiliers attempted to counter-attack in an attempt to take the village of Croix du Bac but the Germans forced them out and they withdrew to Steenwerck Station. Again the Germans advanced in overwhelming numbers and captured Pont de Pierre, with the Fusiliers counter-attacking but having to withdraw to Mont de Lille. After further withdrawal, the Lancashire Fusiliers went into reserve at St. Jans Cappel and on the 18th April felt the severe effect of a heavy German bombardment.

The Battalion had by now lost many men and at St. Jans Cappel, stragglers from other battalions joined the Fusiliers to form a Composite Battalion. However, the German artillery bombardment was still effective and on the 20th April Herbert Wain became another casualty as he was killed in action. His body was never recovered from the battlefield and he is commemorated on the Tyne Cot Memorial, Belgium.

PRIVATE JOHN FREDERICK HANSON, No. 41538, 6th Battalion Leicestershire Regiment (formerly in Sherwood Foresters).
(Died of wounds, aged 20 years, on 28th April 1918.)

Fred had been born in Wirksworth, but for most of his life lived at No. 3 Ryecroft, Two Dales, with his father Joseph and mother Emma. Joseph was a stonemason at Stancliffe Quarries and Fred was employed in the erecting shop at Markham's Works, Chesterfield.

It was at Chesterfield that Fred enlisted, joining first the Foresters and then transferring to the Leicestershire Regiment. It was whilst taking part in the 3rd Battle of Ypres, that Fred was gassed on the 26th September. Mustard gas was used here by the Germans for the first time and Fred was returned to England to recuperate in Horton War Hospital.

He returned to France on the 29th March 1918, eight days after the Germans had launched the first phase of Operation Michael in the Somme area, but the 6th Battalion were not directly involved. Instead they found themselves in the Ypres Salient.

The line on the Somme was eventually held by the British and Commonwealth troops at tremendous cost, but on the 10th April the Germans launched their second phase of the offensive, towards the River Lys. Again, the 6th Battalion were not confronted by the full weight of the thrust, but on this occasion, they found themselves engaged with the enemy. It was decided to withdraw on April 15th in order to straighten the line of the Ypres Salient. A small party of selected men were left behind to hinder the enemy advance as much as they could by rifle fire.

On the 18th April orders were received to prepare all unnecessary bridges for demolition and British artillery engaged many targets during the day. On the 20th a message was sent out for stretcher bearers. The right hand post had been raided about 9p.m. by a strong enemy party who had crept up a trench. After half an hours hard fighting, the enemy was repulsed with considerable casualties and they discarded rifles and equipment. Casualties for the day were three killed, fourteen wounded and one missing..

One of these casualties was Private Fred Hanson, for he had been badly wounded in the arms, hands and thighs. He was taken back to base hospital but died on April 28th. He is buried in grave FR100, Arneke British Cemetery, between Gravelines and Cassel.

PRIVATE ARCHIBALD CARNELL,
No. 260008, 6th Battalion South Staffordshire Regiment.
(Died from wounds, Wednesday 15th May 1918, aged 28 years.)

Archibald had been born at Hackney in 1890 and in 1901 was living with his parents, John, a stone waller, and mother Susan, at Derwent Terrace, Hackney Lane End. By 1918 his parents were living at Flora Cottage, Hackney.

As war broke out in 1914, Archibald, a single man, was working in Lincolnshire and he enlisted at Boston, joining the 1st/6th Battalion, South Staffordshire Regiment. Four other brothers served in the army, including Harold, an army farrier, and Jack Carnell.

During Ludendorff's second offensive, Archibald's Battalion were serving in the Loisne sector, south of the main thrust of the German advance and were not heavily engaged, receiving relatively light casualties of five killed and twenty wounded throughout the whole of April.

On the 30th April the Battalion were relieved and went into support in the Gorre sector, just N.W. of Bethune, entering the lines by the late evening.

At 4a.m. on the 1st May the enemy opened up a gas shell bombardment which lasted for four hours, causing casualties, though the remainder of the day was quiet. On the 2nd May the Headquarters Details suffered heavy casualties from gas, with 90% of those involved reporting to the Dressing Station. As a result of these actions the Battalion was moved into Reserve at Vaudricourt Wood, under canvas.

Archibald was one of those seriously affected by the gas attack and was removed from the Dressing Station and found himself in hospital many miles away at Etaples, a town 27 kilometres south of Boulogne, on the Channel coast. During the war, the area around Etaples was the scene of immense concentrations of reinforcement camps and hospitals. In 1917/1918, 100,000 troops were camped among the sand dunes, and the hospitals, including eleven general, one stationary and four Red Cross could deal with 22,000 wounded.

Archibald had suffered dreadfully from the effects of gas and on the 15th May he died. His body was buried in grave LXV. B. 33 in Etaples Military Cemetery

After his death, John and Susan Carnell heard that another son, Lance Corporal Jack Carnell of the Highland Light Infantry, was wounded in the leg on June 6th 1918. Thankfully he could be brought back to England and recovered from his wounds.

May 27th 1918 saw the third great German offensive on the Rivers Marne and Aisne, mainly against the French positions and by the 30th May they had reached the Marne. At this point the newly arrived American forces were flung against the nose of the German offensive, holding the bridges at Chateau-Thierry against German assaults, then counter-attacking and driving the Germans back across the Marne.

Throughout June and July further German offensives were repulsed, and on July 18th the Allies went onto the offensive themselves on the Aisne and Marne. The initiative had been wrested from the Germans and Ludendorff's gamble to conclude the war successfully had failed. Allied morale soared as that of the Germans dropped.

Towards the end of July, one Darley soldier died as the German offensive began to subside.

CORPORAL JOSEPH SMITH,
No. 41880, 7th Battalion Leicestershire Regiment.
(Died on Thursday 25th July 1918, aged 19 years.)

Joseph was the eldest child of Joseph and Elizabeth Ann Smith of "Westleigh", near the bottom of Northwood Lane. He had four brothers and one sister and his father was in charge of the engine sheds at Rowsley Marshalling Yard. Joseph, junior, had been born at Walton-on-the-Hill, Liverpool, in 1899.

Corporal Joseph Smith

He had joined the Colours in 1917 and had been promoted quite quickly, for by June 1918 Joseph was a Corporal with the 7th Battalion Leicestershire Regiment. By this stage, General Ludendorff's series of offensives against the Allies were grinding to a halt, and, admitting defeat, he now prepared for a general withdrawal.

At 9-30p.m. on the evening of 24th July Joseph's Battalion moved to Englebelmer, a small village 8 kilometres N.W. of Albert, on the Somme Front. They relieved the 1st Battalion of the Artists Rifles in the front line trenches. The village was in Allied hands during the whole of the war, and it was used as a Field Ambulance Station; but in the summer of 1918 it was liable to occasional shelling.

The relief was completed by 1a.m. on the 25th July. However, the unloading party had been shelled, with two soldiers killed and four wounded. One of the wounded was Corporal Joseph Smith and he was rushed to nearby Englebelmer Field Ambulance station, but on the same day he died from his wounds. Joseph was buried at Englebelmer Communal Cemetery Extension in grave D. 8.

Three days later, on the 28th, the Battalion was targeted by gas shells and drenched with mustard gas. Thirty soldiers reported sick, with temporary blindness and sickness on the 29th, when other gas attacks took place. By the 31st July 145 soldiers had been affected by the terrible gas and had been evacuated to the special baths at Acheux.

By this point Joseph was buried and news of his death at 19 years of age had been received by his family in Darley Dale. Later they paid one shilling per letter to have the message "One of the best" written on his gravestone at Englebelmer.

On August 8th the British went onto the offensive themselves when Haig surprised the Germans by launching the great Amiens Offensive. From this point the British and Allied Armies were driving forward in an "Advance to Victory", but the offensive would result in the loss of five more Darley Dale men.

August 8th proved a decisive day on the Western Front for it unhinged the mind and morale of the German Supreme Command, with Ludendorff declaring it to be the "Black Day" of the German Army and taking a view that "The war would have to be ended".

The Amiens Offensive was a complete surprise to the Germans and its foundation was the sudden loosing of a swarm of tanks (456 in all) in place of any preliminary bombardment. The 14 mile long frontal assault was against a relatively weakly held German defensive position, with none of the usual deep dug-outs to safe guard morale until the hour of trial. Thus, when an hour before sunrise on August 8th the tanks swept forward, together with a barrage and infantry advance, the blow had the maximum shock of surprise.

Darley Dale man, Private George Wall, was to die on the 12th August, from wounds received on the opening day of the battle.

PRIVATE GEORGE WALL,
No. 31186, "B" Company 1st/5th Battalion
East Lancashire Regiment.
(Died of wounds on Monday 12th August 1918, aged 19 years.)

George Wall was the son of Walter and Martha Wall, and in 1901 they were living at Stancliffe, where Walter was the foreman of the gardeners. However, by the time of George's death, the family was living at Riversdale, near the bottom of Northwood Lane. At the age of 14 years

George had been employed as a junior porter at Darley Dale Station.

In 1917, George Wall was called up and joined the East Lancashire Regiment. It was involved in the offensive launched by Haig on the 8th August and his Battalion were caught by sniper and machine gun fire as they advanced. George was hit in the head by a bullet and was rushed to a Casualty Clearing Station. Four days later he died from his wounds and was buried in grave IV. A. 29 at Bagneux British Cemetery, Gezaincourt, on the Somme, 2 kilometres S.W. of Doullens.

Henry Holmes, Frank Colley and Sergeant George Wall were next to fall on the battlefield during the second phase of the offensive (21st August to September 4th).

Progressively, the British and French armies took up the assault. Ludendorff ordered a general withdrawal from both the Lys salient in Flanders and the Amiens area. His situation deteriorated even further, necessitating retirement to the final position – the Hindenburg Line. By this time Haig had expended his reserves and could not further exploit his victory. German casualties were more than 100,000, including some 30,000 prisoners. Allied losses were 22,000 British and 20,000 French. Tactically and strategically, the Allies had gained another major victory, cracking German morale.

PRIVATE HENRY HOLMES,
No. 123237, 42nd Battalion Machine Gun Corps (Infantry).
(*Died on Friday 30th August 1918, aged 20 years.*)

In 1901, two year old Henry was living at No. 7 Church Road, Churchtown, with his 41 year old father, Samuel Holmes and mother Ann. His father worked at Abbey Farm where he was the foreman of carters. By 1916 Samuel had died and Ann, his widow, was living at No. 11 Chatsworth Road, Rowsley.

Henry enlisted and joined the Sherwood Foresters but eventually he became a member of the 42nd Battalion, Machine Gun Corps. In any advance, the machine gunners were employed on the flanks of the

Battalion of assaulting infantry, providing covering fire and attempting to keep the heads of the defending troops down low. They advanced with the infantry, finding protection in the shell holes in No Mans Land, where they set up their guns.

On the 30th August Henry was advancing to the south of Bapaume on the day the ANZACS penetrated across the Somme, taking Peronne and threatening St. Quentin. On that same day Henry Holmes was killed attacking the German defences. He is buried in grave IV. G. 28 at Beaulencourt British Cemetery, south of Bapaume.

SERGEANT GEORGE WILLIAM WALL, No. 240220, 1st/6th Battalion Sherwood Foresters.

(Died on Monday 2nd September 1918, aged 25 years.)

George Wall lived with his father, William, a carter, and mother Annie, at Northwood. Enlisting at Matlock, he had served so well that he had been promoted to sergeant and was undergoing training for a commission when he was called to the new British advances in France and fell bravely for his country.

He was involved in the Allied counter-offensive (Amiens Offensive of August 8th to September 4th), in which the entire German situation would deteriorate, necessitating retirement to the final position – the Hindenburg Line.

Between August 8th to 11th Haig threw his forces against the Germans, who were caught off guard by a well mounted assault, secretly prepared. More than 15,000 prisoners and 400 guns were captured. Haig cautiously paused on August 11th to regroup.

However, between August 21st and September 4th the second phase of the assault took place. Ludendorff ordered a general withdrawal. By the 26th August the 1st/6th Battalion and Sergeant George Wall were in the Gorre sector, near Bethune. "D" Company captured Epinette Keep and pushed forward to posts in front.

By 1st September "B" Company in the centre pushed on across the Loisne River and captured Scott and Hunters Posts after strong opposition. "A" Company attacked and captured Richebourg post after also crossing the river in the face of considerable opposition.

It was during these actions, performed between the 26th August and September 1st, that Sergeant George Wall was severely wounded and he succumbed to his injuries on the 2nd September. He is buried in grave VI. A. 6. In Pernes British Cemetery, between Lillers and Bethune.

PRIVATE FRANK COLLEY,
No. 70019, 1st Battalion Cheshire Regiment
(formerly with the Lancashire Fusiliers).
(*Died on Monday 2nd September 1918.*)

Frank's father, George Colley, came from Ellesmere, Shropshire, to work as a joiner for Hackney building contractor Thomas Bowler. George married his employer's daughter, Mary Jane Bowler and they lived on Matlock Bank. A son, Frank, was born in 1898 but sadly Mary Jane died shortly after his birth. By the early 1900's George's sister, Mary Ann Colley, was acting as house keeper and helping to raise young Frank.

By the time Frank was called up into the army he was working in Lancashire and he enlisted at Seaforth, joining the Lancashire Fusiliers, before transferring to the 1st Battalion Cheshire Regiment.

On the 8th August, 1918, Haig struck his first great blow in the counter-offensive, the Amiens Offensive, and recaptured a large area of ground. The 1st Battalion arrived at the front on 14th August in time to take part in further actions. Its objective on the 21st August was to take the railway line S.E. of Achiet-le-Petit, just west of Bapaume.

There was no artillery support, but six tanks moved with them. It was now broad daylight, but the fog still held. Achiet was captured without heavy casualties and they pushed on through the village to the railway line.

As they did so the fog lifted and they came under very heavy machine gun fire from beyond the railway, but they fought their way up the hill, reaching the railway and holding it. Most of the tanks were knocked out before they could support the leading companies. Within fifteen minutes of reaching their objectives the Battalion successfully repulsed a counter-attack.

The Battalion went into action 600 strong and lost no less than 300 killed and wounded on this day. The 1st Battalion, with Frank Colley, was relieved in the evening.

Between the 31st August and 3rd September the attack continued around Bapaume. Here the enemy was now fighting carefully staged rear-guard actions over ground that was terribly battle scarred and in which machine guns played a decisive part.

On the 2nd September, the 1st Battalion took part in the capture of Beugny village and high ground, a few kilometres east of Bapaume. The village was known to be strongly held by the enemy, a previous attack by another Division having failed.

A barrage began at 5-08a.m. which brought down a heavy retaliatory barrage on the assembling companies. This caused many casualties, especially amongst the officers and N.C.O's. Great shells fell right into the trenches, causing at least 50% casualties before they even started forward.

The surviving men were told to lie in No Mans Land till the time was up. In spite of these difficulties, "A" Company went on through the village, capturing several prisoners. The left company advanced about a thousand yards and were then held up by very heavy hostile machine gun fire. An enemy counter-attack later in the day drove back the left flank of "A" Company. An immediate counter-attack by the Cheshires re-established the position on the high ground.

Casualties were again extremely high in the attack on Beugny and Frank was one of those who had been killed by the hideous affect of the German shelling. His body was never recovered and his name is found on Panel 16 of the Vis-en-Artois Memorial, S.E. of Arras.

Thus, on the 2nd September 1918, Darley Dale had lost two men on the same day.

Another Darley man to die, but only after the war had ended, was:

SAPPER GILBERT PREECE,
No. WR/275474, Railway Operating Division, Royal Engineers.
(*Died on Sunday 1st December 1918, aged 24 years.*)

Gilbert was born at Llandaff, Glamorgan, but by the age of seven, in 1901, he was living with his parents, William and Mary Preece and nine month old brother Donald at " The Knabb", Ladygrove, where his father was a domestic gardener. By 1915, William Preece's family was living at the East Lodge, Stancliffe, but by 1916 he was in "Vraynor", on Station Road.

Gilbert found employment on the Midland Railway, as did his younger brother Donald. Tragedy struck the family when, on the afternoon of March 19th 1915, fifteen year old Donald was killed by a train on the track between Darley Station and Churchtown Crossing, whilst carrying out his duties of putting the signal lamp in for the Church Lane signal box.

By this time Gilbert was in France, having volunteered to serve as a sapper in the Railway Operating Division of the Royal Engineers. Towards the end of the war this had become a huge organisation, with the object of getting men, munitions, artillery and food to the front line. It operated on both narrow and standard gauge track and the work on the narrow gauge could be very dangerous, for it was often targeted by enemy artillery.

Gilbert survived to the end of the war, but by late 1918 and early 1919 a flu epidemic throughout the world was claiming more victims than had been killed during the Great War. Gilbert became one of these victims and he died in hospital in France on 1st December 1918.

He was buried in the Tourlaville Communal Cemetery, on the outskirts of Cherbourg.

Unfortunately, I have been unable to find with certainty the identity of three of the Great War servicemen on the Darley memorial. They are HARRY GREY, WILLIAM A. OWEN and LEONARD HOUGHTON. Their names, however, will not be forgotten.

A month before Gilbert Preece's death, inspired by the Communists and sparked by a mutiny of the High Seas Fleet, disorders, revolts and mutinies flared inside Germany between October 29th and 10th November,1918. A new Socialist government took power and proclaimed a republic on November 9th, whilst the Kaiser fled to Holland on November 10th.

A German delegation negotiated an armistice at Compiegne, France, at 5a.m. on November 11th, 1918, and hostilities ceased at 11a.m. After nearly four and a half years of fighting the war had come to an end.

There has probably never been a more prolonged and appalling experience for ordinary soldiers in all the history of the British Army than the four years of trench warfare, 1914-1918. This was a war in which the noise of the artillery was so tremendous it could occasionally be heard in London; that left 65,000 British veterans in mental hospitals, still suffering from shell shock in 1929; in which – in winter, when it rained – 40 British soldiers a night were reckoned to drown in the mud; and in which the front line was at times drenched in poison gases ("Gas cases are terrible," recalled an eye witness. "Their lungs are gone – literally burnt out. Some have their eyes and faces entirely eaten away by gas and their bodies covered with first-degree burns.").

And now, after living through such nightmare conditions, the survivors could look forward to returning to the beautiful parish of Darley Dale.

CHAPTER SEVEN

DARLEY DALE –
LIFE BETWEEN THE WARS

The Armistice became effective on the 11th November 1918. Victory had been achieved but the cost was enormous in both manpower and material, with 900,000 Empire troops killed and a further two million wounded. Those who survived came back to "a land fit for heroes" and were promised that the Great War had been "the war to end all wars". The sentiments seemed appropriate at the time but history would make a mockery of them.

As a silence fell over the distant battlefields, Darley Dale counted its loss of 63 parishioners, but those who arrived safely back into the Derwent Valley gave thanks that they had survived the horror of war. A saddened parish was also grateful for the war's end and wished to see the survivors take up their civilian lives again.

The feeling of a return to normal circumstances was provided by the closing down of the **Whitworth Institute Red Cross Hospital** in early June 1919. A letter printed in the High Peak News of May 24th reads;

"I hear the closing down of one of the finest War Hospitals in the County is expected in a few days at Darley Dale and the nursing staff is to have a good time on Friday this week, to celebrate the same. The village people are looking forward to the gates of the Park being flung open as in other years, seeing the Railway Company is likely to issue cheap tickets for school treats during June and July."

Setting out on a misty morning, the staff of the Whitworth Red Cross Hospital and soldier patients, had a days holiday on Monday 26th May, motoring to Monsal Dale. En route there was a call to go through Haddon Hall and the return journey was past Chatsworth House. The

Hospital was to close at the end of that week, with a dinner and dance provided for the staff on Friday evening. The gates of the Park would then be thrown open to the public as in pre-war years.

The curtain finally came down on the Hospital when, on Sunday 29th June 1919 in St. Helen's Church, there was a dismissal service of the nursing staff. Special prayers for peace were said and the flag that had flown over the Whitworth Institute during its occupation was taken up and placed over the altar, the first flag to be placed in the ancient church of Darley.

On Saturday 19th July 1919, **Peace celebrations** took place throughout the whole country and flags and bunting were found in profusion hanging in the streets of Darley Dale. North Darley Peace celebrations began with teas being provided in the local areas of the parish (Hillside, Green Lane, etc.). Darley Dale United Band marched from Stancliffe West Lodge and then from Two Dales bridge to the Park, and at 6p.m. a short united Thanksgiving Service was held. Sports were open to all residents of North Darley and at a later time dancing took place on the lawn, the whole programme concluding with flares and rockets.

Balloons were sent up during the evening; 80 prizes were competed for and light refreshments were provided in the grounds. At the subsequent sports there were 33 events, commencing with flat races for both girls and boys and later included a bandsmen's race whilst playing an instrument, a bike race on planks for men and ladies, a soldier's flat race and a tug-of-war.

Two Dales had its own peace celebrations and welcome home for the returning servicemen when local farmers such as the Wagstaffes, and the Fearns of Tax Farm, used large tarpaulins to erect marquees in the field next to the Blacksmith's Arms. A tea was provided for Two Dales folk and races were held.

Almost a year later, sadder and more poignant events took place, in November 1920. At 7-15p.m., on Friday November 19th, a crowded St. Helen's Church witnessed the unveiling and dedication of a beautiful stone wall tablet honouring the names of those from the parish who had fallen during the Great War. It had been designed by Matlock sculptor J.W. Boden and cost £150. The dedication was led by the Right Reverend Bishop Taylor Smith, the Chaplain General to the Forces.

Unveiling and dedication of the wall tablet to the First World War dead of Darley Dale, in St. Helen's Church, on Friday November 19th, 1920.

The newly commemorated Darley Dale War Memorial in the Whitworth Institute Park, unveiled on Sunday 21st November 1920.

Two days later, on Sunday afternoon, November 21st, a handsome **War Memorial**, consisting of an 11 foot high Celtic Cross of Stancliffe stone was unveiled and dedicated in the Whitworth Institute grounds. At least 500 people assembled to witness the unveiling by Colonel H. Brooke-Taylor, in the absence through illness of Colonel Goodman of Buxton, and to hear the names of the fallen read out. The memorial cost £500 and was the work of Messrs Robert Lehane and Company, to the design of W.F. Wills of Derby. This was a sad occasion because it would bring back memories of the many who had fallen during the war, but the shared experience of loss would perhaps unite and strengthen them.

Memories of the Great War, tinged with sadness, must have come flooding back to those gathered in the Institute grounds but at least they had the comfort of knowing that Darley Dale had honoured its dead. Now the people could look forward to continued years of peace and building fresh lives, unfettered by the harsh grip of war. Little did they know that just nineteen years later they and their families would face the grim prospects of involvement in another violent world conflict, the

Second World War, resulting in the loss of 30 more lives.

We have already taken a glimpse at the experiences of day to day life in pre-Great War Darley Dale, shared by those who fell during the war. What was peacetime life like during the 1920's/1930's in Darley Dale for those families who would send loved ones off to fight and die in the years 1939 to 1945?

For all the future combatants, a significant number of these inter-war years were spent within the confines of either **Darley Council or Darley Churchtown Schools**.

By 1921, at the Greenaway Lane school, the wartime gardening lessons for the older boys were continuing on the allotment plot, with Mrs. Sharpe, Dr. Sharpe's wife at the Red House, giving a penknife each year for the best kept plot. Around the perimeter of the school garden were general plots, but each lad also had his own area to tend. Each pupil gardener contributed a shilling a year, with the County providing the seed, and the boys could then take home the produce.

Gardening lesson at Darley Council School, c.1921.
Mr. Child, Clifford Allsop.
Tom Needham, Tant Wildgoose, Tant Smith, Harry Pearson, Tom Ollerenshaw,
John Turner, Tom Pilkington, Harold Pearson, Harold Thomas, Dyson Charlesworth,
Rockcliffe Boam, Harry Gentle, Lewis Barker, Joe Waterfall, Robin Wildgoose,
Walter Jackson.

North Darley Council School teachers 1920.
Back row: Miss Edith Pugh, Mrs. J. Smith, Mrs. Child, Mrs. Jessie Agutter.
Front row: Miss Renee Smith, Mr. A. H. Child, Miss Fanny Gregory.

Football was popular amongst the boys, but the school at this stage lacked a team kit and a field to play on. In the close season of 1920/1921 each boy paid one penny a week to school mates Harry and Harold Pearson, and made house to house collections, until £2-15-6d was raised and the head teacher, Mr. Child, could send off to P.B. Mays of Birmingham for the team shirts.

John Gregory of Hackney, and owner of Victoria Mill Timber Yard on Old Road, was approached to see if he would allow the team to play on one of his fields across the road from the school. He was ill at the time and confined to the house. He agreed that if schoolboy Harold Pearson, a junior member of Darley Band, would play the cornet for him, they could make use of the field. When goal posts were required, the procedure was repeated (almost a case of "playing for your supper"). On May 8th 1925, the managers gave a half day holiday to celebrate the school winning the Matlock and District Schools Football Cup. By this stage the lads were playing their matches in the field along Oddford Lane which now contains the allotments.

During the 1928 season, when Horace Smith (the Two Dales shoemaker of later years) was a team member and they acquired a new kit, they were made to wash it themselves in the boy's cloakroom. The shirts shrank and unknown to Mr. Child they attempted to stretch them back into shape by nailing them out on the playground fence. The idea was not a success.

December 3rd 1923 witnessed fourteen of the girls over 12 years of

Darley Council School football team 1920-1921 season,
when they were without a football kit.
Back row: Harold Pearson, Harry Pearson, Jack (Nugget) Wagstaffe, Fred Hallows,
Harold Thomas, Joe Waterfall, Mr. Child.
Front row: Walter Jackson, John Turner, Monty Turner, Stan Ollerenshaw,
Harry Gentle, Lewis Barker.

Darley Council School football team 1921-1922 with their new kit.
Back row: Mr. Child, Harold Thomas, Joe Waterfall, Lewis Barker, Harold Pearson,
Joe Knowles (Wensley).
Centre row: Ralph Gregory, Bert Webster (Wensley), Jack (Nugget) Wagstaffe.
Front: Bill Wragg, X, Harry Pearson.

Darley Council School 1924-1925 season.
Winners of the Matlock and District Schools Football Cup.
Back row: Ken Grafton, X, X, Horace Woodhouse, Charlie Bark, Jimmy Slack.
Middle row: X, X, Mr. Child, X, X.
Front row: X, X.

Darley Council School football team 1928-1929.
Back row: Owen Williams, Fred Fawley, X, Mr. Child, Horace Smith, X, X.
Middle row: Ken Grafton, Cecil Woodhouse, X.
Front row: X, X.

age beginning cookery lessons for the first time in the Two Dales Wesleyan Sunday School, under the supervision of Miss Morris. (During lessons on a Monday, a small queue would form in the same building, as the elderly and needy arrived to collect parish relief). These lessons would continue throughout the 1920's and 30's, under the supervision of Mrs. Smith and later Miss Oldfield, but would be transferred into the old Anglican school room (now Hayes bake house), where a couple of ovens were provided. It became known as the Special Resources Centre and the boys were not allowed to feel left out, for they began woodwork lessons with Mr. Vallender in the same building, The girls would take their own ingredients for cookery, but on some occasions, instead, they learned the rudiments of washing, ironing and starching clothes, using the correct procedures. Perhaps the lads in the 1928 school football team could have benefited from such lessons?

In the early 1920's, swimming lessons for older children recommenced at the Whitworth Institute. Different schools went on different days and it was always the hope of many children that their lesson would be early in the week, for by Friday the water was becoming dirty and "muddy". It would certainly not have passed the Health and

Girl swimmers from Darley Council School c.1926.
Back row: Lilian Crooks, Vera Allen, Kathleen Harris, Gladys Kirkham,
Alice Wildgoose, Phyllis Staton, Audrey Smith.
Middle row: Edna Barker, Kathleen Wagstaffe, X, Ivy Holland, Margaret Sheldon.
Front row: Clarice Holland, Clara Howe, Hughna Lane.

Darley Dale Council School swimming team 1929.
Winners of the Whitworth Challenge Cup.
Back row: X, Fred Wagstaffe, Clifford Barker, Mrs. Agutter, Olive Woodhouse,
Mr. Child, X, X, Phyllis Lane.
Middle row: Clara Howe, X, Edna Barker, Hughna Lane, Margaret Sheldon, X, X, X.
Front row: Fred Harlow, John Charlesworth, Dennis Lane, Howard Wagstaffe, X,
Marjorie Soppitt.

Darley Council School swimming team 1931.
Winners of the Whitworth Challenge Shield.
Back row: Edith Coleman, Sybil Salt, Mrs. Agutter, Joan Chapman, Mr. Child,
Peggy Begnall, Nelly Waterfall.
Next row: Harry Dalton, X, Howard Homewood, Arthur Brown, Tom Talbot, X, X,
Fred Harlow.
Next row: Sidone Donelan, Ethel Wagstaffe, Isabella Jago, ? Smith, Marjorie Soppitt,
Edith Hole, Joan Wagstaffe.
Front row: X, Olive Woodhouse, Jean Bawley.

Darley Churchtown School swimming team 1932.
Winners of the Whitworth Challenge Cup taken by the poolside.
Back row: Arnold Kingman, Dick Corfield, Jack Atkinson, ? Gill, Les Bramwall,
Harold Mayall, (swimming instructor).
Front row: ? Marsden, Norah Taylor, Arthur Ayre, Florence Webber, Vera Corfield,
? Duggins.

Safety laws and regulations of today. The Supervisor for the pool was Tom Smith.

The first swimming gala between local schools was held at the Institute, on October 4th 1927, when Darley Council, Darley Churchtown, Rowsley and Matlock All Saints Schools competed. On October 12th 1928 the competition was held again and the Whitworth Swimming Challenge Shield was awarded to the Council School. Good swimmers abounded, for during the following three years Darley Council School teams would again prove triumphant. Their four year hold on the trophy was broken on October 4th 1932, however, when Darley Churchtown School won it for the first time. On that occasion the winners of the individual trophies were Norah Taylor and Arthur Ayre.

The social conscience of the children was not neglected, for during the Great War, they had helped to raise money for the servicemen

Darley Dale Council School 1921-1922 football team.
Back row: X, Mr. Child, Wilburn Boam, Dyson Charlesworth, George Allwood, Tom Smedley.
Middle row: Fred Waller, Charlie Bark, X.
Front row: Cecil Allsop, Horace Woodhouse, ? Wood.

Darley Council School c.1921.
Back row: Tom Needham, Rockcliffe Boam, Matthew Smith, Anthony Smith,
Dyson Charlesworth, Robin Wildgoose, Clifford Allsop, George Woodhouse, Lewis Barker.
Next row: Mary Allwood, Frances Bond, Olive Bowler, Florence Smedley, Elsie Fearn,
Marjory Morris, Minnie Kirkham, Elsie Wardman, Jessie Sharp (later Mrs. Agutter).
Next row: Lucy (Totty) Hodson, Florence Warren, Rose Woodhouse, Nancy Allsop,
Edna Holland, Beryl Goodwin, Madge Holland, Hannah Charlesworth, Linda Holland.
Front row: Harold Pearson, Tommy White, Jack Wagstaffe, Fred Walker, Bill Wragg,
Ralph Gregory, Ronnie Burnett, Harold Thomas.

Darley Council School 1923-1924.
Back row: X, X, X, X, X, Horace Woodhouse, Wilburn Boam.
Next row: X, X, X, X, Dorothy Allen, Mary Fawley, X.
Next row: Mr. Child, X, X, X, teacher.
Front row: X, X, X, X, Charlie Bark.

Darley Council School c.1925.
Back row: Sam Wlliams, X, ? Devanney, X, Walter Wilson, X, X, Percy Wagstaffe, George Roberts.
Next row: Renee Smith (teacher), Audrey Smith, Ena Goodwin, X, X, Marion Wildgoose, Alice Wildgoose, Kathleen Harris, Vera Allen.
Next row: X, Vera Charlesworth, Wilfred Fearn, X, Ivy Holland.
Front row: Charlie Maddocks, Jim Turberville, Eric Hallows, ? Mullett, Derek Redfern.

Darley Council School c.1925.
Back row: Fred Ollerenshaw, Fred Waterfall, Walter Boam, Wilfred Woodhouse, Dick Hodge, Charlie Dunn, Berty Fletcher, Ronald Gage, Harold Burnett.
Next row: Alice Howe, Mary Wood, Ida Sheldon, Joan Beaumont, Lois Milner, Mary Wildgoose, Gladys Kirkham, Alice Wildgoose, Daisy Reed, Marjorie Bailey, Kathleen Harris.
Next row: Horace Smith, Edna Hawley, Ivy Holland, Arthur Vardy, Victor Brightmore, Dennis Marshall, Jean Wagstaffe, Miss Woodhouse.
Front row: Ken Ward, Harold Ward, Colin McDowell, Eric Hallows, Len Wilmot, Joe Walker, Ronald Gage.

Darley Council School c.1928.
Back row: X, X, Dick Syson, X, John Howe, X, X, X, X.
Next row: X, Winnie Travis, X, X, X, X, Gladys Staton, Marion White, X.
Next row: X, Nancy Smith, X, X, X, X, Jean Wragg, Renee Smith (teacher).
Next row: X, X, X, X, Billy Wagstaffe, Fred Gill, X, X, X.
Front row: X, X, X, X, Freddy Wildgoose, X.

Darley Council School x.1930-1931.
Back row: X, Fred Fawley, Cecil Woodhouse, Walter Wilson, Leslie Fearn,
Horace Smith, X.
Front row: X, Vera Charlesworth, Edna Hawley, Gladys Kirkham, Valery Evans,
Phyllis Staton, Mr. Child.

fighting overseas and for the convalescent soldiers at the Red Cross Hospital. Thought for the welfare of others was encouraged during the 1920's and 30's when the children were asked each year to collect eggs that could be presented to the Whitworth Hospital (in 1927, 466 eggs were sent, in 1929 – 452 eggs, in 1931 – 773 eggs, and in 1932 – 677 eggs).

It was a sad occasion, however, when well respected head teacher, Mr. Arthur Child and his school mistress wife, terminated their engagement with the school on January 31st 1934, after nearly 22 years service since the opening of the school. He was replaced by Joseph Hancock, late headmaster of Blackwell Newton Council School, who began his duties the following day.

"A new broom sweeps clean" and exciting events for the children took place during his first year in office. On Thursday 5th July 1934 an afternoon holiday was given by the managers for the first annual school sports, to be held in the Whitworth Institute Park, whilst on the 18th July the presentation of sports prizes and trophies were held in the school yard at 3-30p.m. On the 3rd August 1934 Miss Griffiths and Mr. Leslie Fearn accompanied a party of five boys and six girls attending a Derbyshire Schools' Camping Association Camp at Sutton-on-Sea. Mr. Hancock had been a founder member of the organisation.

However, these experiences were the exception rather than the rule and more hum-drum events formed the basis of day to day school life. On 19th December 1934 Eric Carey got a piece of cardboard in his ear. He was taken to Dr. Wills and Dr. Phillips for it to be removed. It was not just pupils, however, who required the good doctors' attention. An accident to the head teacher occurred during a science lesson when a gas jar rose suddenly while collecting gas and struck him above the left eye. He went to the Whitworth Hospital and stitches were inserted by Dr. Phillips.

Darley Churchtown School had continued to be run successfully by the well respected head teacher, Mr. Scott Anthony, throughout the 1920's. His discipline was firm, some might say robust, for woe betide any lad who "stepped over the mark". James Smith and Sons had a nursery of willows growing in the field behind the school and this was very convenient for the head teacher. Mr. Anthony often asked a lad to

Darley Council School football team, 1939,
winners of the Bunting Cup against Darley Churchtown.
Back row: Ken Marsden, Dennis Brailsford, Harold Toplis, Dick Wagstaffe, John Wilson.
Middle row: Leslie Fearn (teacher), Gene Woodhouse, Ron Broome, Jim Charlesworth,
Joe Hancock (head teacher).
Front row: Jack Hayes, Bill Smith, Brian Boam.

go and cut him a willow stick when punishment needed to be meted out.

During the 1920's the school classrooms were separated by a house in which the Fearns lived (the building now contains the head teacher's study). Mrs. Fearn was a kind lady who allowed certain children to bring eggs to school, which she would boil, so that they did not have to go home for lunch. It was only later, in 1933, that an extension was built on to the school.

On the 2nd May 1929 Sylvia Marsden, aged 13 years, was presented with a set of 10 volumes of childrens' encyclopoedias for the best essay sent in from Lancashire, Cheshire and Derbyshire schools on "The qualities of Ovaltine".

In July 1929, Mr. Anthony's long reign at Darley Churchtown came to an end and on October 23rd Mr. John Charles Bartram arrived from his previous post at Great Longsone to take over the helm. Though strict, his regime was a little more liberal and the school continued to prosper.

The allotment at the side of the school, next to the church, continued

Darley Churchtown School 1925.
Back row: Cecil Jackson, Billy Taylor, Arnold Taylor, Alan Forbes, Billy Gill, Alan Knifton, X, X, Colin Cowley, X, X, ? Geeson, ? Fletcher, X, X, X, Alfie Taylor, Roy Walls. Next row: X, X, X, X, Nancy Fletcher, Gladys Smedley, Gwen Fearn, X, X, Miriam White, X, Mabel Wilson, Marjorie Walker, Dennis Holland, X, Cissy Morton, Joyce Taylor,Gladys Fairclough, Amy Price. Next row: X, X, X, X, X, X, X, X, X, X, X, X, X, Miss Fox, Mr, Scott Anthony, X. Next row: X, X, X, X, X, X, X, ? Ainscough, X, X, X, X, X, X, X, X, Norah O'Connor, X, X, X, X.Front row: X, X, X, X, X, X, X, X, X, Jack Greaves, Ernest Poulson, X, X, X, X, X, X, X, X.

Darley Churchtown School 1925.
Back row: X, Alfie Taylor, Roy Watts, X, Jack Coe, Jim Jackson, X, X, Leslie Walker, Roy Hibbs, ? Howson, Fred Taylor, Bill Grinly, ? Fielding, Clifford Jackson, Sam Morton, X. Next row: Joyce Taylor, Gladys Fairclough, Amy Price, Beatie Lomas, Mona Wilson, Chloe Brassington, Violet O'Connor, X, Adele Lomas, Molly Bailey, Agnes Morton, Maurice ?, Gwen Bowler, X, X, X, X, X, X. Next Row: Mr. Scott Anthony, Miss Priestley, Ivy Lovell, X, X, Vera Slater, May White, X, X, Daisy Charlesworth, X, Evelyne Woosnam, Renee Ainscough, Ethel Ainscough, X. Next row: X, Elsie Taylor, X, Marie Haynes, X, X, X, X, X, X, Ethel Haynes, X, Sidone Donelan, Lexie Hibbs, X, Nancy Burton, X. Next row: X, X, X, X, X, X, X, X, X, X.Front row: X, X, X, X, Jack Atkinson, X, X, X, Ernie Bellfield, X, X, Jeff Fearn, ? Bark, Jim Slater, X, X, X.

Darley Churchtown 1928.
Back row: X, X, X, X, X, X, Jack Greaves. Next row: X, X, X, X, Norah Whitehead, X, X,
X, Florence Webber, Ethel Haynes, Mrs. Hooker. Next row: X, X, X, X, Gerald Fletcher,
X, X, X, X, X, X, X, X. Front row: X, X, Louise Watts, Joyce Holland, Vera Corfield,
Nancy Burton, Alice Greatorex, X, X, Irene Browne, X, X.

to be well tended, but Mr. Bartram also introduced new, interesting ingredients to the teaching process. A new person quite often brings new ideas and Darley Churchtown was the first school in the locality to receive a pottery wheel and microscope, whilst book binding and weaving lessons were introduced.

On March 29th 1933 work began on a new classroom extension, which was opened formally by Judge Harold Newell of Darley Hall on December 9th 1933. The scholars gave an entertainment and there was an exhibition of the work done in school.

On July 5th 1933 the School was given the opportunity of seeing the King and Queen on their way from Chatsworth to the Royal Show, at Derby. The scholars left school for the main road at 11-35a.m. but their majesties passed through Darley Dale ten minutes before the time announced, resulting in the children not being able to see them. On the following day the Rector made arrangements for the children to be accommodated in the Station Yard, Rowsley, to see the departure of their majesties by the Royal Train. The infants went to the Churchtown Crossings to view the train.

According to the school log book, January 21st "was a miserable day with snow and rain, and attendance was poor. At 9-00a.m those present listened to the announcement on the wireless of the passing of our beloved King. The children stood for a few moments in silence. The hymn "Let Saints on earth" was sung and a commemoration prayer included in the morning service. The headmaster spoke of the mourning of an Empire-wide family."

At nearby Abbey House, Matthew Walker and his wife continued to be benefactors to the school and local community. Throughout the 1920's the businessman allowed classes to attend his jam and Christmas pudding factories at Derby on educational visits near Christmas time and the children came away with a small pudding and pot of jam. At Christmas, all the children received a shiny new penny and a pudding, whilst in Autumn, the school children were always allowed to visit his orchard and collect the windfalls. By the mid-1930's free milk was issued to the children and monitors would walk on to Abbey Farm, where Mr. Goodwin provided bottled milk, fresh from the farm.

September 29th 1936 again saw Darley Churchtown winning the Whitworth Swimming Shield, with Eileen Devaney and Harry Johnson winning the individual cups, whilst on July 13th 1937 the school defeated Wirksworth Grammar School on the Whitworth ground and won the Warney Lea Cricket Championship Shield. In the year that war began with Germany the final of the Bunting Cup was contested by the football teams of Darley Churchtown and Darley Council School. At Wirksworth, on May 10th 1939, Darley Council School were the victors by one goal to nil.

When the children of Darley Dale left school, most of them at the age of 14 years, they found work mainly in the local parish or adjacent districts. The large majority of employment opportunities were the same as had existed before the Great War and so son would often follow father into the same workplace.

The nurseries still continued to flourish, with **James Smith and Sons** remaining the largest. However, the demands of the Great War 1914-1918 had brought the number of employees down to 22 from 149.

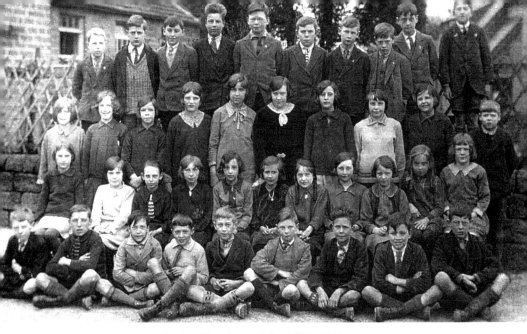

Darley Churchtown School 1929-1930.
Back row: ? Geeson, Frank Knifton, Billy Jones, ? Gill, Stanley Hitchman, Jack Greaves,
Maurice Lane, George Clarricotes, X, Dick Corfield. Next row: Bessie Thompson, Nellie
Whitehead, Norah Taylor, Lexie Stone, X, Vera Greatorex, Joyce Allsop, X, Joyce
Fentem, Sam Stringer. Next row: Ethel Haynes, Dorris Greaves, Joyce Holland, Vera
Corfield, Florence Webber, Alice Greatorex, Louise Watts, ? Tipper, Margaret Witham,
Gwen Taylor, Norah Whitehead. Front row: Jack Price, Gerry Fletcher, Harry Bispham,
Alwyn Wain, ? Fearn, Ronnie Allsop, Walter Cropper, ? Taylor, X.

Darley Churchtown School 1930-1931.
Back row: Dennis Scot, X, Dennis Allen, Alan Knifton, Charlie Thompson, Vernon Gill,
John Tunnicliffe. Second row: O. Corfield, G. Morgan, Leonard Jackson, Marie White,
Maurice Buck, Gwen Fentem, C. Thraves. X. Front row: Kathleen Devaney, Betty
Woosnam, Betty Ainscough, X, Ethel Johnson, X, Cynthia Brown, X.

Darley Churchtown School c.1932.
Back row: X, Sam Stringer, John Evans, Jack Allsop, Louis Holmes, X, Eric Lees, Sidney Taylor. Next row: X, Dorothy Wall, Isabelle Fearn, Audrey Holmes, Margery Webster, Joan Burgess, Thelma Lomas, Renee Brown, Rita Bradshaw. Next row: Dorothy Thompson, Alec Thompson, Harold Gill, Dudley Welch, Aubrey Bowler, John Thompson, Arnold Kingman, Les Bramwall, Harry Knifton, Frank Taylor. Next row: Margaret Bispham, Winnie Price, ? Harris, Marguerite Allsop, X, Florence Percival, Louie Johnson, Renee Gould, Mary Briddon. Front row: X, Albert Hallows, Haydn Kingman, Harry Hibbs, Roland Corfield, Selwyn Ricketts. (Both Aubrey Bowler and John Thompson were killed in the Second World War.)

Darley Churchtown School netball team c.1935 1935.
Back row: Marguerite Allsop, Connie Marsden, Renee Brown, Joyce Fentem, Joan Burgess, Joan Wilson, Louie Fletcher. Middle row: Barbara Fentem, Louie Johnson, Rita Bradshaw, Dorothy Wall. Front row: Eileen Devaney, Milly Hibbs.

Darley Churchtown football team 1938-1939 season.
Back row: Frank Fletcher, Tom Goodwin, Alan Wigley, Reg Parks, Peter Wells.
Middle row: Alan Fletcher, Peter Thompson, David Holness, Mr. R. Wragg.
Front row: Maurice Kingman, Colin Burgess, Henry Mellor.
For three successive years the boys had headed the Northern Cricket Section. Owing to difficulties in obtaining a suitable field, this was their first year in the football section of the Association and they were indebted to the L.M.S. Railway Sports Club for the loan of their sports ground. The girls last year headed the Northern Section Rounders League.

With the post war development of machinery, fewer men were required and the number employed at James Smith in 1932 was 55.

The Nursery consisted of three groups in 1932; the Home Group of 26 acres consisting of Home and Wheatley Nurseries, the Hall Moor Group of 88 acres and the famous Siberia Nurseries of 80 acres. They were still the largest growers of hardy heaths in the world, with saleable stock carried of 500,000 plants every year. Stock was grown for forests, game cover, fox cover and gardens, and many thousands of hedging plants were cultivated. There was a stock of 200,000 English Yews in various stages of growth, with 30,000 laid down each year.

During the Second World War, when certain of the skilled workers were away fighting, some of the land was used for growing essential food and women workers were employed for this. They grew turnips,

James Smith and Sons Nurseries c.1920, showing Wheatley Nursery and Wheatley House.

James Smith and Sons Nurseries, c.1920, showing Wheatley Nursery.

carrots and potatoes. The turnips were sent to the Bolsover Jam Factory in which Eric (James's second son) had shares. Other people also went from the nursery to the newly built shadow factory of Firth Derihon in 1942.

However, the decline had already set in during the mid 1930's. We have seen that well before the Great War, Matthew Smith, the second son of the family, had been given, rather reluctantly, 50 acres of land at Sydnope to set up Forest Nurseries. During the 1930's this nursery began to prosper, helped by Wilfred Smith, who, although still working for James, took cuttings secretly and gave them to Forest Nurseries, so putting the business back on its feet. As the years progressed, Forest Nurseries continued to develop and still continues to operate today in the form of a garden centre.

Further along the slopes of the valley, at Upper Hackney, another Smith family continued to develop their nursery during the inter-war years. **Gervase Smith** had begun his nursery in the 19th century and was helped by his sons Gervase, junior, Harry, Sid and Dick, whilst the daughters helped in either the shop or in the Hackney post-office that they ran.

Top two photographs: Gervase Smith's nursery stall on Chesterfield market, late 1920's.
Bottom photograph: Eric Smith, Jenny? and Sydney Smith at the bottom nursery, 1930's.

We have already seen in chapter one how young Gervase was employed as a licensed hawker, taking his horse and cart around the district, selling soap, Brasso, rubbing stones, as well as paraffin from a metal container. This he continued to do well into the 1920's.

However, the main work was performed in the Top Nursery and Fairfield Nursery on Old Hackney Lane, which provided work for 15 people, altogether. The produce was taken to Bakewell market on a Monday, Matlock on a Friday and Chesterfield market on a Saturday, with the cart acting as the stall. Their horse and cart carried the produce to Chesterfield via Farley Hill, and an extra horse helped it up the steep slope, before it was unhitched and sent back to find its own way home. The horses were stabled underneath the shop. By the start of the 1930's, however, a lorry had been bought to replace the horses.

The main speciality was rose growing, with Harry Gill doing the grafting, but conifers and fruit trees were also grown. The period after Christmas was also hard work, for a lorry delivered lawn seed and vegetable seed in bulk. These had to be sorted and weighed by hand, in order to be put into individual packets, which then had to have labels put on them by means of a hand operated printing machine. It was a tedious, time consuming business.

The **London Midland Railway Company's Rowsley marshalling yards** continued to operate and provided work for many men from Darley and adjacent parishes. Those youths leaving school at 14 and wishing to become firemen on the railway would have to work their way up to that position.

Some of the youths began their careers as a "caller up", with the task of ensuring that engine drivers and firemen would arrive at Rowsley on time to take out their locomotive. There were three shifts and during the night shift, from 10-30p.m. to 7a.m., there would be three "caller ups" operating. Two youths would arrive at 10-30p.m. and one at midnight.

The foreman in the loco department provided the two youths with a book of names of Darley men to be "knocked up" and a book for Rowsley men. Bicycles were also provided, with oil operated lamps, and in the darkness a "caller up" would cycle to an engine driver's house and either throw a handful of gravel at the bedroom window or tap on the window with a clothes prop, left lying there for the purpose. The details of the locomotive to be used and the destination were handed over and the cyclist then pedalled rapidly to the fireman's house to give the same information. All of this was accomplished an hour before the loco men were due on their shift.

The lad who came on at midnight had first to clean out the offices and then relieved the other two at 2-30a.m., while they took a well earned "snap break". Whenever there was a lull in the work load, the Darley "caller ups" took their rest in the Church Lane signal box and those for Rowsley in the North Junction box.

On the two separate day shifts, only one "caller up" was required and instead of a book they were issued with tickets by the foreman, with drivers' and firemen's names on them, the time and also the destination. If an accident had occurred on the line or if it became foggy, the "caller up" also had to wake up the plate-layers. On a foggy day these men went to their cabin by the side of a signal and placed detonators on the lines, if a distant signal was set at danger, thus allowing the engine driver a warning to slow down.

At 14/15 years of age, some of the lads became "bar boys", helping to change the fire bars in the fire boxes of the locomotives when they were burnt out, and cleaning the fire boxes and smoke boxes, but only under the supervision of the boiler man. Most lads progressed to be cleaners, another filthy job, entailing cleaning of the outside of the engine with a cleaning material that smelled terribly.

At 16 years of age

Circa. 1930. A Kirkby class 2 outside frame freight locomotive underneath the Coaling Plant at the new Rowsley Shed, built in 1926. Coal is being hauled up the gantry and tipped into the hopper, ready for discharging into the tenders. In the foreground is the ash disposal pit, where engines had their fires cleaned after arriving at the shed.

(Fred Morton via Rowsley Association Collection.)

223

Rowsley Loco football team c.1930. Back row: X, A. Wain, X, J. Wain, X, X, Les Wright, X, X. Middle row: Harry Davies, Walter Smith, Stirling Wragg, X, X, Arthur Haslam, X. Seated: X, X, X, Eric Lane, X.

(Fred Morton via Rowsley Association Collection.)

Rowsley Loco cleaners 1944. Back row: Jack Hibbs, Sam Briddon, Doug Goodall, Madge ?, Rosie ?, Rosie ?, Harriett ?, Pat Esplin, Mrs. Marshall, Daphne Evans, Mrs. Evans, X, Ken Lill, Tom Thorpe. Front row: X, Mrs. Hiden, Mrs. Wager, Olive Fearn, X, Edna Barnes, X, X, Madge Poundall, Mrs. Gold, Harriett ?, X, Ivy ?, X, XX.

they went on to become "pass cleaners", subject to passing an examination by the inspector, enabling them to work on the footplate. The main work for them was on shunting engines in the sidings, though sometimes they were allowed onto the main line with the permission of the driver.

Eventually, they were made up to fireman for work on the main line, especially on the banking engines that pushed the goods trains to Peak Forest, for the coast down the other side. The inspector, wearing a bowler hat and navy blue suit, might come on board for the ride up to Chinley and ask the new fireman questions about firing and about rules and regulations.

Meanwhile, with 800 jobs provided by **Mill Close Lead Mine** during the 1920's and 30's, either underground, on the surface workings or in the laboratory, the South Darley company remained the biggest employer in the district and helped to offset the problems caused by the "Depression Years" of the early 1930's.

Even in the late 1920's and early 1930's the miners from Bonsall and further afield were still using the "miners' track" that slanted across Wensley hillside, into Wensley and across the "Clouds" to Mill Close. In all weathers, the twinkling lights from their lamps or torches could be seen snaking up or down the hillside during the evening or near the commencement of the dawn shift. It was not until a little later that Frank Loxley, haulage contractor from Bonsall, operated a bus that brought Bonsall and Winster men for the early morning shift and returned those miners home who were "knocking off".

The large majority of the employees worked underground on a three shift system during the 1930's, but considerable numbers of men and youths were employed on the surface, especially on the dressing and flotation plants, which, by the late 1930's, were extremely modern.

Danger was always present underground and accidents were much less frequent at the surface. But danger there was for the surface workers, especially if the safety precautions were relaxed by anyone. 18 year old Ferdinand White of Darley was killed in 1934 whilst working on the jigs, when his scarf became tangled in the machinery as he was oiling it and he was dragged to his death in the mechanism.

On Friday 25th February 1938, following the firing of a shot in the lower levels of the mine, water burst through and flooded to a considerable depth, causing complete stoppage of work underground and over 300 men temporarily out of work. Many of the surface men continued working however.

Shortly after the mine was reopened just two months later, an even more serious accident happened near the working of the flotation and dressing plant. On a Tuesday afternoon, at 3p.m. on 10th May 1938, three men were killed and one severely injured in an accident on a large tip of waste "slime", near the entrance to the mine.

Four men were engaged in loading Frank Toplis's lorry with material that was being taken away to the dressing plant for re-treatment for the discovery of lead deposits. James Byatt (aged 50) of Old Hackney Lane, Thomas Ball of Elton, Victor Barnes (19 years) of Ashford and Arthur Bond (18 years) of Bonsall were the men involved.

While engaged in shovelling the waste, the men noticed a fall from the face of the tip, and one of their number was buried. The other three were seen to dash to his aid but at that moment there was a further, heavier fall and all four were completely buried.

A rescue gang of 30 men was at once formed and attacked the "slime". After a few minutes James Byatt was dragged clear in a semi-conscious state and with a broken leg. He was taken to the Whitworth Hospital in the Matlock motor ambulance.

Men attacked the waste frantically in an effort to save the other men, and after a few more minutes, Barnes and Ball were brought to light. Dr. Phillips and Dr. Wills arrived on the scene and took charge of the attempts to revive the men, but, after about an hour, they were forced to give up their efforts.

It was over two hours later that Arthur Bond's body was found. The three bodies were taken to the mortuary to await an inquest. Arthur Bond had only just recommenced work at the mine the day before, after recently being involved in a motor-cycle accident and receiving a broken leg. Victor Barnes was found with his arm around Thomas Ball's shoulder.

Fortunately, such tragedies were few and far between.

By 1938, **Stancliffe Stone Quarry** was still prospering, with approximately 280 men employed in the different departments. A great

1929. The 300 yard steam operated rope-hauled inclined tramway from Lees Shaft to the dressing plant. 'Jumbo' headgear and engine house is in the background.

New headgear has been built onto Jumbo Engine House and shaft c.1934. The two hopper bins are for Haddon and Stancliffe Estates ore. In the foreground is Mill Close Mine Laboratory.

Lees Shaft headgear at Mill Close Lead Mine. Ore was pushed in tubs from the shaft, and tipped into two stone hoppers, then drawn via the tramway shown to the dressing floor at Warren Carr Shaft.

Mill Close Mine suspension bridge over the River Derwent, between the cricket ground and St Helen's Church. It eventually became a short cut to the mine for Darley miners. It was demolished in the 1960's.

Dismantling 'Jumbo' pumping engine at Mill Close Lead Mine 1933.
Back row: Derek Lane (lorry driver), J. Grimshaw (foreman), J. Slack, F. Hardy.
Front row: N. Porter, M. Bowen, T. Evans, H. Cook, H. Grimshaw.

Harry Sheldon driving the battery powered electric engine on the 70 fathom level. Harry was to die in a Japanese P.O.W. camp near the end of the Second World War.

deal of that prosperity was down to the good management of **Charles Dawson**, managing director during the war years and the 1920's. He was one of the most popular and well respected figures in the parish and it was with deep shock and sadness that Darley folk learned of his death in 1928, at the age of 45 years. It resulted in one of the largest funerals seen in Darley Dale.

Charles Dawson, Managing Director of Stancliffe Estates Company Limited.

Returning from Cheadle Hulme with his wife and daughter, he died in a car accident in Ashwood Dale, Buxton, at 10-30p.m. on Thursday May 31st 1928 The back tyre burst and the car left the road, crashing into a tree and overhung the river.

A much respected man, "Charlie" Dawson had a smile for everyone and his workforce virtually knew him as a friend. Amongst many other positions held, he was

229

Funeral procession of Charles Dawson, Managing Director of Stancliffe Estates Company Limited, killed in a car accident near Buxton on 31st May 1928. Procession led by Darley Band, is at the bottom of Whitworth Road.

Funeral procession of Charles Dawson, led by Stancliffe foreman George Charlesworth, reaches Church Lane crossing, Church Road, 1928.

*Funeral cortege for Charles Dawson about to arrive at St Helen's Church,
Darley Dale, 1928.*

*Stancliffe Stone Quarry in the late 1920's.
Alf Holland stands at the extreme left on the back row.*

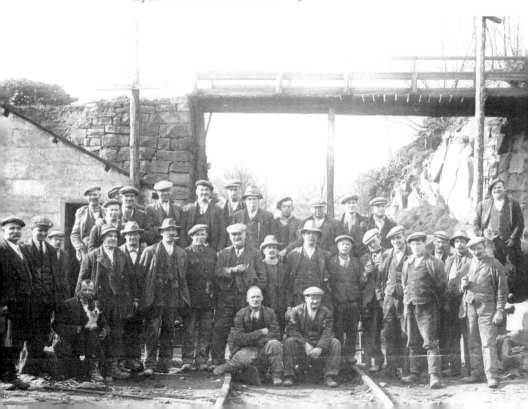

Above left: Workers in the quarry at Stancliffe Stone, c.1931.

Above right: Doug Marsden, from Oker Road, South Darley, Stancliffe Quarry steam crane driver, in 1929. He would light the boiler early in the morning, to raise a head of steam. The crane moved across the quarry bottom on rails.

Group of workers at Stancliffe Stone Yard in 1934. They mixed the precast stone that was placed in the wooden moulds to make the assorted shapes shown in the foreground. Wilburn Boam is fourth from the right and Jack Ayre is sixth from the right.

the Chairman of the Committee of the 1st Darley Dale Troop of Boy Scouts and vice-captain of Darley Cricket Club's 1st Eleven. Saturday's cricket match at Darley was postponed and the flag flew at half-mast.

The simple and impressive funeral service at St. Helen's Church on Monday afternoon was attended by hundreds of people from all parts of the district. The cortege of many cars was headed by Darley Band and 200 Stancliffe employees, led by foreman George Charlesworth. They proceeded down Whitworth Road and along Church Road to the church.

At **John Gregory's Victoria Saw Mill and Timber Yard**, throughout the 1920's and early 1930's, teams of woodcutters still travelled to the woodland areas owned by the company. Hardwick Wood had been bought by John as well as areas of timber near Ashboune. Three horses used for pulling out the timber were stabled in farm buildings on Hackney. Steam engines, coiling in a steel rope, were also used at Hardwick Woods and Ashbourne to drag the timber out.

Some timber was taken to the nearby sidings to be loaded onto rail wagons for the journey to Darley Station. At other times a Robey steam traction engine, nicknamed "Big Bertha", would bring quantities back by road. This engine was replaced by a smaller Foden engine that would travel as far as Gainsborough and Peterborough to collect the timber. These engines were driven by Sammy Crooks and Bill Greenough.

In 1936 the Foden went off the road, to be replaced by a petrol driven French Latil tractor which could go further afield at a faster pace.

Twenty men were employed at the timber yard, with two men out driving the engine and three wood cutters away felling timber. Wood was never cut in the summer, because the sap was "up", and during this period the wood cutters helped out at the timber yard. During the 1920's and 30's the majority of the timber brought into the mill was made into pit props for the coal mining industry. All the machinery in the Old Road yard was worked by their own power source, a steam boiler and generator.

On Wednesday evening 4th May 1938, Victoria Sawmills was gutted by fire as 50 feet flames spread rapidly, despite the efforts of Matlock and Chesterfield fire brigades. The only piece of machinery to escape the fire was the steam boiler, whilst the only building left in use was the office.

Gregory's Timber Yard. A gang is felling and hauling the timber at Hardwick Woods, in the 1920's.

Timber being transported along the A6, near Matlock, late 1920's, by the steam engine known as 'Big Bertha".

234

Gregory's Saw Mills, c.1920's. The traction engine was used for drawing in the timber.

Felling and haulage operations by John Gregory and Sons taking place at Hardwick Woods in the 1920's.

Caravan accommodation for some of John Gregory's workers at Hardwick Woods, 1920's. It appears that someone has been out getting meat for the 'pot'.

Gregory's Timber Mill. A load on its way home, in the late 1920's.

Matlock Fire Brigade on duty c.1935 at Oddford Lane Bridge, Two Dales. Part of the field on the left is now a car park for Forest Nurseries.
The by-standers are, left to right:
Tommy Allwood, Tom Smith, X, George Woodhouse (driver on the Silver Service).
In May 1938 the engine was used to combat the disastrous fire
at Gregory's Saw Mill, Old Road

The saw mill employees worked hard at crushing all the fallen masonry and put it back into the floor as cement. Outside contractors built new working premises, but meanwhile, Big Bertha was used to drive a portable rack bench and circular saw, so that business could be maintained. It took three months of hard work to complete the task of refurbishment.

During the Second World War, the depleted work force was helped by the use of P.O.W. labour, when Italian prisoners from the camp at Harpur Hill, Buxton, were brought by Silver Service bus drivers Vic Carter, Bill Haynes or Harry Bailey.

Between 1924 and 1932 **Bakelite Limited** was sited next door to the woodyard and made laminates and plastics for the electrical and radio industries, using petroleum based raw materials brought into the nearby sidings by railway tankers. It provided much welcome employment, and the firm even boasted their own football team. However, in 1932 Bakelite relocated to Birmingham but in March 1941 they returned to the Darley site in order to escape the ravages of the German Blitz. The production of laminates for the aircraft industry was of major importance to the British war effort, especially in the construction of the renowned Mosquito fighter-bomber.

The milling firm of **A. Johnson and Sons (later S. and E. Johnson)** arrived in Two Dales in late 1924 and set up business in the Ladygrove Mills. A large area of land and many properties within the Two Dales, Ladygrove and Hackney area belonged to the Dakeyne Estate, based at Holt House, Two Dales. On June 18th 1924 the Dakeyne Estate came onto the market and amongst those properties being sold were the Ladygrove Mills.

The property consisted of a three storey factory, with old mill adjoining, commodious warehousing and stabling and ample water supply, a 60 horsepower water turbine and a steam powered main shafting hoist. The sale also included the 35 acres of Ladygrove, including valuable sporting property, dams and capital fishing.

The property was withdrawn on the day at £2200 but was sold a little later in the year to Ernest and Sidney Johnson for £2400. The business of A. Johnson and Sons had originated in a small mill near Birchover in 1860 and was carried on at Alport Mill, near Youlgreave, from 1896.

The works team of Bakelite Limited, c.1932, playing in the Matlock and District League.
Included are: L. Barker, T. Riley, H. Thompson, Dick Fentem, Bill Wood, Bill Salt,
R. Geeson, E. Wood, Mr. Bramall, Mr. Mountney, R. Aspinal, W. Holmes.

View of Ladygrove Mill, Two Dales, the home of A. Johnson and Sons, corn millers. On
the extreme right is a distant view of Loscoe Row.

Johnson's Mill steam lorry in 1928 at Fairclough's Mill, Warrington.
Driver and mate Edgar Pashley and George Green.

Frank Hodgkinson, driver of a Johnson's Mill lorry, taking grain from the riverside
wharf at Gainsborough to Ladygrove Mill, Two Dales. During the war years he would
sometimes make the 'trip' twice a day.

The two brothers were very different in character, with Sidney dressed in suit and "hard" hat and Ernest in overalls, always prepared to get his hands dirty. He was skilled in preparing stone work and could dress his own mill stones. Just before his marriage to Beryl Gould in 1925, Ernest would travel in his motor cycle and sidecar from Alport and get down to physical work in restoring Ladygrove Mills to a reasonable state.

Another brother, Joseph, worked at Ladygrove as an employee, while a fourth brother, Alfred, remained at Alport to run that mill on behalf of Ernest and Sidney. For a number of years the Alport Mill was used to grind corn, which was sold as crushed barley or rolled oats for animal feed for local farmers, who collected it in sacks. (The Alport Mill was kept on until the 1960's).

When Ernest and Sidney arrived at Ladygrove in 1925 they concentrated purely on flour milling, but in 1932, when Bakelite Limited left their premises on Old Road to go to Birmingham, A. Johnson and Sons took over the site and after a while Ernest began to concentrate on producing cattle and poultry food at the new premises. Other activities of the firm covered maize flaking and barley flaking for the brewing industry.

The Second World War saw ancillary plants at Ladygrove Mills manufacturing oatmeal and producing porridge oats, called "Ladygrove" Breakfast Oats. Puffed wheat was manufactured, with the pieces being blasted out of a large, "gun-like" mechanism, set upon a tripod. During this period and after the war the firm was contracted by the war office and prison service to provide them with breakfast oats and cereals.

It was during the war years that women such as Rose Grafton, Marjorie Webster, Joan Barker, Elsie Ethelstone, Dolly White, Joyce Briddon, Winnie Allsop and Mrs. Yates came to work on the conveyor belts, glueing together the boxes of cereal food. In the sack room, Doris Elliot, Dolly White, Mrs. Grafton and the McNevin girls helped to clean the hessian sacks that were returned by the local farmers, after they had received a credit note. A powerful pneumatic suction machine sucked out unwanted particles and the women patched the holes and sewed the seams together. This work was carried out until the 1960's, when paper and synthetic fibres were used instead. Canadian wheat also arrived at the mill in linen sacks during the war years and because of the shortage of linen due to rationing, some women made tea towels and bed linen out of this material..

During these difficult times, whilst Ernest was attempting to improve the mill, he travelled to various parts of the country to buy reclaimed material and second hand machinery. On one such expedition, hollow wooden tubing (called trunking) was salvaged from the bomb damaged Tate and Lyle sugar factory at Liverpool. Lorry loads of "trunking" arrived and before fitting it inside the mill, the compacted icing sugar inside had to be chiselled out by the locals, who were allowed to take it away to supplement their sugar ration.

Wartime rationing was supplemented in other ways. Treacle was occasionally obtained when the large tanker wagon arrived with molasses treacle to mix with the cattle food. At the tail of the tanker valve was more refined treacle that was certainly edible during such periods of hardship. Another ingredient of the cattle feed was monkey nuts and although they were rather musty when they arrived in bulk delivery, many workers would eat them during their twelve hour shift.

The 1920's saw a **revolution in road transport** in the area, with the

James Henry Woolliscroft, founder of the Silver Service Bus Company. He stands by his Green Lane home in the 1920's.

development of bus services, especially in the rapid expansion of passenger services operated by the **Silver Service Bus Company**. James Henry Woolliscroft acquired a Model-T-Ford with a convertible flat lorry waggonette body for his business at the green grocers shop on Stancliffe View in 1920. It doubled as a taxi and a makeshift charabanc and was followed by a 12 seater charabanc on a Model-T-Ford chassis and a 14 seater Napier. These vehicles were parked in the Stancliffe Stone Quarry Yard and painted silver. In 1924 the first regular schedule services were begun with a 20 seater Dennis bus.

The year 1929 saw the company moving from Stancliffe Yard to a purpose built

One of the early fleet of Silver Service buses. A BAT No.7.

Driver Eric Froggatt and his conductor on the Matlock to Rowsley route, late 1920's.

R.A.C. man Billy Wheeldon on left.

Interior of the Silver Service Bus Company garage c.1934.

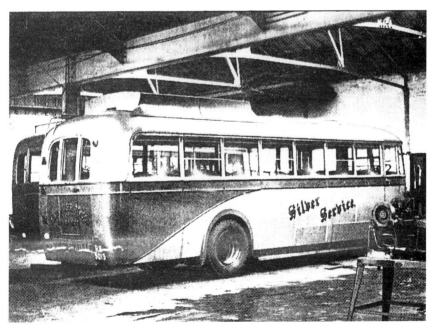

243

Silver Service Bus Company garage c.1934. A corner of the workshop, showing a drilling machine and, part of the welding equipment.

Silver Service Garage c.1938 (now Milner Conversions).
The notice board offers a Saturday trip to Nottingham Goose Fair for four shillings and Blackpool Illuminations for eight shillings and sixpence.
Left to right: Geoff Birkett, Oliver Marsden, David Lowe, Felix Boam.

Silver Service bus drivers in the 1940's.
Bill Haynes, Wilf Woodhouse, Harry Bailey.

Silver Service bus on the A6 in front of Darley House, c.1948.
Jimmy Woolliscroft, May Wayne, Elsa Stuart, Joyce Pennington.

Church Inn charabanc trip c.1924 by Hands Bus Company.
Back row: Jim Jackson, X, Alf Waller, X, X, X, X, X, X, X, X, X.
Seated: Enoch Lomas, Ernie Smith, William Cope, X, X, X, Joe Thomas, X, Kye Gilbert,
Rhoda Hughes, driver Sam Slack.
Rhoda Hughes worked for the landlord and landlady of the Church Inn, Mr. and Mrs.
John Alston,

Tommy Slack's bus from Green Lane, Darley Dale (an early competitor to the Silver
Service bus company), outside Billy Needham's shop at Darley Bridge, in the late
1920's. In the background is Len Riley's greengrocer's horse and cart.

Darley Bridge. South Darley.

garage at the junction of Hackney Lane with the main A6 (containing Milner Off-Road at the time of writing), where repairs were effected. A lathe, pillar drill, grinding wheel, electric welder and an oxy-acetylene welding plant allowed day to day repairs to be carried out, whilst a 600 gallon tank of fuel oil was built behind the garage.

The hilly roads of the district were subject to heavy snow falls and frosts in winter and tyre chains were therefore used very frequently in winter. The damage to chains was always a problem and the bill for new chains or repairs was considerable. The welding plant was invaluable and was kept very busy on this job alone in severe winter conditions.

A Darley man who knew all about the roads in the district was **Frank Toplis**, who, together with his brother Jim, a skilled mechanic, operated a haulage business during the 20's, 30's and 40's.

On the site of the present Loggins mini-market and petrol station, by the side of the A6 and opposite the entrance to DFS Furniture Store, Ernest Henstock had sold and repaired wireless sets and charged batteries from a wooden shed, during the early 1920's. He began

Frank Toplis's garage and haulage lorries c.1938. Now the site of TwoDales Petrol Station and Loggins supermarket at Warney Road.

Frank Toplis in his taxi, late 1930's.

building a house on the site but could not complete it and sold the ground to Frank Toplis of Chesterfield Road, Two Dales.

Frank had been given the valuable contract to haul lead ore from Mill Close Mine to the Lea Mills smelter and he needed parking and garage space for his increasingly large fleet of lorries. Ernest Henstock's partially completed home was now converted into a garage, from where Frank Toplis operated his haulage firm and taxi. Long distance tramping lorries were also run by the firm and drivers included Ernie Walker, Harry Bispham, Bill Grindy, Jack Cowley and Fred Walker.

Another highly gifted Two Dales motor mechanic during this period was **Richard (Dick) Lane**. Born at Northwood in 1884, Dick attended Churchtown School and at 14 years went to work in the Stancliffe Hall gardens and nurseries when the Reverend Owen started a boys' preparatory school at Stancliffe.

In 1905 Dick was selected to be chauffeur of Reverend Owen's Humber car, followed in turn by an Armstrong Whitworth, and Dick was sent on a mechanics' course to their Manchester works. He drove his employer and later his successor, Mr. Conway, many miles whilst touring the country.

*Richard (Dick) Lane, chauffeur to Reverend Owen, outside Stancliffe Hall
front entrance in 1906, at the wheel of a Humber 1905 Tourer.
Leyland Foster (the valet) is in the background.*

*Derek Lane in 1926 Austin 20 Saloon car, outside his father's garage, Two Dales, 1930.
Nancy Smith, Ena Gregory, Hughna Lane, Betty Lane, Dennis Lane.*

Harry Gregory, driver for Dick Lane, with Morris Commercial lorry, c.1931-1932, outside the garage, Two Dales. In the later 1930's he went to Gainsborough to run the dockside warehouse on behalf of Sydney and Ernest Johnson of Ladygrove Mill.

During the First World War he worked at Chesterfield Tube Works as a furnace tender, making cannon shells, and came home to Darley Hillside every other Sunday on his Rudge-Whitworth motor bike.

After the war Dick Lane went to the Stancliffe Stone Quarry Yard, where his first job was in charge of a huge gas engine that supplied the motive power via belts and pulleys throughout the works. He became the founder mechanic of Stancliffe Garage, but in 1921 he decided to branch out on his own account and erected at Darley Hillside a large wooden workshop purchased from R. Lehane and Company, delivered by steam wagon.

He also invested in a Ford-T-model taxi-cab, which he bought in London and drove back to Darley Dale, with only oil lamps for illumination. Largely he concentrated on motor and cycle repairs, especially for Ford-T models, with which he had become a local expert.

In 1924 he decided to expand and took over the former butchers shop on Chesterfield Road, Two Dales, that had been run by William and Stanley Wagstaffe. On land adjacent to these rented premises he used a large shed for working purposes and for storage and started his Two Dales garage. Two more Ford taxi-cabs were added as well as a lorry and help was provided by drivers Harry Gregory and George Turkington, with George maintaining the vehicles in good repair, and putting his skills as a sign writer to good use.

"Pratts" petrol was sold and was delivered to Dick's garage in two gallon cans. These had to be emptied by hand into the fuel tanks of clients vehicles. Eventually, a petrol pump was provided on the roadside, selling fuel at one shilling, eight and a half pence a gallon and was often operated by Linda Slack (nee Holland).

Dick Lane would turn his hand to most things, including selling scrap, lorry loads of flagstones and timber. During the 1926 Miners and General Strike, there were numerous small open cast and underground coal mines working in the Clay Cross and Chesterfield area, needing timber for pit props. Dick therefore decided to cut timber during this period and asked Two Dales blacksmith Arthur Watts to provide him with a couple of horses, for Arthur had good contacts with ex army sales of horses.

When the trade slump of the early thirties came, Dick decided to dispense with the garage business and in 1932 left Two Dales, after buying land near Gas Cottages and established a small haulage and timber trade with scrap metal and second hand machinery.

The state of the roads for such motorised transport was not good. Even the main roads in the early 1920's were fairly narrow and of limestone macadam, muddy and slippery in winter and appallingly dusty in dry summer periods. By 1930 the A6 was being laid with tarmac, obtained from a plant in Derbyshire Stone Quarry, but many secondary roads simply consisted of large stones bonded with limestone grit and dust. A machine with spikes on it, pulled by a horse, came along and cut up the surface of the road, which was then rolled flat again after more dust and gravel had been added.

Some of these secondary roads were now being treated by tar spraying. A horse pulled a cart with a large metal cylinder in the back, containing tar, and a chimney on top. The compartment below contained a fire to keep the tar viscous and it would be sprayed onto the surface of the road to bind it together

Although gangs of council workmen were now being formed to lay a tarmac surface, aided by lorries and steam rollers, the tar spraying on the minor roads was often dealt with by the local farmer, using his horse and cart, after tendering for the job with the Urban District Council. The same procedure applied when snow ploughing duties were required during the heavy falls of the winter months.

Another task, and an unpleasant one at that, which was often tendered out by the council to local carters or farmers, was the removal of night soil from the earth closets of local residents. When an accumulation of night soil, mixed with ash and cinders, built up, the older residents of Ryecroft could remember their fathers shovelling it out into the open, ready to be collected by the sanitation cart or wagon at night time. It would often be left there overnight and householders were required by the council to mark it out by putting down white lime or newspaper, so enabling unwary pedestrians from stepping in it during the hours of

Road lengthmen for North Darley Urban District Council, Wilf Taylor, at Broadwalk, 1937. His 'patch' was from Gas Cottages to Northwood.

darkness. It would seem that there are certain things that have changed for the better over the years.

The day to day maintenance and cleaning of the roads and pavements was still dealt with by local "lengthmen", performing similar duties as those of the pre-Great War council employees, Miles Fox and Sammy Cardin.

Throughout the 1920's, 30's, 40's and 50's, my father, Wilf Taylor, was a familiar sight along the A6 as he tended his "length" between Gas Cottages and Northwood, armed with just a large wheelbarrow, brush and shovel. Often working in the worst of weather conditions, he would seek protection from the elements in the early years by wearing a potato sack around his shoulders and certain kindly residents would replenish him with dry sacks at intervals along his length. He certainly had neither the time nor inclination to rest, as Miles Fox had been able to do in earlier times, high on the moors beyond Sydnope.

This particular stretch of the A6 worked by my father saw much change during the two decades after the ending of the Great War, particularly in **the development of housing** in the fields alongside the road. Housing on Northwood Lane, Broadwalk, the triangle of land between the A6, Chesterfield Road and Warney Road, and on Darley House Estate and Hooleys Estate changed the physical appearance of the valley side.

Ezra Toft's building firm constructed housing on both sides of the steeply sloping Northwood Lane during the 1920's and 30's, from the A6 to just short of Lumb Lane.

Arthur Morton of Bakewell, managing director of Stancliffe Stone after the death of Charles Dawson, together with his brother Ben, bought land from off the Stancliffe Estates Company Limited in 1924. The following year he began the work of constructing 155 houses, six villas and eight shops in his South Park Estate development, now known as Broadwalk. By September 1925 the building of the first six rows began and then they took out a mortgage to buy more land for the top six rows.

Arthur had connections with the building trade in Manchester and brought over the three Ainscough brothers, Harry, Tommy and Bob, together with labourer Jack Roberts, to build the houses. With his Stancliffe Stone connections, Arthur was able to benefit by getting good quality off-cuts from the pulping stones in the quarry yard. It also helped to have the standard gauge railway running from the quarry right alongside the development, enabling easy off loading of the materials. Other requirements, such as plumbing materials, could also be obtained cheaply from Manchester, because of his good connections.

The shops at Broadwalk were constructed from one of the first artificial stones, "Stancrete", made by the quarrying company at Darley Dale. A gap was left between the six villas at Broadwalk to allow road access for a further planned development in the fields behind. Nothing came of this idea and in the 1970's the empty space was filled with two further buildings.

In 1928/29 Charles Wildgoose of Darley House, farmer and building contractor, began constructing houses and bungalows on his land at Holt Road, Hackney, and especially on land adjacent to Darley House. The farming slump of the late 1920's and early 30's had persuaded him to diversify. Plots of land were on sale at Darley House Estate and when a person bought a plot, Charles Wildgoose would construct a dwelling. This resulted in piecemeal development over the following decade.

The photograph shows the first few bungalows on Darley House Estate, c.1932, built by Charlie Wildgoose. More and more plots were developed over the years, on a 'piecemeal' basis.

254

At Hooleys Estate, Long Eaton building contractor Mr. Hooley employed two brick-laying brothers by the name of Kemp to build an estate of nearly 190 houses over a period of five years. The first houses were built in 1932/33 and the Holt Drive area was finally completed in 1937. An identical estate had been developed by Mr. Hooley at Long Eaton.

A final piece of infilling was achieved along the A6 during the 1920's and early 1930's when the land bordering Warney Road and Chesterfield Road was developed in partnership by Richard Alan Twyford, the Two Dales building contractor, and joiner Frederick Anthony Gregory. The joinery business had begun in earlier times on Wheatley Road, where coffins were made in a shed and carpentry undertaken.

The Twyfords lived at Hazel House, on Chesterfield Road, and in the adjacent yard was a large **mortar mill**, with two revolving gritstone mill stones, set into a pit. They were eventually operated by electricity and as they turned round and round they ground up the ashes and cinders to be added to the lime. This mortar did not set quickly and so there was a constant supply to be collected by horse and cart and later by lorry. Bernard Mastin looked after the two black horses and the big dray cart, one horse being used for pulling and the other for slinging (holding the loaded cart back on steep slopes). Jack Mills from Brook Bottom drove the motor lorry during the late 1920's. Bernard would go to the local quarries and "muck them out" (clear the waste for free).

On this one small, triangular field, a bank, post-office, hairdressers, general provisions shop and a cafe were built by Twyfords in the 1920's, as well as domestic housing, with a new carpenters and undertakers premises provided for Fred Gregory and a garage constructed, both of these on adjacent land. The expanding population of Darley parish was therefore receiving new services and infrastructure to cater for their needs, whilst at the same time enhancing the existing feeling of self suf-ficiency.

In 1924, the existing corrugated iron hut belonging to the London County Westminster Parrs Bank Limited, at the junction of Chesterfield Road and the A6, was removed and a new stone branch office built, renamed the National Westminster Bank (at the time of writing, Hibbard's Chemist)

London County Westminster and Parr's Bank Ltd., branch office in 1920,
at the junction of Chesterfield Road with the A6.

National Westminster Bank branch office, built in 1924 to replace the former hut.
(Hibbard's chemist shop at the time of writing.)

Chesterfield Road, Two Dales, mid 1930's.
Note the barber's pole outside Reginald Jago' shop and the sign for Two Dales Cafe,
run by the Duke sisters. The area of trees now houses the doctors' surgery.

The following year, a new Two Dales post-office was built by Twyfords and Frederick Dobson, the post master, moved there from his former premises (where Coates the butchers is presently situated), with his sister-in-law, Miss Sibley, running it for him. The old post-office was now converted into a butchers shop when William Wagstaffe and son Ernest Stanley moved their business 300 yards along the street. Following on from the pre-war years when the Wagstaffes operated a carriage hiring business, and using his newly developed skills as a lorry driver in the wartime Royal Flying Corps, Sidney was now supplementing the family income by operating a taxi, one of the first in the parish. We have already seen that it was into the Wagstaffe's vacated property that Dick Lane transferred his garage and taxi business in 1924.

In the mid-1920's Captain Charles Ward of Sitch Lane, Oker,

257

Stanley Wagstaffe and father William outside the butchers shop on Chesterfield Road (now Coates), on Carnival Day, in the late 1920's/early 1930's.

Stan Wagstaffe and Fred Elliott outside the butchers shop (now Coates butchers) in the late 1920's.

Ernest Stanley Wagstaffe driving early taxi, (1920's). He was also the Two Dales butcher. The taxi is parked next to his slaughter house at the bottom of Sydnope Hill.

Early Two Dales taxi, 1920's, possibly near the Blacksmith's Arms pub.

259

employed Twyfords to build **Two Dales Cafe** for three of his wife's spinster sisters, on the site of present day "Westmoreland Flats", at the junction of Chesterfield Road, Oddford Lane and Warney Road. Laura Duke, who had been trained in the bakery and catering trade, was joined by her invalid sister Clara and sister Mary, to build up a thriving bake-house and cafe that operated into the mid 1950's, and was renowned for its milk loaves.

The bake-house was at the back of the building with a room for wedding receptions upstairs and a downstairs cafe for parties. Rosie Horrobin (nee Woodhouse) was employed to help the sisters in those early days and at the age of 14 she worked from 6-30a.m., with the first task being to grease the tins. She and Laura then knelt on flour bags on the concrete floor in front of a huge bowl, full of dough, ready to knead it, before pushing it towards the huge oven and covering it with flour bags to make it rise. The dough was cut, weighed and moulded and put into rows of tins, which were placed into the oven on a huge wooden shovel.

The present day hairdressers of Andrew Wild was originally built for retired Royal Navy man, Reginald Jago, in 1928, who started a hairdressing business there, and although Reg Jago enjoyed a drink or two, he always had a steady hand when performing his cutting duties.

After the Great War, James Squires from Park Lane, returned to baking but now produced his bread and cakes in the converted old chapel building at the top of Northwood Lane. Competition for the Duke's Two Dales Cafe bakehouse now came from the Hayes family at No. 2 Park Lane, just above Ryecroft.

Jessie Hayes, founder of Hayes Bakery. In the First World War she was a nurse at the Whitworth Institute Red Cross Hospital and later received a black 'wound stripe' when in action near the trenches in France and Belgium.

In 1918/1919, **Jessie Hayes**, aged 30 years, had returned from the Western Front after serving as a Red Cross nurse near the front line, where

260

Artist's impression of the green corrugated iron shed in Phoebe Barker's garden near Brook Side, Two Dales, 1942, that was used as Hayes Bakery throughout the late 1920's, 30's and 40's. When no longer used as a bake house, it was taken by Roy Jaquest of Loscoe Row and placed in the nearby nursery, where it was used as a garage to repair vehicles.

The shop at 4 Brookside, Two Dales, showing Mrs. Mary Ann Knifton and Charlotte Charlesworth (nee Hollamd), about 1922. Mrs. Knifton ran the shop for a few years, before Jessie Hayes used it to sell bread and cakes from Hayes Bakery.

Adrian Charlesworth and Roberta Maddocks by the site of Hayes bakehouse hut c.1950-1951.

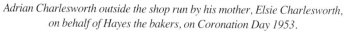

*Adrian Charlesworth outside the shop run by his mother, Elsie Charlesworth,
on behalf of Hayes the bakers, on Coronation Day 1953.*

Gunner Walter Hayes, Royal Artillery, on horseback, first left, in the Vosges Mountains area of France c.1918. He was a member of the Hayes 'Bakery' family.

she had been wounded in the process. Earlier, she had nursed convalescing soldiers at the Whitworth Institute, together with her two sisters. She was one of the nine children of John and Esther Hayes and was determined to provide for her elderly parents and invalid sister, Lilly.

Starting in 1919 she used the side oven in their house to bake bread and sell it. Shortly afterwards a small tin shed was erected in the back garden, containing an oven. She had no formal training and all the recipes were worked out by herself. A tiny woman in stature, she was extremely hard working and could be seen delivering bread in her basket or pushing it around the area in a green four wheeled cart, with a rounded, domed top, made by the local joiner, Fred Gregory.

In 1925/26, after her sister Lucy married Bill Silverwood from Cross Green, the firm became known as Hayes and Silverwood, and a larger green corrugated iron shed was built opposite Brook Side, near to the Plough Inn, in the back garden of Joe and Phoebe Barker's cottage. A large baking oven was installed and large wooden bread racks on wheels were used.

Jessie Hayes and Albert Girling from Sydnope were the bakers, producing bread, cakes, tea cakes and wedding cakes, with Freda Bainbridge from Hooleys Estate, Joan Barker from Loscoe Row and also Lexie Holland helping out. Lilly Hayes, a polio victim, would sit in her wheelchair and help in washing up at the sink. During hot summer weather, they would set up a striped canvas tent with an open front, over a metal frame, on the road in front of the bakehouse, where they ate their lunch, away from the overpowering heat of the enclosed oven.

The small shop which had operated from the front room of Hannah and George Charlesworth's cottage at Brookside, opposite the bakehouse, had been rented and used by shopkeeper Mary Ann Knifton during the early 1920's, until in 1927 her daughter Agnes Needham and husband Bernard had a house and shop, selling general provisions, built next to Reg Jago's hairdressers. The empty shop was now rented from the Charlesworths by Jessie Hayes and from it she began selling bakery produce, under the control of her sister, Polly Hayes. One speciality amongst many were cornish pasties and residents in the locality would take along their jugs to collect gravy, specially made at the bakery.

The business prospered and in 1930, Jessie's brother, Walter Hayes, left his job as engineer at the Markham Chesterfield and Stavely Works and came into the business in partnership with Jessie Hayes and Bill Silverwood, though Bill left soon afterwards.

A red, second hand Trojan van from P.G. Tips was bought and during the 1930's Walter acted as the van driver, delivering as far afield as Beeley, Rowsley, Wensley and Northwood. The flour was supplied from Cauldwell's Mill at Rowsley and was stored in a shed at the back of the Plough Inn.

The bakehouse shed continued to be in use until 1947, when work was transferred to the old Methodist Chapel, near the Blacksmith's Arms, before the present premises in the old Anglican School room was bought in 1968.

Brook Side in the 1920's was quite a hive of activity, for Fred and Agnes Waterfall continued to run their butcher's business and the Derwent Cooperative Stores still provided a fine, wide ranging service to their customers. George and Polly Norman could be found in their shop

*Fred and Agnes Waterfall outside their butcher's shop, Brookside, Two Dales,
on Darley Carnival Day c.1930.*

next to the Nags Head Pub in 1928 but by 1930 it was being run by Miss
Dagmar Lowe.

Mr. and Mrs. Harry Barker no longer sold fish and chips from their
lean to extension, although May Charlesworth, by the side of the Plough
Inn, took over for a few years, selling tripe and cow heels and delivering
wet fish in a basket. However, in the early 1920's, alongside Chesterfield
Road, **Hilda Burnett** opened her **fish and chip shop** in the cottage by
the trough, at the entrance to Brook Side, and earned the well deserved
praise of selling the finest fare in the district.

A spinster, Hilda was a squat, powerfully built woman, who, during the
Great War, had worked in Stancliffe Quarry, performing the same work as
the men and wearing clogs in bad weather. Her front room was made into
a shop, with a counter on the left side and a coal-fired fat frier. Although
her friend, Kathleen Wragg, lived with her, she was helped in the shop at
night by Stancliffe quarry worker, Arthur Mason, nicknamed "Tickler".
Hilda also operated a small lending library from these premises.

A zinc bath full of potatoes would need peeling each day and very
often, farmer Bert Dalton from Woodside Farm, Sydnope, would deliver

Agnes Waterfall is standing by the side of Hilda Burnett's fish and chip shop, Two Dales, c.1929. Dick Lane's taxi is parked next to the Blacksmith's Arms and Dick Lane himself is standing in the road, in the far distance.

Chesterfield Road, Two Dales, c.1943, showing Hilda Burnett's fish and chip shop on the right and the Blacksmith's Arms on the left. The Smithy is also on the left.

a load of Majestics, her favouite selection, on his horse and cart.

The popularity of Hilda's fish and chips was widespread. Every so often, the Miss Dukes from the cafe sent for young Daisy Reed from Ryecroft to collect an order for their brother-in-law, Captain Ward at Oker, and his chauffeur, Herbert Chell, would then deliver them to the family home, "Dale View", at South Darley.

Hilda would tolerate no swearing or unseemly behaviour in her shop. Once, when a drunken customer refused to stop his swearing, it was Hilda, not Arthur, who led him out by the scruff of his collar and immersed his face in the nearby trough of water. You were wise not to argue with Hilda. The popularity of her business meant that she prospered and when she retired around 1947, she was able to buy a car and move to a large house on Hackney.

Between 1930 and 1936, May Charlesworth started an **eiderdown factory** in a corrugated iron shed on land between her cottage and the Plough Inn. Six electric sewing machines were installed and inside the shed was a large air blower, used for filling the eiderdowns with feathers. The whole process could be quite dusty with feathers flying in all directions on occasions. Work was let out to women working in their own homes and then it was brought into the shed. For those difficult years of the early 1930's the business provided useful money to supplement the family income of women such as Una Lane, Annie

Mick Payne and Ursula Brookhouse at Brookside, Two Dales. In the background is part of the Plough Inn and the shed that housed the eiderdown factory during the 1930's.

Grafton, Marjorie Saunders and Hannah Charlesworth.

It was during the inter-war years that respected Matlock **furniture dealer, Micky Morris**, arrived in Darley Dale from Sheffield, after walking all the way. During the early 1920's his father, Michael, operated a small business in Sheffield, selling socks, vests and other clothes from a room in his house. His son, Micky, and his daughter Raye, helped by taking samples from door to door in a suitcase.

Eventually, in the late 1920's, young Micky decided to branch out further afield, and, with his great love for the Peak District, walked the area around Bradwell, Hope and Hathersage, selling his wares from his suitcase and often sleeping rough. Gradually, he travelled further south into the Tideswell, Youlgreave, Winster, Darley Dale and Matlock areas. Having arrived in the Darley district he fell in love with the area and did not wish to return to Sheffield.

Micky slept rough, lodging at farms or sleeping in barns. Whilst in the Two Dales area in the late 1920's he found useful accommodation when James Gabbitas, at the bottom of Sydnope Hill, allowed him to sleep in his son's tent, pitched in their garden. The Gabbitas family sold fruit and vegetables from their tiny house, Yew Tree Cottage, and Micky would buy a large bunch of bananas from them at breakfast and this provided nourishment for him during the long day's work. Eventually, Micky bought an old, drecrepit bus/caravan and Elton farmer, Mr. Bibby, agreed for Micky to keep it on his land in return for the salesman helping on the farm.

He would often hitch a lift on one of Tom Smith's milk wagons from Oker Side, South Darley, which travelled to the Sheffield Co-op milk depot, and later that day he returned on the lorry with items of clothes that he had purchased. Micky was a kind hearted business man, who, despite his own difficult circumstances in those early days, would often take pity on those with low wages, who found difficulty in paying for their goods. The people took him to their hearts because they knew that they could trust him.

In 1936 he married Tess, a girl from Sheffield, and lived for a time at Wirksworth before settling down at Northwood Lane. He began branching out into selling small items of furniture from his Northwood home but the war interrupted this venture, as Micky volunteered for

Chesterfield Road, Two Dales, c.1912, showing Wagstaffe's butchers shop on the left, under the canopy. The large shed on the left was used in the 1920's and 1930's by Dick Lane and then by Micky Morris in the late 1940's to store his furniture.

service and became a physical training instructor in the army.

After being demobbed, he continued running his furniture business from his home, but in 1946 he began renting from the Wagstaffes the large shed on Chesterfield Road, which, as we have seen, had been used by garage man and haulier Dick Lane in the 1920's and early 30's. In this shed Micky Morris stored his furniture.

Cyril Bowler, the Two Dales newsagent and shopkeeper, was born on Hackney in 1904 and after leaving school, worked for W.H. Smith on Chesterfield Railway Station. In the 1930's he started up his own business at Two Dales in a small wooden hut, by the side of the old Anglican school and Sunday school (now Hayes bakery). The business had previously been run by Miss Wilson.

Sometime after his marriage in 1929, he moved to Hazel View on

Cyril Bowler, newsagent and shopkeeper, outside his 'hut', c.1935. It was sited next door to the Church of England Sunday School (now Hayes Bakery) and was used from the early 1930's to the early 1950's.

Horace Smith, Two Dales shoemaker and cobbler, in his workshop.

Horace Smith's shoemaker's shop, Two Dales, next door to the Old Two Dales Chapel.

Chesterfield Road and from his wooden shop he sold sweets, papers, cigarettes and also started a lending library. During the war years he served in the fire service and continued in business in the hut until the mid

1950's. As a young child I have pleasant memories of visiting the shop in those later years to collect my comic. In 1955 Laura Duke retired from Two Dales Cafe and Cyril Bowler transferred his business into the more modern premises, where he continued working for the next twenty years.

During the 1920's **shoemaker and cobbler** George Simmons took over the responsibility of looking after the footwear of Two Dales folk. Living on Park Lane, his cobblers shop was first established in the lean to building on Brook Side, where Harry Barker had once dispensed portions of fish and chips, but by the 1930's he had moved across into a shop at No. 3 Ashbrook, on Chesterfield Road.

Meanwhile, young Horace Smith, from Laburnum Cottage, Wheatley Road, had joined his father Anthony, a foreman at Flash Nurseries, and his two brothers, in working for James Smith and Son. Horace disliked the nurseryman's life and soon afterwards went to serve an apprenticeship with the Wensley shoe maker and cobbler, John Devaney.

Starting work on the surface workings at Mill Close Mine in the mid 1930's he mended shoes in his spare time in the backyard shed at Laburnum Cottage. His family was well versed in shoe repairing for his maternal grandfather, Thomas Burnett, and his great grandfather were both shoe makers at Two Dales in their time.

In 1939, George Simmons left Two Dales and Anthony Smith bought the shop and Horace moved in, paying his father rent. He now took up shoe repairing full time, but in 1940 he was called up into the 13th Battalion Sherwood Foresters and fought against the Japanese in Burma, where he was wounded.

After recovering, Horace joined a tank regiment, but was back in England in February 1946 and began work in his shop on the 1st March 1946, where his fine craftsmanship was much appreciated by all who did business with him over the next four decades.

In the first chapter we saw that Rose Wood of Park Lane, Two Dales, had been in charge of the fledgling telephone service for the parish in pre-war years, with the branch headquarters at her home. When Frederick Dobson, the post master, had moved into his new premises in 1925, a room was set aside in the post-office for a crude switch board to be operated by Miriam White over the next few years.

However, by 1932, **Darley Telephone Exchange** was to be found in the front room of William and Mabel Hallows's home, "Westwood", on Warney Road. Their daughter Freda was the lone operator, for very few customers existed in Darley Dale, but by 1934/1935 help was required and she was joined by 17 year old Winnie Travis from Holmes Terrace, Chesterfield Road.

Former switch board operator Winnie (later Winnie Holmes) remembers the telephone numbers for Walton's Mill (No. 1), Alfred Smith (No. 2), Stanton Woodhouse (No. 3), butcher Stan Wagstaffe (No. 4), Robert Lehane (No. 5), Gregory's Woodyard (No. 6), James Smith's Nursery (No. 7), Ackroyds Quarries (No. 8), Silver Service (No. 25), Stancliffe Stone (No. 29), F.A. Gregory, joiners (No. 48) and Johnson's Mill (No. 54).

The bay windowed room contained no furniture, simply a switch board in the centre, a table in the bay and equipment and wires in the corner of the room. When a call came in during daytime hours, a small white flap came down on the board to indicate the need for action. The operator plugged the caller in and after three minutes, turned a key and cut into the conversation to say that three minutes had elapsed, and then repeated the procedure at three minute intervals.

Winnie only worked there in the mornings until war broke out, but then worked full time. At night, Mabel Hallows took over as caretaker operator, but a bell rang instead, to warn of a call coming through and Mabel or any other person in the house would assist in making the connection.

Mabel's son, Ron Hallows, remembered the confusion caused one night in the 1930's when Dr. Phillips rang through to ask to be connected so that he could make an international call. His daughter, working in China at the time, had been kidnapped by Chinese war lords, together with several missionaries and a ransom was being demanded for their release. The doctor wished to make a call to China and Ron somehow managed to make the connection.

The onset of war greatly increased the workload, for soldiers arrived at Darley Dale from Dunkirk and wished to use the kiosk on the A6 to get in touch with their families, whilst many soldiers arrived at the Whitworth Institute when it was turned into a Royal Army Service Corps camp. They too used the public phone boxes a great deal and by this time

Telephone Exchange supervisor Joan Gibbs by the front of the wooden hut.

Winnie was working on her own, even though two switch boards had now been installed

The Darley Dale operations were continued from "Westwood" until circa 1947/1948, when a large wooden hut was constructed on a small vacant plot of land between " Westwood" and the A6. Three switchboard panels were now in operation, with the day shift personnel being Joan Gibbs (supervisor), Iris Woodhouse (nee Fearn) and Audrey Kirk (nee Dale), with Ann Saunders (nee Marsden) as the relief operator. The night shift consisted of Harry Salt, Eric Boden and Ken Orridge. Everything was done manually by the operators, even to the timing and costing of each individual call, which were written on tickets and collected by the supervisor.

Christmas time in Darley Telephone Exchange Hut c.1952.
Left to right: Audrey Dale, Iris Fearn, Joan Gibbs.

Brook Side, Two Dales, showing the Plough and the Nag's Head, c.1926.

Frank Hodgkinson's butchers van at Churchtown during the mid 1920's,
with Kitty the horse.

These premises were finally closed in February, 1955.

From Broadwalk to Northwood Lane, the increase in population during the inter-war years resulted in more business for the **shopkeepers on Dale Road North**. At the top of Green Lane the six shops continued to provide service for their customers. Nearest to the Grouse Inn, John Henry Fearn the draper would measure customers for suits but also sold carpets, lino and even knitting needles. Next door, Henry Fielding the cobbler had his work shed at the bottom of his garden, where he repaired shoes, and in earlier days made clogs, while Mrs. Hannah Siddall's post-office and grocery shop was being run by her daughter Ada throughout the 1930's. The shop was also used unofficially as a place to put your bets on the horses, for Ada would take bets from people on behalf of Green Lane "bookie", Charlie Gill.

Across Green Lane, Nellie Boam ran the newsagents shop for her brother-in-law, Lionel Fairclough, with the support of her brother Joe. In the early 1920's Lionel would go very early in the morning with a sugar box on carriage wheels to Darley Station to get the national papers from off the train. The shop did very well from supplying the Stancliffe Quarry workers with cigarettes and an errand boy would be sent from the Stancliffe offices to collect the order for "fags" and mineral water. Although closed during the evenings, the shop received a good deal of extra trade during these hours as people called to make a purchase at the back door.

Woolliscroft's shop next door sold bread, cakes and clothing until 1935, when it was taken over by the Soppits as a drapers shop, whilst at the far end of Stancliffe View, John Price, grocer and tea dealer, had taken over from Mr. Morten of pre-war years. During the early 1920's John Price also ran a bakery at the back of the shop and on Sundays, locals could take their joints of meat to be cooked in the hot oven.

On the present day site of Crowder's petrol station, opposite Firth Rixson, Thomas Brookes and his son Harry operated both a cycle agency and repair shop and dealt with wireless sets (radios). The house and shop were old army huts and in another shed, further back, bicycle repairs were carried out. A petrol pump was attached to the wall and they sold bicycles, wirelesses and charged wireless batteries.

However, the store in Stancliffe Stone Quarry yard, with Billy Bell in charge, was the place where many Churchtown and Green Lane inhabitants went to charge their wireless batteries. At this store, locals could buy a wide range of goods, including nails, nuts and bolts.

Along the A6, near Northwood, mention could be made of Annie Elliot and daughter Emmy who ran an off-licence and grocers, or old Johnny Boden, who sold groceries from his front room, whilst Reg Hibbs and Lewis Boden also had shops in the vicinity, and Charlie Wall and his brother repaired shoes at Riversdale.

It was on the present site of the Shalimar Indian Restaurant, alongside the A6 at the bottom of Northwood Lane, that in the 1920's Mr. and Mrs. Gregory catered for customers at the **Aerial Tea Room**, which in the 1930's was taken over by Mrs. Mary (Polly) White. It received its name from the fact that Mr. Gregory was interested in the new wireless sets and children and adults were encouraged to go across in the evenings to listen to the new device through ear phones, being charged a penny or two for the privilege. When Polly White took over, she was helped by Jessie Brassington, who did the baking in a tiny kitchen. They catered

The Aerial Tea Rooms, Northwood, during the 1930's. Mrs. Mary (Polly) White stands with two visitors. The wireless aerial can be seen on the roof, in the background.

The Aerial Tea Room, Northwood. Owned by the Gregory's and then by Mary (Polly)
White. It was run by Mr. and Mrs. Stuart as a transport cafe from 1960
with its closure in May 1977. At the time of publication (2002),
it is the site of Shalimar Indian Restaurant.

for a sparse trade in passing cyclists, horse and cart drivers and increasingly, motor vehicle drivers.

At Broadwalk, F. Chapman the butcher traded by the side of the

Dunkirk evacuee soldiers at Charles Bower's bakery,
Broadwalk, June 1940.
Soldier, X, Margaret Bonsall, Charles Bower,
Mrs. Bower, Eric Bower, soldier.

villas, with Audrey Hayto running a sweets and tobacconist shop next door, and sister Rita established in the room above as a ladies hairdresser. F.H. Jackson, the master baker, came next, until he left in 1938 and the bakery was taken over by Charles Bower from Darley Bridge. Mr. Gibson had run the chemist shop next door, but by the 1930's, Miss Dorothy Cartledge was the chemist, with Mr.

and Mrs. Wilson serving fish and chips from the shop alongside.

Saxonholme, the end house on Lime Tree Avenue, was the home of Walter Lomas and from these premises Ernest and Walter Lomas ran a painting and decorating business. Brother Ernest was a sleeping partner and Walter was helped by his sons, Harry, Reynold and Jack. The store was a green corrugated iron shed, across the road from the side of the house, where the trimming of wall paper was dealt with on a hand operated machine. People came to the house to buy paper and paint and were served by Walter's wife, Jane.

Milk **could be obtained from most of the local farmers**, whether they kept a large herd or just a few cows. Bert Dalton from Sydnope delivered milk from churn and ladle, on the back of his cart, as did Maggie Waterfall, from Hazel Farm, in her pony and trap. (At 14 years of age, her younger sister, Tessie, had walked in earlier times to school at Churchtown and dropped milk off in a four pint container at the Blacksmith's Arms. On her way home she would collect the container, but by now it was filled with beer for her father at Hazel Farm).

Sam Wagstaffe also had a milk round and was helped by children Percy, Kathleen and Jean. During the 1920's and early 1930's Sam Wagstaffe delivered milk locally from Holt Farm in buckets suspended from a yoke across his shoulders. For journeys further afield a pony and trap was used.

Whilst attending Darley Council School, his daughter Kathleen regularly took a two gallon can of milk, with measure, to the houses in Ryecroft, before the school day started, and left the empty container in the hedgerow, ready to be collected on her way home at lunch time. During the summer months, a second delivery was often made at night time because there were no refrigerators and the milk soon turned sour. Another task for her during these summer months was to take the cows to graze on the grass verges of the public highways and tend them whilst they fed.

During the early 1930's, the Wagstaffes kept cows in the field between Dale Road Methodist Chapel and what eventually became the New Estate and in the field next to St. Helen's Rectory. Kathlene would travel in the horse and trap with her father Sam and it was a common sight to see them sat on milking stools in these fields, milking the cows by hand and filling the milk churns. The churns were then transported to Holt Farm and placed in the troughs of water to cool.

However, by the late 1930's Sam had invested in a small bottling plant on his farm and was providing milk for Darley Council School pupils. Joe Hancock, the new head teacher, had been instrumental in introducing The Milk for School Children Scheme to the area.

It was a busy life for another young son of Sam Wagstaffe, for in the 1920's seven year old Howard Wagstaffe milked the cows early in the morning, before school, pulped the turnips for cattle fodder in his dinner break and again helped with the milking at night. Charlie Wildgoose

Outside Arthur Watt's blacksmith's shop c.1930. Molly Littlewood and Gwendoline Watts.

from Darley House also had a large milk round in the Darley, Hackney and Matlock districts.

Smallholders, such as building contractor Richard Alan Twyford, who kept a few cows and pigs in barns and pens near his mortar mill at Two Dales, produced milk for sale on a much smaller scale. Daisy Reed from Ryecroft remembers often being sent to Twyfords with a jug, and on occasions she would bring back the "beastings". This was the first milk from a cow after it had calved and was more

Farming group between Butcher Lane and Sydnope Hill 1920's.
Back row: X, X, X. Front row: Harry Woodhouse, X, Bob Watts.

Farming at Two Dales in the 1920's and 1930's.
Below: Everard and Sidney Waterfall at Hazel Farm, Sydnope.

284

Joe Harry Allsop from Yew Tree Farm (used to be at the bottom of Sydnope Hill)
cutting hay on Oddford Lane in the late 1920's,
where the Primary School playing fields are now.

yellow and thicker than ordinary milk and richer in protein. Her mother would use the "beastings" to make custard puddings.

In earlier times Daddy Watts could be seen delivering milk on his large tricycle, whilst in the late 1920's and 30's the Watts family made their own ice cream and sold it from the shop attached to Arthur Watts' smithy, near the Blacksmith's Arms.

Life was not all hard work, however, and what little spare time was available was put to use in **leisure time pursuits and entertainments**. A number of older residents can still remember when, in the years just after the Great War, they went to see the small fair that came annually into the field by the side of the Blacksmith's Arms at Two Dales.

Darley Dale Cricket Club continued to flourish during the 20's and 30's, under the watchful eyes of the Smith brothers, Alfred and Fred. The first and second elevens played at Darley Bridge, whilst Charlie Hallows from Two Dales ran the Third Eleven on the Whitworth Institute ground. By 1928, one in sixteen of the Darley menfolk were involved in some way with the club and reports were given in the local press that the ground was the best small club ground in the county. By 1937 the club was in a healthy condition, with Alfred Smith providing a splendid new scoring pavilion in the same year,opened on May 12th 1937 in commemoration of the coronation of George VI and Queen Elizabeth. Local football clubs also allowed the men of the parish to parade their sporting skills, with the likes of Darley Harriers winning the Cavendish Cup in 1919 and the Mill Close Mine team repeating the feat in the 1930's.

The Whitworth Institute never quite returned to its pre-war glory

Darley Dale Football Team. Winners of the Cavendish Cup 1919/1920.
Back row: W. Freeman, D. Petts, L, Riley, T. Wright, B. Gregory.
Middle row: H. Walker, S. Wilkinson, B. Walker, J. Bark, W. Allsop.
Front row: J.S. Carter, J. Twyford, J. Webster, J. Phillips, H. Flint, S. Crossland, W. Gregory.

Mill Close Mine Football Team c.1938.
Back row, left to right: Mr. Mitchell (surface manager), Alan Dakin, Herbert Webster,
Lew Barker, Vic Dakin, Don Taylor, Edmund Shimwell, Arnie Shimwell,
Charlie Shimwell, Jack Phillips, Jim Bark.
Front row: Maurice Wild, Harry Evans, Frank Bates, Bill Bates, Cliff Webster,
Arnie Webster, Bert Webster, Wilf Dakin.

Mill Close Mine Football Team, winners of the Cavendish Cup 1938.
Standing: ? Shimwell, Peter Donelan, Tom Evans, Charlie Shimwell, Vic Dakin,
Horace Webster, Tommy Concannon, Herbert Webster, ? Wilson, Frank Staton, Arnold
(Keker) Webster, Ike Evans, Joe Webster, Eric Wild, Eric Evans, Jack Pugh.
Seated: X, Frank Bates, Bert Webster, Bill Bates, Alan Dakin, Wilf Dakin, trainer.

Darley Dale Cricket Club First Eleven, 1925 season.
Back row: Ben Gregory, Joe Wall, ? Duckmanton, Louis Jacques, Walter Bingham,
Noel Jacques, X, Charlie Hallows.
Front row: George Wall, Reg Boden, Arthur Morton (captain, he had Broadwalk built in
the 1920's), Alfred Smith, Charlie Dawson (Managing Director of Stancliffe Quarries).

Darley Dale Cricket Club 2nd Eleven 1934 season.
Back row: Fred Smith, George Holland, Herbert Taylor, Norman Lees, Jack Wilmot,
Cyril Taylor, Wilfred Taylor, J. Siddall.
Front row: W. Mitchell, Barry Sharmon, C.R. Lymn (captain), J.R. Taylor, Alfred Smith,
Arnie Bland.
Results: Played 1/ matches, won 11, lost 2, drew 4.

Boating lake at the Whitworth Institute Park 1930's.
The water came from an underground hillside reservoir. It was drained and became a
sunken garden in 1948/1949.

Tea Rooms Pavilion, Whitworth Park, during happy times in the 1930's. It had originally
been the large cow shed on Sir Joseph Whitworth's model farm in the 1880's. During the
Second World War it became the R.A.S.C. cookhouse and soldiers' mess. It was
demolished in the 1960's.

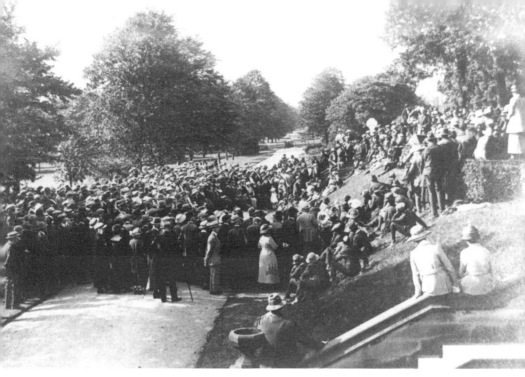

Political rally at the Whitworth Institute Park, in the 1920's.
Note the captured German artillery gun on display in the far distance.

Darley Dale's 1935 Silver Jubilee Celebrations Committee at the Whitworth Institute.
J. Agutter, J.A. Smith, J. Hancock, J.W. Hibbs, Fred Smith, J.C. Bartram, F.A. Gregory,
G.W. Burton.
The Silver Jubilee celebrations for George V and Queen Mary were held on May6th
1935 with a party for the children in the Tea Room at the Whitworth Institute, where they
were presented with Commemorative silver teaspoons.

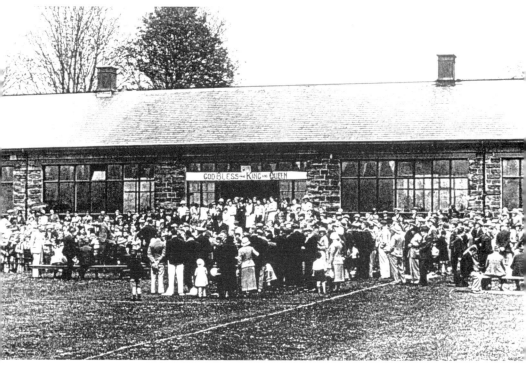

Tea Rooms Pavilion on May 12th 1937 showing celebrations marking the coronation of George VI and Queen Elizabeth.

days but parties still came by train and charabanc and enjoyed the pleasures of the boating lake and their meals in the Tea Room, catered for by Moores of Dale Road, Matlock. Harry Pearson, a member of Darley Band, remembered that one Thursday in 1926, he and his father finished work early at 3p.m. to go and play in the Institute grounds for a large excursion party from Birds Custard Company, Birmingham.

One aspect of life at the Whitworth Institute that faded from the scene in the year before the Second World War began was the use of the indoor swimming pool. It was superceded by the fine modern pool at the Matlock Lido, which was opened on Thursday 26th May 1938, by Brigadier General G.M. Jackson of Clay Cross Hall.

It had been built, at a cost of £12,000, on the site of the old Imperial Road Gardens and consisted of a large open air pool, smaller indoor pool, accommodation for sun bathers, a cafe, slipper baths and contained a system for amplification of musical programmes. At the deep end, three diving stages swept out in a curve over the centre of the pool.

After the opening speeches, there was a display of the latest bathing wear by professional mannequins, as well as a humorous item that brought roars of laughter in the form of "Matlock's own mannequin Victoria", in the guise of Remo Tinti. Finally, a diving exhibition by the Scott brothers, well known North of England champions, was well appreciated.

The Council had certainly been very forward looking. Just eleven years after the closure of the Bank Road Tramway, in 1927, a splendid new baths had been presented to the town, only months after the Council had also provided the boating lake on the Hall Leys. At the Whitsuntide Holiday both venues were extremely busy.

In 1938, the Whitworth Swimming Pool could still be used, but by the middle of 1940, the water had been drained away, a wooden floor constructed over it and Royal Army Service Corps personnel were making use of the room as a dormitory throughout the rest of the war years.

Whitworth Institute Swimming Pool. In the Great War it became a hospital ward and in the Second World War it became a soldiers' dormitory.

Darley Dale residents could now visit the Matlock Lido (opened May 1938)instead of the Whitworth Institute indoor pool.

For many social occasions throughout the 1920's and 30's, **Darley Band** provided welcome entertainment. Each Christmas Day, carols were played by the band throughout the day. There was no going home for Christmas dinner, which was had in the Crown Inn at Wensley, after the Secretary had purchased bread, butter, cheese and pickles from John Keane Colman's shop in the square.

Christmas morning was started at the Rectory, then progressed to Abbey House, the home of Mr. and Mrs. Matthew Walker. These calls were made early so that the playing did not clash with the pealing of the church bells. The band then went on to the Square and Compass Inn, where Henry Martin had hot drinks and mince pies waiting for them.

In 1922 the band decided to have their instruments silver-plated and the name changed to Darley Dale United Silver Band, though in 1926 "United" was ommitted from the title and it was eventually called Darley Dale Public Band. 1934 saw much progress when Jack Fletcher, late solo player of Cresswell Colliery Band became director and Fred Slater joined as assistant conductor, with Luther Britton his assistant. For the first time ever the band performed on the Hall Leys Band Stand, Matlock, where they gave a concert.

Jack Fletcher was no stranger to Two Dales, for during the 1920's he

293

Darley Dale Band c.1912.
Harry Fielding (senior), Ambrose Turner, Billy Fawley, Benn Pearson, Billy Holmes,
Dick Thraves, Andrew Pearson, Charlie Hallows, Harold Bennett, Tommy Holmes,
Herbert Fawley, William Waterfall, Harry Fielding (junior).

Darley Band c.1919.
Back row: Albert Evans, Charlie Hallows, Harry Pearson, Herbert Fawley,
Charlie Hayto, Charlie Fletcher, X, Cyril Goodwin, Harold Pearson.
Front row: Harry Fielding, Vic Wilson, Dan Wagstaffe, Ambry Turner, Billy Holness,
Benn Pearson.

worked at the Bakelite factory on Old Road and lodged with Mr. Hallows, one of the band's senior members. He practised for one or two hours every day on the cornet and this he often did in Hall Dale Wood. His practice was varied and people in Darley Dale could hear his playing all along the valley. In 1936 Harold Pearson was elected to take over the duties as bandmaster and at Christmas 1936 the band as usual made their first call at the Rectory. It was a beautiful sunny morning and the rector's son, Eric Griffiths, took a photograph of the band.

Darley Dale Silver Band at the Rectory, St Helen's, on Christmas Day, 1936.
Dan Wagstaffe, Cyril Sheldon, Billy Walker, George Gilberthorpe, Harry Pearson,
Percy Gladwin, Colin Wild, Charlie Maddox, Freddy Fawley, Harold Pearson,
Arthur Marsden, Benn Pearson, Harold Bennett, Dick Maddox, Eric Hallows,
Johnny Siddons.

The Band of Hope was still meeting in the old methodist chapel at Two Dales, as in pre-war years, and one or two of the older residents have mentioned that as children they "took the pledge" against the demon drink, even though they had no real understanding. Meat and pie suppers were also held there by the methodists, and by the anglicans a few yards further along Chesterfield Road, and some children would attend on each occasion, a case of "pick and mix". Throughout the 1920's and well into the 30's both Sunday schools were still marching with their banners on Whit Walks and school anniversaries.

295

DARLEY DALE

ANNUAL CARNIVAL

Official.
Programme

6d.

Sep. 1st,
1928.

Fancy dress competition in the Carnival field, Two Dales, c.1928.
Back row: Mrs. Wilson, Mrs. Crooks, Lilian Crooks, Nelly Fielding, Maggie Gill,
Mrs. White, X.
Middle row: Roy Swift, Saga Swift, Rita Fielding, Winnie Haynes, X, X, X, X, X, X, X,
Gladys Staton, Barbara White.
Front row: Dorothy Crooks, Ann Crooks, Olive Crooks, Alma Swift, Florrie Swift,
Nora Fielding, Gwynneth Wragg.

C.1931 Church Inn at Churchtown during Darley Carnival Week, early September.
Albert Allsop, Enoch Lomas, Jim Taylor, Sam Stringer, Owen Lane, Rachel Stringer,
William Stringer, Joe McNeven, Mary Tilston, Joe Stringer.

The Bazooka Band, Darley Carnival, c.1932, at Two Dales. The members practised for the event in Knabb Quarry.
Standing: Kathleen Blair (nee Wagstaffe), Clarice Wright (nee Holland), Connie Maddocks, Alfie Grafton, ? Wright, Hannah Hibbs, Edna Williams (nee Barker), Laura Smith (nee Holland).
Seated: Winnie Holmes (nee Travis), Linda Slack (nee Holland), Lena Storer (nee Holland), Rose Horobin (nee Woodhouse).

Darley Band was certainly to be found to the fore when, in 1927, the first **Darley Carnival** was held in the first week of September. Between 1927 and the start of the war in 1939, **Carnival Week** in early September became the main social event of the year, and the money raised went to help the local hospital. Bunting was strung from buildings and the lime trees lining the A6 were also festooned with flags and bunting.

The 1928 Carnival commenced on Thursday with a balloon race from near the Westminster Bank (now Hibbard's chemist), with three balloons reaching Belgium. On Saturday, a quarter mile of pennies was assembled by the side of the A6 and sprigs of lucky white heather sold. At 2p.m., 200 competitors assembled for the fancy dress parade in Holt House grounds, Two Dales, and decorated lorries, push bikes and prams were included.

The procession, led by Darley and other bands, went from Two Dales bridge, along Chesterfield Road, Dale Road North, Green Lane, Derwent View, and returned by way of the A6, Park Lane, Wheatley Road and then to the field by the Blacksmith's Arms, where prizes were awarded. The winners of the shop window competition were 1st, Jacksons, 2nd, Wagstaffe and Sons, 3rd, Kniftons and 4th Orme and Sons, grocers. Winster Morris Men and the Longstone Folk Dancers entertained at intervals in the proceedings.

The Carnival Ball in the Whitworth Institute during the evening was overcrowded, and those assembled were splendidly entertained by the local dance band "The Frollies". Alternative entertainment could be found at the Whist Drive, where 15 tables were in use.

During Carnival Day, a mock police court, led by the Judge, John Wood, was set up to prosecute and fine would be breakers of Carnival law. Throughout the previous week the judge and jury had judged the pub landlords, fining them for any misdemeanours. On one occasion at the Grouse Inn, landlord Harry Johnson was fined £5 for keeping a grouse without any feathers.

Darley Dale Carnival c.1939.
Members of the 'Mock Court' on top of the lorry belonging to the Ladygrove corn milling business of A. Johnson and Sons. They claimed fines for the 'misdeeds' of Darley residents during Carnival week. Lew Barker is seated on the left and Bill Horrobin is seated on the right.

From the late 1920's to the mid 1930's, Mr. Goodison, the landlord of the Plough Inn, Two Dales, incorporated a walking race into the varied events of Carnival Week, with the winner receiving the Challenge Cup. The route varied, but in later years went from the Plough Inn, up Sydnope Hill to the cross roads, turned left along Mile Lane to Gladwins Mark, circled round onto the Beeley Bar Road, then over by Burley Fields and back down Long Hill and Wheatley Road into Two Dales.

Sammy Crooks, the traction engine driver for Gregory's Saw Mill, and a fine walker, won the cup for the first three years, with Derbyshire cross country runner Herbert Hardy winning it outright over the following four years. According to Herbert, although officially a walking race, the competitors would at times break into a run. Herbert was therefore well placed to hold off any challenge.

Crowning ceremony at Darley Dale Carnival
in the Two Dales carnival field in the early 1930's.
? Sheldon, X, (child ?), Doris Wood, Miriam White, X, Queen Miss John,
Mrs. Dawson (widow of Charlie Dawson.

Darley Carnival Queen Miss John and attendants at the junction of
Park Lane and Chesterfield Road, Two Dales, in the early 1930's.
Percy Wagstaffe is seen leading the horse.

1935 Carnival in Chesterfield Road field, Two Dales.
A float called 'The Garden Party' on Tom Wright's coal lorry.
Rosie Horobin, Monica Burton, Lilian Crooks, Dorothy Crooks, Laura Holland,
Nelly Fielding, Mrs. Hall, Mrs. Smith.

Fancy dress competition at Darley Carnival in the Carnival Field at Two Dales, 1935.
Back row: Extreme right, Phoebe Barker, third adult from the right, Mrs. Charlesworth.
Front row: Jack Hayes advertising 'Soaps you need'.

By September 1938, the Carnival had added another event to the proceedings, with the Derbyshire Supreme Baby Show taking place at the Institute on the Thursday, with a Tramps Supper on the Two Dales Carnival field in the evening. 300 people waited for the "Hobos" at the Grouse, to parade to the field, with Darley Band playing. On the Friday evening 1000 spectators watched a comic football match between men and women played on the same field, with the women fielding two goalkeepers. The final of a 6-a-side knockout football competition was also held between Johnson's Mill and Darley Dale Public Prize Band, with the mill team winning the match 7-2, and receiving a silver cup.

On Saturday, the usual events took place during the day, with the crowning of Queen Amy Holmes taking precedence. Displays by the carnival band, Darley Public Band and "The Matlockians" entertained the crowds. A large tent had been erected on the field for teas and the tent was also used for presenting a talkie cinema show. The Queen attended the Whitworth Hospital during the afternoon, having a word with the patients and presenting a basket of fruit. In the evening people flocked to the Institute to dance to the music of J. Crich and his Mikado Dance Band, or to play a hand of whist at the Grand Whist Drive.

Since April 1936 the Darley Dale Carnival Charities Committee had distributed £211 to hospitals and associations and £112 to benefit and distress cases.

302

Crowning of 1936 Darley Dale Carnival Queen by Miss Evans, Housekeeper at Chatsworth Hydro, Matlock, in Darley Hall field.
Margaret Smith, Miss Evans, Lilian Crooks, Sylvia Marsden.
X, Margaret Wildgoose.

Darley Dale Carnival Queen and attendants on R.A. Twyford's lorry.
Rita Hayto, X, Nancy Boden, Queen ?, X.
John Samson Wain, Mrs Wain, X, X, X.

Darley Carnival Queen on float at Two Dales 1938.
Gladys Taylor, Eunice Bunting, Ada Travis, Queen Amy Holmes, Rose Winthrope.
June Woodhouse, Norma Barker.

Darley Dale Carnival Queen and attendants,
visiting the Whitworth Hospital and patients 1939.
Back row: X, X, X, X, X, X, Bill Webster.
Front row: George Roberts, X, X, Ivy Coney, Dorothy Thompson, Joan Salt, the Matron,
Vera Hawley, X.

The Frollies Dance Band at the New Bath Hotel, early 1930's.
Lesley Pearson, Matthew Ball, Harold Pearson, Luther Briddon, Aubrey Knowles,
Hedley Pearson.

One group of children who participated with gusto in all of these proceedings during the late 1930's were the young girls of the Churchtown/Green Lane Triangle. Three mothers in particular, Mrs. Howes, Mrs. Muir and Mrs. Spencer organised the girls to form tableaux on decorated floats for the carnival processions, with Mrs. Howes, a dressmaker, making many of the costumes. They were always determined not to be outdone by the "Two Dales end" of the parish.

They also formed a **concert party**, called **"The Fairies Concert Party"**,

Herbert Hardy, winner of the Challenge Walking Cup c.1931. Sam Crooks had won the cup in 1925, 1926 and 1927.

305

with the edition of one young lad, Herbert Siddons, from Ryecroft. The round of the village carnivals was made in summer and concerts were performed during the winter months. They sang, danced (the clog dance was in their repertoire) and performed acrobatic displays at the Whitworth Institute and in villages all around, including Youlgreave, Wirksworth, Bonsall and Brassington. Silver Service bus driver Felix Boam delivered them to their venue and returned them home.

Though the best of friends, the two women had a difference of opinion at one stage and Eunice Muir went off to form her own extremely successful concert party, called **"Rhyme and Rhythm"**. They were allowed to practice in the Club Room of the Grouse Inn by kind permission of landlady, Ethel Johnson. An added attraction with this concert party was the ability of a number of the troupe to play the accordion, ably supported by young pianist Marie White. The two concert parties became friendly "rivals" for a while, with one side calling the other "Rhyme with no Rhythm" and the other retaliating with "Fairies with clogs on". The two ladies still remained friends.

The Churchtown triangle carnival group performing as 'Henry Hall and his band' c.1935.
Standing: Jean Crawford, Ethel Johnson, Louie Muir, Audrey Howes, Jean Dunn, Marie White.
Seated: Avis Gladwin, Margaret Hallam, Norma Howes, Betty White, Joan Muir,
Winifred Spencer, Mavis Allen, Lilly Gill, Molly Hallam, Jean Fletcher, Doris Wigley,
Kathleen Devaney, Gwen Fentem.

The Fairies Concert Party c.1938.
Back row: Connie Waller, Doris Wigley, Betty Waller, Florence Hibbert,
Herbert Siddons, Norma Howes, Winnifred Spencer, Elsie Parks, Audrey Howes.
Front row: Joan Lewis, Audrey Fox, Marjorie Parks, Phylis Ward, Sylvia Atkin.

Rhyme and Rhythm Concert Party c.1938.
Back row: Jean Wardle, Louie Fletcher, Louie Johnson, Mrs. Muir, Jean Crawford, X,
Annie Gill.
Middle row: Len Gilbert, Jean Dunn, Ethel Johnson, Herbert Siddons, Marie White.
Front row: Renee Toft, Jean Fletcher, Kathleen Devaney, Lillian Gill, Louie Muir.

Rhyme and Rhythm Concert Party at the Grouse Inn c.1937.
Back row: Henry Mellor, Doris Chatburn, Frank Fletcher, Jean Fletcher,
Kathleen Wilson, Eunice Muir, Jean Evans, Doris Harris, Diana Mellor,
Donald Chatburn, Irene Harris, Alan Fletcher.
Front row: Ethel Johnson, Louie Muir, Renee Toft, Marie White, Mona Toft,
Leonard Gilbert, Lillian Gill, Kathleen Devaney.

Charity football team 'Mrs. Johnson's Amazons' led out from the Grouse Inn by
accordian players Louie Muir and Marie White.

*Comic football match to raise funds for charity in the 1930's, organised by the Grouse
Inn landlady, Ethel Johnson. The game against the men was held by the side of the
railway line, near Churchtown. The women were nicknamed ' Mrs. Johnson's Amazons'.
Back row: X, Wilfred Boam, ? Greatorex, Dick White, X, X, X.
Front row: X, X, Olive Woodhouse, X, Ethel Johnson, ? Wood, Agnes Morten, Hetty Hanson.*

Two other leisure time outlets for Darley children were provided by
the **Darley Cubs/Scouts organisation** and a club for boys organised by
Eric Griffiths, the Rector's son, during the mid 1930's. The cubs and
scouts, under the leadership of Mr. Geeson, met in one of the buildings
in Stancliffe Stone Quarry yard and each year would travel to their
annual camp, either near the sea, or in the countryside.

Eric Griffiths organised a club for choir boys and others, in an
upstairs room of the Rectory Cottage at Churchtown. A snooker table
and table tennis table were provided and a splendid model electric
railway line was built and operated, incorporating all the details of the
stretch of line from Darley Dale to Bakewell. Eric was also interested in
cine-photography and, with the permission of head teacher Mr. Bartram,
would get the boys in the club and children from the school to act out
plays before the movie camera.

Darley Dale Cubs in Stancliffe Stone Quarry Yard c.1930.
Back row: X, X, ? Geeson, X.
Middle row: X, ? Knifton,Neville Siddall.
Front row: X, X.

Darley Dale Scouts at annual camp early 1930's.
John Roland Corfield, X, Dick Corfield, X, X.

St. Helen's Church Choir 1933.
A number of these chidren were in Eric Griffith's club.
Back row: Tom Rhodes, Dennis Sellers, Vernon Cull, Phillip Willett, Harry ?,
George Potter (choir master), Reg West.
Front row: Alan Young, Arthur Gilbert, Desmond Soppitt, Dennis Gregory,
Lesley Bramhall, Walter Boden, Edwin Willett, Mervyn Corfield.

Local outing clubs held their annual trip on August 25th 1928 when 200 enjoyed a trip to
Blackpool. (Plough Inn, Crown Inn, Blacksmith's Arms and John Gregory and Sons
timber merchants.) This is part of the Blacksmith's Arms contingent.
Back row: John Wood, Walter Walker (plumber and landlady's son).
Middle row: Sid Waterfall, X, Sam Wood, Frank Carter, X, X, Sapp Carter, X, X.
Front row: X, X, X, X.

The Girls' Life Brigade outside Hackney Methodist Chapel 1936/1937. Founded in 1902 by the National Sunday School Union, members were admitted at the age of six. Bible and Missionary study were stressed and instruction provided in camping, swimming, first aid, hygiene and home nursery.
Back row: Phyllis Staton, Edna Hawley.
Next row: Gwen Downes, Enid Brooks, Maud Cook, Eileen Croft.
Next row: Barbara White, Peggy Milner, Sonia Cooke, Gwen Degge, Jean Boden, Gwyneth Wragg, Edna Degge, Jean Smith, Olwyn Waterfall, Gwen Knowles, Monica Waterfall.
Next row: Audrey Brooks, Mrs. Essie Clarke, Mrs. Millie Smith, Reverend Tom Greener Gardner, Enid Wragg.
Front row: Enid Oldfield, Joyce Smith, Margery Phillips, Barbara Croft, Vera Smith.

When nowadays looking at these cine-films of Darley in the 1930's, and enjoying the scenes of yesteryear, there comes a poignant reminder that it would not be long before many of these young lads would be plucked from the safety of their rural environment and thrust into the dangers endemic in any world wide conflict. A young John Thompson is captured on film, taking part in one of Eric Griffith's adventures on film. A few years later, he would be facing danger in real life, during the Second World War, and be killed in the skies over Europe.

It now seems appropriate, therefore, to tell the stories of those Darley Dale men who worked and played in the parish during the inter-war years, but did not survive the dangers and perils of wartime.

CHAPTER EIGHT

THE SECOND WORLD WAR

The early years of the 1930's had been the "Depression Years". The bottom had fallen out of the Wall Street stock market of late 1929, resulting in a faltering in investment, less money for people to spend, factories closing due to a lack of markets, with demand reduced still further as men were thrown out of work. Whilst people "tightened their belts", farmers found that no one could afford the food they had grown. As Great Britain abandoned her policy of free trade, international trade virtually collapsed and more men were thrown out of work as more factories, shipbuilding yards and industries were closed down.

Darley Dale people could not avoid being affected by these national and international ramifications in the business and industrial world, but, as we have already seen, the availability of jobs in the lead mine, various quarries, nurseries, the wood yard, railway marshalling yard, at Bakelite and in other businesses, helped to ward off the worst ravages of the "Depression".

What could not be avoided in Darley Dale or elsewhere, were the repercussions from the growing tensions on the international diplomatic scene. The political climate in Europe was changing and "war clouds" loomed on the horizon. The strains imposed by economic collapse and the bitterness caused by the outcome of the Versailles Peace Treaty, imposed in 1920, had found certain country's democratic institutions wanting. Fascist and Nazi regimes had won favour, determined to push their aggressive foreign policies in the belief that the remaining democracies were ill-prepared to defend their rights.

The likely victory of Fascism on the Iberian Peninsula, during the Spanish Civil War of 1936-1939, only emboldened the aggressive plans of Adolph Hitler's Nazi Germany. In 1938 a German ultimatum led to the appointment of several Nazi representatives in the Austrian cabinet. On March 11th German troops entered Austria and the Anschluss, or forbidden union of Austria with Germany, was established.

Tension increased in Czechoslavakia, where Hitler demanded the handing over of areas of Bohemia to Germany, particularly those occupied by Sudetan Germans. Czechoslavakia agreed to this demand, under pressure from France and Britain, but Hitler demanded further considerable concessions by October 1st 1938, in default of which Germany would "march". The Czech army mobilised on September 23rd, France on the next day, whilst on the 28th the British fleet was mobilised.

Prime Minister Neville Chamberlain visited Hitler at Bad Godesberg and Berchtesgaden, without result, and on September 28th Hitler invited the British and French premiers to meet with Mussolini at Munich the next day. At this meeting, to which no Czech representative was admitted, it was agreed that German occupation of the areas demanded should proceed in stages between October 1st and the 10th. Chamberlain was able to return to London, claiming "Peace in our time" and most of Britain breathed a collective sigh of relief.

Relief turned to concern, when, in March 1939, Hitler ignored certain conditions of the Munich Agreement and occupied Bohemia and Moravia without British or French government intervention. Sensing a weakness of resolve throughout the European democracies, Hitler turned his attention to Poland during the summer months. War clouds were looming once again over Europe, for at last, Chamberlain spelt out clearly in Parliament British condemnation of Hitler's latest aggression and made it clear that an attack on Poland would not be tolerated. On April 26th Britain reintroduced conscription.

There was an unprecedented fear in 1939 of devastating air attack, with immediate dangers and horrors in store. When air raid sirens at Mill Close Mine were tested throughout Darley Dale in April 1939, the occasion was not a success, for they were difficult to hear and three months later three more sirens were introduced to improve the situation. At the end of July an Air Raid Precaution exercise took place to test the blackout, when, at midnight on Thursday 20th, wardens and special constables were called out.

The weakness displayed by Britain and France in Munich was

Hitler's most powerful incentive to plan the attack on Poland, first for August, then for September 1939. He believed that Poland could be defeated in isolation, as Czechoslavakia and Austria had been before, especially when, on August 23rd Germany and Soviet Russia signed a Non-Aggression Pact. Hitler's way to Poland seemed open, but on August 25th the signing of the Anglo-Polish alliance was announced in London and Hitler realised that his attempt to isolate Poland had failed.

In the week before the announcement of war, Matlock and Darley Dale had almost a wartime appearance at night, with their extinguished street lamps, darkened windows and white painted kerbs and posts. On Friday 1st September pupils from Ladybarn Girls and Boys Schools, Manchester, arrived at Darley Dale Station and the locals saw the seriousness of the situation as the evacuee children were billeted throughout the district. **** (For a comprehensive insight into life in Darley on the "Home Front", see "A Derbyshire Parish at Peace and War – South Darley 1925 – 1955" by Keith Taylor and Trevor Brown.)

On Sunday September 3rd 1939, at 11-15a.m., Neville Chamberlain announced to a hushed nation that Britain was at war with Germany. Darley Dale families once again faced the prospects of losing loved ones for the second time within living memory.

Thirty Darley Dale men were to die during the Second World War, compared to the 63 combatants who perished in the Great War. The 1939-1945 conflict was spread even more world wide, but did not suffer from the stalemate conditions of trench warfare experienced on the Western Front. Nevertheless, thirty more families would receive the sad news of bereavement and the war would be brought closer home to the civilian population by the ever present threat of aerial bombardment during the "Blitz".

Besides the lower number of deaths recorded within the parish during the Second World War, compared to those of the previous conflict, the next most significant difference was in the range of service organisations that these men represented at the times of their deaths. Between 1914 and 1918 only one of the fallen served in the Royal Navy and none served in the newly established Royal Flying Corps. Instead, they were members of the British Army and the majority served in the local regiment, the Sherwood Foresters.

The widening of horizons generated by travel during the Great War, an improvement in education for the young within the parish during the 1920's and 30's and the rapid development of science and technology resulted in considerable numbers of those who were to die in the Second World War serving in the Royal Air Force and Royal Navy. During this war, all three services were therefore well represented.

If anyone still doubted the serious implications for families within Darley Dale, resulting from the new world wide conflict, any such false hopes were dashed when news came just days into the war, that the first parishioner from Darley had lost his life whilst serving Crown and Country:

STOKER 1ST CLASS JOHN WILLIAM JACKSON, No. D/KX76978, H.M. Submarine "Oxley", Royal Navy.
(Died on Sunday 10th September 1939, aged 31 years.)

John Jackson was born at 3 Vineyard Terrace on Darley Hillside in 1908, the son of railway engine driver James Jackson and wife Kate. In 1928 he joined the Royal Navy and for two years was involved in general training, becoming a stoker on a large surface vessel.

In 1930 he transferred to the submarine branch as a stoker, first on submarine L26 and then H56, whilst stationed in the Mediterranean Sea. Around 1933 he married Bertha Fearn from Hallmoor Road. A child, Geoffrey, was born but soon afterwards John was posted to the China Sea Station on the submarine "Pandora".

Stoker 1st Class John William Jackson.

He was away from wife and son for three years and when he returned

316

Geoffrey greeted him by calling him "that man". The "Pandora" was based at Wei-Hai-Wei Naval Base on the North China coast, and life was quite hectic due to the Far Eastern political situation. 1931 had seen the beginning of the Japanese conquest of Manchuria, in Northern China, and by 1932 it was a virtual colony, with Japan withdrawing from the League of Nations on May 27th 1933. There was therefore growing tension between China and Japan during John Jackson's period of service in the Far East. The Chinese Nationalist leader Chiang Kai-Shek attempted to unify and modernise his backward nation, while simultaneously fighting Communist and dissident warlords, in the face of increasingly aggressive Japanese actions.

At the end of his period of duty, John sailed back to England on the submarine "Osiris", to the Submarine land training base H.M.S. Dolphin, near Gosport, and began a period of training. Eventually he was discharged from service in the Royal Navy, and on to the Naval Reserve, in June 1938, and went to live with his wife and son in a house at the top of Gill Lane and Hallmoor Road.

On leaving the navy he got a job at Mill Close Lead Mine, using his skills as a stoker by working on the pumps with Pat Devaney.

However, in the late summer and autumn of 1938 the Munich Crisis caused great tension in Europe and almost straight away he was recalled to serve for a while. Returning to Mill Close after the crisis was averted, he was called up once again, in August 1939, as war threatened to break out.

At the moment of recall, Bertha was heavily pregnant. John said farewell to wife and son, travelling to Gosport and then boarding his vessel, H.M. Submarine "Oxley", before sailing with two other submarines to Rosythe naval base in Scotland, en route to patrol the North Sea naval bases of Nazi Germany and the Skagerrak, the narrow entrance to the Baltic Sea.

As the three submarines left Rosythe, one day before war was declared, news had arrived for John of the birth of his second son, also named John. By 10th September, however, the submarines were in position on the surface, when, in the darkness, currents caused one to become detached. A failure in the signalling equipment resulted in a torpedo being fired at the "Oxley", believing it to be an enemy vessel.

The submarine, hit by "friendly fire", sank to the sea bed with only two survivors being plucked to safety. John lost his life and became the first Darley casualty in the Second World War.

The postman, Wallace Young, arrived at John's mother's house to ask her to accompany him with the telegram for Bertha. The first war widow to receive such tragic news in Darley Dale would not be the last, unfortunately.

John William Jackson's name is commemorated on Panel 34, column 2 of the Plymouth Naval Memorial, Devon.

Between September 10th 1939 and July 5th 1941, Darley was fortunate to be spared any other losses. During the Autumn the British Expeditionary Force embarked for France, but no hostile action was pursued, as the opposing sides faced each other across the Siegfied Line during the winter of 1939/1940, in the period known as the "Phoney War".

Back home in Darley Dale, rationing was introduced in January 1940, although the ration books had been ready ever since 1938. Butter, sugar, bacon and ham were first on the list, but things did not get really bad until 1942.

At 3-30a.m. on Monday 4th September 1939 air raid sirens went off in the district but the false alarm only revealed the need for a more adequate siren warning in this hilly area. The Warden Post was at the Grouse Inn and the First Aid Dressing Station was at the Stancliffe Works Cabin.

The first large co-ordinated A.R.P. practice took place at 9a.m. on Sunday 22nd October 1939. Reports came in from the wardens of imaginary phosgene gas attacks at Darley Bridge, high explosives at Two Dales and mustard gas at Church Lane, Darley. Electric sirens were now fitted at Mill Close Lead Mine, at Stancliffe and on a tall metal frame fixed to one of the buildings in the Council Depot Yard on Station Road.

On May 14th, Anthony Eden broadcast to the nation that volunteers were required for a new force called the Local Defence Volunteers, later to be known as the Home Guard. The headquarters of "B" Company, Darley Home Guard, was in the Stancliffe Quarry Yard, whilst its night time communications centre was at Darley Hall, Two Dales (now an old people's residential home) and Darley Dale parishioners, young and old, rallied to the cause.

Dick Lane, then living near Gas Cottages, was a respected pigeon fancier and breeder and became involved with the Home Guard when he joined "The Pigeon Reserve". He provided pigeons to supplement the communications network, if ever the radio or telephone systems broke down. During training manoeuvres, three pigeons would be collected by a Home Guard motor cycle dispatch rider and taken into the Peak District, to be released with a message contained in cannisters attached to their legs. Another dispatch rider collected the message from Dick's home and rushed it to the local Home Guard Headquarters. Dick also bred 30 pigeons each year to be sent to the Royal Navy, for them to be used on board ship.

Another creature, somewhat larger than a pigeon, was used by Matlock Home Guard. William Smith organised a small mounted troop of Home Guard members to patrol the countryside on either side of the valley, riding across the Bonsall to Winster hillside and from Matlock towards Flash Dam.

William and Edna Smith had come to live at the Red House, Darley

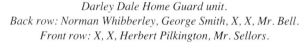

Darley Dale Home Guard unit.
Back row: Norman Whibberley, George Smith, X, X, Mr. Bell.
Front row: X, X, Herbert Pilkington, Mr. Sellors.

Matlock Home Guard members outside the old Starkholmes School, near St. Giles Church. Winners of a .22 shooting competition. Randolph Booth won the cup for the highest points total, with Danny Furniss second.
Back row: Sam Lewis, X, Roy Land, X, Dennis Martin.
Next row: X, X, Harold Bradshaw, X, X, Horace Bowler, Herbert White.
Next row: X, Ron Pugh, X, Herbert Walker, Bill Astbury, X, Vic Carter, Colin McDowell, Cyril Crowder.
Front row: Randolph Booth, Danny Furniss, Mr. Van Raalte, X, Vincent Hobbs, X, Ken Hadfield, Tom Bucklow.

Dale, in the late 1930's, after the departure of Dr. Sharpe. William owned the open cast mines and quarries in the Eyam area, but his great love and passionate hobby was horses and horse riding. His Irish ancestors had bred horses and during the First World War he had been a captain in the Royal Horse Artillery.

It was in 1940 that the Red House and stable block was requisitioned by

William Smith of the Red House, Darley Dale, a member of the small mounted group in Matlock Home Guard, in late 1940.

320

the army and became the headquarters and domestic quarters for the women's A.T.S. The Smith family had to move out and for the remainder of the war lived near Matlock Green, at Huntsbridge House (now the headquarters of the Red Cross). Beds were placed in the stable block and in most of the downstairs and upper rooms of the Red House, providing dormitory accommodation for many women soldiers.

During the period of late Spring 1940, the Whitworth Institute and its grounds were closed to the public. It too was requisitioned, in this case as an army base for the Royal Army Service Corps. For the remainder of the war, batches of trainee soldiers learned drill in the grounds and driving skills on the hilly roads of the district, whilst shooting practice took place on the Oker Hill firing range. The large input of soldiers into the parish resulted in extra customers for the local public houses. Rationing meant that there was less beer available to the pubs and so they opened officially on a rota basis, with one pub opening between 7p.m. and 8p.m., another from 8p.m. to 9p.m. and so on. One problem resulting from this procedure was that each soldier would take the beer mug from the first pub on his round of the pubs and the next morning the landlord would have to attempt to reclaim them from the other hostelries.

The dire military situation of the Allies and the British Army was brought home to Darley folk in early June of 1940, when soldiers who had been evacuated from the beaches at Dunkirk arrived by train at Darley Station, or by lorry. In a dirty, dishevelled state, they rested by the roadside on Station Road and the A6, before being billeted in Bell tents in the fields near Broadwalk.

As the Dunkirk soldiers departed and the R.A.S.C. troops arrived at the Whitworth Institute, the local ladies of the Dale Road Methodist Chapel, including baker James Squires' daughter, Muriel Walters, set up a canteen for their benefit at the back of the chapel building, close to the boiler room. Cups of tea and sandwiches were served to the Dunkirk soldiers in June, but later, the ladies became even busier in providing refreshments for the R.A.S.C. troops. Between July 28th and September 22nd 1940, ten thousand and forty six cups of tea were served.

Other women from the parish were doing their part for the war effort, with many taking up the jobs of the men who had gone off to fight in the war. Mrs. Violet Goodall from Hooleys Estate, for example, became a porter at Matlock Station from 1940 to 1945, whilst some ladies took over the jobs of loco cleaners at Rowsley Railway Marshalling Yard and many more were able to join the work force at Firth Derihon (Firth Rixson) when the shadow factory was built in 1942 by Lehane, Mackenzie and Shand Limited.

Firth Derihon were drop forgers and stampers, specialising in forgings for the motor and aircraft trade and the firm wished to escape from the threat of possible damage in further German air raids over the city of Sheffield. (see "A Derbyshire Parish at Peace and War"). The factory site was on the former sports ground of the London Midland Railway Company, where pre-war football and cricket matches had been played and teas served in the converted railway carriages that were used as a pavilion. Many people still remember with fondness the meat and pie suppers, domino drives and whist drives held there to raise money for the Sports Club.

Violet Goodall from Hooleys Estate. Porteress at Matlock Station 1940-45.

The railway carriage pavilion at the L.M.S. sports field. The area became the site of Firth Dehiron in 1942.

322

Lehane Mackenzie and Shand Ltd., begin work on the foundations of Firth Derihon 1942.

Artist's impression of newly constructed 'Shadow Factory' of Firth Derihon Stampings Limited, built by Lehane, Mackenzie and Shand Ltd., in 1942. The main bays of the factory housed a number of heavy forge hammers which required deep and massive foundations insulated with hardwood packings to minimise transmission of vibration into the surrounding ground.

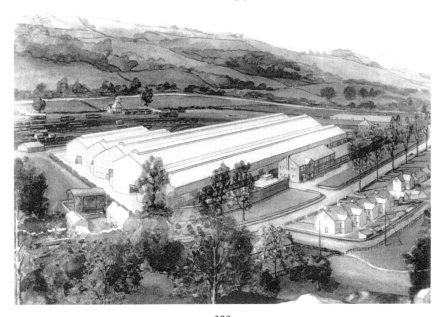

The workforce of Firth Derihon in 1943.
the three men standing in the centre of the second row are:
Mr. Hargeaves (manager), Mr. Julian (owner), Mr. Wolper.
The group of workers include local men and women, people from Sheffield
who lodged in local homes and Irish men, who were housed
in a specially built hostel, now part of the Cobb-Slater factory.

Workers enjoying a break in the canteen at Firth Derihon during the war years.
Extra rations were allowed for the factory canteen. During the war an ENSA concert
party entertained the workforce in the canteen and the show was broadcast on the
BBC 'wireless'. On most days of the week a bus load of Italian prisoners of war were
brought from the P.O.W. camp at Heage to work at the 'shadow factory'.
One Italian sailor worked in the stores, using his skills to make large ropes
which could be used in the stamp side.

Firth Derihon c.1943. A group photograph of the stamp side at the 'shadow factory'.

Back row: X, X, Horace Hyde, Cliff Byard, George Grant, Gena Astles, Eunice Astles, Mrs. Taylor, Matthew Pattison, X, X, X, X, X, X, X, X, George Poultney, X, X, Arthur Lees.

Middle row: X, X, C'arlie Porter, Joan Lewis, Gwen Fentem, Enid Batterley, Billy Gill, Kath Cooper, X, X, ? Hough, Ety Briddon, X.

Front row: X, Marie White, ? Gill, X, Arthur ? ? Kithcen, X, Jean Scriven, X.

Firth Derihon c.1943.
A group photograph of the die shop workers, who made the moulds.
Back row: X, X, Bill Wheeldon, Mr. Housley, X, X, Mr. James.
Middle row: Eric Lees, X, X, Rex Wheeldon, X, Sidone Donelan, Olive Woodhouse,
Geoff Mee, Lucy Pitt, X.
Front row: X, Jimmy O'Brian, Arthur Stoppard, Mr. Wolper, X, Frank Harrop, X, X.

When it came to raising funds for providing comforts for the servicemen or for helping bring in the harvest or crops on the farms, the women and children again "came into their own". This fact is encapsulated in the photographs of Darley House Estate residents taking part in pageants and fancy dress football matches, organised by women such as Queenie Wheeldon, or collecting the potato crop on the farms of Mr. Charlie Wildgoose. Dances were held at Darley House, with music being provided by Joe Vallence on the drums and his daughter Gloria on the accordion. The money raised from these events helped boost the total collected in the district for the Spitfire Fund or for Matlock War Weapons Week.

Darley House Estate residents potato picking 1942 in Charles Wildgoose's field near the Red House, Old Road, Darley Dale.
Back row: Nellie Hayes, Annie White, Sam Hayes, Jenny Marsden, Mrs. Artless, Queenie Wheeldon, Sidney Wildgoose, Ann Andrews, Fred Wildgoose, Charlie Wildgoose, Ada Merritt, Albert Marsden, Doris Smith, Bertha Oldfield, Gordon Winder, Lizzie Gregory, Roy Smith.
Bertha Robinson, Bill Smith, Jessie Wood, Mrs. Harris.
Front row: Rose Winder, Joan Moore, Jean Wood, Audrey Marsden, Margaret Wildgoose, Rita Marsden, Joan Smith, Ann Winder, Ivor Smith, Derek Marsden, Ann Rhodes, John Cooke, Owen Moore.

Fund raising for the war effort by Darley House Estate residents 1941, on St. Elphins School grounds.
? Kenworthy, John Merritt, Alf Clarke, Walter Bradley, Vic Toft, Joe Marsden, Miss Stopford (headmistress of St. Elphins), Cyril Cook, Ada Merritt.

Darley House Estate residents taking part in a comic football match on St. Elphins sports field 1941 to raise funds for the war effort.
Back row: Margaret Wildgoose, Rita Marsden, Fred Williams, Charlie Smith, John Merritt, Jim Kenworthy, Isaac Oldfield, Joe Marsden, Walter Bradley.
Middle row: May Knowles, Florence Moore, Joe Lichfield, Cyril Cook, Sam Crooks, Ena Clarke, Charlie Gregory, Vic Toft, Kenneth Toft, Marion Wildgoose, Jessie Wood, Olive Crooks.
Front row: Ada Merritt, Louie Cowley, Ann Andrews, Jenny Marsden, Joyce Allwood, Alf Clarke, Queenie Wheeldon, Lizzie Gregory.

*Raising money for Matlock War Weapons Week 1941
by Darley House Estate children at Darley House.*

1. *Una Wheeldon,*
2. *Joan Moore,*
3. *Jean Wood,*
4. *Margaret Wildgoose,*
5. *Barbara Marsden,*
6. *Joan Smith,*
7. *Maureen Clough,*
8. *Rita Marsden,*
9. *Joyce Jackson,*
10. *Barbara Marsden,*
11. *Audrey Marsden,*
12. *Margaret Jolly,*
13. *Iris Vallence,*
14. *Margaret Smith,*
15. *Enid Oldfield.*

Nursery Rhyme Pageant by Darley House Estate residents
to raise money for the war effort at Darley House 1942.
Back row: Margaret Smith, Audrey Marsden, Margaret Jolly, Jean Wood, Joan Moore.
Next Row: Joyce Jackson, Maurice Wright, Derek Marsden, Peter Wood, Jean Marsden.
Next Row: Victor Berresford, Maureen Clough, Rita Marsden, Margaret Wildgoose,
Mary Randell, Vernon Moore.
Next row: Joy Roose, Michael Jolly, Barbara Robinson, Enid Oldfield, Una Wheeldon,
Margaret Smith, Barbara Marsden, Joy Toft, Joan Smith.
Front row: Bob Roose, Ann Woodhouse, Alan Robinson, Eunice Woodhouse,
Colleen Worrall, Sheila Clough, Janet Howe, Deana Andrews, Cynthia Smith,
Maureen Smith, John Cooke, Graham Moore, Vera Wright, Owen Moore.

Though Darley Dale men were participating in the fighting in
Belgium and France during May/June 1940, and one was flying in the
skies of Southern England during the Battle of Britain
(August/September 1940), others in the North African campaign against
the Italians in 1940/1941 or in naval actions on the High Seas, it was not

until July 1941 that word arrived confirming the death of a second person from the parish:

PRIVATE HARRY RAYMOND TAYLOR,
No. 10537235, Royal Army Ordnance Corps.
(Died on Saturday 5th July 1941, aged 37 years.)

The son of railway man Harry Taylor and wife Edith, living at Number 3 Derwent View, Harry junior left Churchtown School at the age of 14 to start his working life as a "caller up" on the Midland Railway at Rowsley. His job was to go around the houses and make certain that engine drivers and firemen were woken up on time. He progressed to

Private Harry Taylor's wedding day.
Harry Taylor (senior), Florence Webber, Charlie Taylor, Harry Taylor, Elsie Wardman,
George Wardman, Marjorie Wardman, Sam Wardman.
Edith Taylor, Mrs. Wardman.

becoming a loco cleaner and occasional fireman, until he became a regular fireman.

Later he married Elsie Wardman, from a strong "chapel going" Darley family, and they settled down to married life at Number 12 Derwent View, Church Road. One day after work he went collecting pea sticks for his garden and by accident his eye was poked and he lost the sight of one eye, it being replaced by an artificial one.

He could no longer work as a fireman but the railway company found him other duties to perform. Unhappy with this situation, because his disability and the early wartime blackout restrictions made it difficult for him to see clearly, he became the caretaker at the National Westminster Bank in Matlock, living with his wife in a flat on Dale Road.

It was a great surprise to everyone when, in early 1941, Harry, at the age of 36 and with only one eye, received his call up papers. Just before taking his medical examination it had been suggested by people that he should attend without wearing his artificial eye, but Harry was truthful and wore it on the day. He was passed and was told he would be joining the Royal Army Ordnance Corps.

After three months training, he received seven days leave, but this was extended by a few days when notification arrived that the Battalion was to form part of an overseas draft, bound for North Africa.

During January and early February of 1941 the British and Empire troops of the Western Desert Force had advanced 500 miles in North Africa, destroying nine Italian Divisions and taking 130,000 prisoners, 400 tanks and 1290 guns. British casualties amongst the "Desert Rats" amounted to 500 killed and 1373 wounded. It was a remarkable demonstration of fire and movement, aided by effective naval and air support, against an inept passive defence, greatly superior in numbers.

By the end of February 1941, however, the German Luftwaffe had arrived in Sicily with 500 planes, and by their actions, barred the use of the port of Benghazi as a base for the Western Desert Force. The "Desert Rats" were also weakened by many troops being sent to intervene in Greece against German invasion forces.

General Erwin Rommel arrived in North Africa with his Afrika Korps in March 1941 and drove back the British forces between the 24th March and May 30th. The isolated fortress of Tobruk was reinforced by the

Australians and held out against the Germans and Italians, in order to deprive Rommel of a base port to support further advance into Egypt.

In early July 1941, the Western Desert Force, renamed the Eighth Army, began reinforcing and preparing for a counter-offensive against Rommel, proposed for November. One of the many service men sent out from England to join the Eighth Army was Harry Taylor. Sadly, he was never to arrive.

Harry left Liverpool on the troopship S.S. "Anslem", en route to Egypt, but whilst in convoy in the Atlantic the ship was torpedoed by a German U-boat. Elsie Taylor received a telegram reporting him missing and yet hope remained, for Harry had always been a strong swimmer, but another telegram later arrived to say he was missing, presumed killed. As this news was delivered, Harry's parents were on the station platform on their way to a holiday in Blackpool, but were allowed to go off without being told. His mother, Edith, died soon afterwards of a broken heart.

Some time later, Elsie heard of a survivor from the ship returning to Chesterfield and she visited him. He could only tell her that 200 survived out of a complement of 2000 men. Harry's name is commemorated at the Brookwood Memorial, Surrey, thirty miles from London, on Panel 19 Column 3, commemorating over 3000 men and women of the land forces who died at sea.

A few years after the war, Elsie Taylor married Tant Wigley from Number 4 Derwent View, a widower with two children, Alan and Doris.

Throughout the rest of 1941, the world witnessed the evacuation of British forces from Greece and the German conquest of the Mediterranean island of Crete. However, 1941 saw important developments in widening the war into a truly world wide conflict. The main new German sphere of interest now became Russia, when, on June 22nd 1941 Operation "Barbarossa" was launched against the Soviet Union, and towards the close of the year America was drawn into the war when the Japanese launched their surprise attack on Pearl Harbour, on December 7th 1941.

As 1942 dawned, two years of war had so far resulted in two fatalities amongst Darley's servicemen. However, the coming year, with its ever widening spheres of conflict, witnessed six more deaths of men from the parish. The Japanese advance through Malaya and their capture of Singapore claimed one victim, three R.A.F. fliers lost their lives, one in the fight against the U-boat menace in the Atlantic, another over Germany as embattled Britain carried the war to the enemy by air bombardment, whilst the third airman was lost when defending these shores from enemy bombers and the two remaining victims lost their lives in the battle for supremacy in North Africa and the Mediterranean Sea.

FLIGHT SERGEANT NORMAN CLARE, No. 644121, 201 Squadron, Royal Air Force.
(Died on Friday 6th February 1942, aged 20 years.)

Unfortunately, I know little about the background of Norman Clare's life, except to report that he was the son of Thomas and Jane Annie Clare of Matlock.

He entered the war quite early and in 1942, at the age of 20, was a Fight Sergeant with No. 201 Squadron, R.A.F. The squadron was part of Coastal Command and had flown Southampton flying-boats upto 1936, when they were replaced by "Londons", which were still in service by the start of the war.

In April 1940, 201 Squadron converted to Sunderland flying-boats and in October 1941 moved to the R.A.F. base at Castle Archdale in Northern Ireland. Their duty was to carry out anti-submarine patrols over a large expanse of the North Atlantic, a vital task, since the U-boats were wreaking havoc throughout the vital convoy routes.

1941 had been a critical year with shipping losses rising all the time with 1300 ships sunk in that year alone, worth a staggering 4,328,000 tonnes. The Short Sunderland flying-boat was Britain's most important aerial weapon against the U-boats, especially those submarines whose bases were on the French coast and so had to cross the Bay of Biscay to reach the convoy lanes. Using depth charges and guns when attacking U-boats on the surface, or those just submerging, the Sunderland could be very effective, but the patrols could be exhausting and dangerous.

On one such mission, on the 6th February 1942, Norman Clare's flying-boat did not return to base. No bodies were recovered and his name is commemorated on Panel 73 of the R.A.F. Memorial at Runneymede, in Surrey.

GUNNER BERTRAM EDWARD CONQUEST,
No. 1502871, 12 Battery,
6th Heavy Anti Aircraft Regiment, Royal Artillery.
(Died on Sunday 1st March 1942, aged 23 years.)

Bert Conquest, together with brothers Ray and Len, were born at Holloway, but in 1938 they moved to the recently built Hooleys Estate at Darley Dale, with their parents Harry and Martha. Their father Harry worked as a Derbyshire County Council lengthman, whilst Bert worked for the Silver Service Bus Company as a conductor.

Private Bertram Conquest.

Bert was a militia man (Territorial) and was called up into the Royal Artillery before the war started. Going out to France as part of the British Expeditionary Force in the winter of 1939/1940 he was involved in attempting to stem the German invasion of the Low Countries and France in May/June 1940, but was evacuated from Dunkirk in June.

During the Autumn of 1940 and for most of 1941 his battery of heavy anti-aircraft guns was involved in defending British towns and cities against the aerial threat of the Luftwatte during the Blitz. They defended Bristol, Birmingham, Manchester, Barnard Castle, Tenby and Wolverhampton from attack, and it was in the latter town that Bert met and married a local girl.

Shortly after his marriage, he sailed from Liverpool on November 11th 1941, heading for the fortress naval base of Singapore, at the southern tip

335

of the Malayan Peninsula, arriving on 29th January 1942. Whilst on the journey, the Japanese launched their attack on Pearl Harbour on December 7th 1941, resulting in the entry of the United States of America into the war.

During January 1942 the British retreated southwards in Malaya, as the Japanese outfought and outmanoeuvred them and the defenders were forced back into the island fortress, where they were joined by Bert Conquest.

The attack on Singapore began on 8th February after a protracted air bombardment. Crossings of the stretch of water in armoured barges were covered by intense artillery and machine gun fire and British counter-attacks were broken up by dive bombers. Tanks began moving across the causeway, which Japanese engineers had repaired, and, despite desperate resistance, the city's reservoirs were captured. The 70,000 man garrison thereupon surrendered unconditionally on February 15th.

During the fighting of 8th to 15th February, Bert Conquest was wounded. He never recovered and died on the 1st March 1942, aged 23 years. He was buried in Kranji War Cemetery, 22 kilometres north of Singapore, on the northern side of the island, overlooking the Straits of Johore.

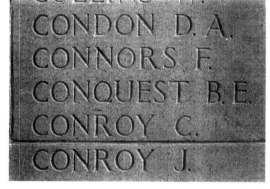

Bert's two brothers, Ray and Len Conquest, also joined the British Army, and were fortunate to survive the war. Ray joined the Kings Own Royal Regiment, serving in the 10th Indian Division in Egypt and Palestine, just after the Battle of Alamein. Afterwards he transferred to the 24th Guards

Changi Cemetary, Singapore.

336

Brigade H.Q. and landed with them near Naples, Italy, and continued with them in their advance northwards throughout 1944 and 1945.

Meanwhile, brother Len had joined the Light Anti-Aircraft Battery of the Leicestershire Yeomanry and saw service in Belgium, Holland and Germany after D-Day. It was whilst in Germany, near the Russian sector, that Len and his fellow soldiers of the Yeomanry had the traumatic experience of witnessing the terrible conditions and sights within a number of concentration camps in the area.

The first two weeks of August 1942 brought great sadness, when, within the space of twelve days, three more Darley servicemen were reported killed:

SERGEANT PETER JOHN HENRY DONELAN, No. 1378642, Royal Air Force Volunteer Reserve, Air gunner 9 Squadron.

(Died on Saturday 1st August 1942, aged 20 years.)

Peter's father and mother, John Henry and Grace Donelan, lived at Ware in the Hertfordshire countryside. Mr. Donelan was de-mobbed from the army after the First World War and was sent as a signal man on the railway to Rowsley Marshalling Yard. They lived at Number 8 Meadow Cottages (now demolished), near to the bottom of Northwood Lane, where a daughter, Sidone, was born in 1920 and a son, Peter, twenty months later. Their father was proficient in first aid and took teams of young men to competitions in Derby.

Peter and Sidone went to Darley Churchtown School, but eventually Mr. Donelan was promoted and was

Sergeant Peter Donelan.

sent to Stockport, where the children attended Alexander Park School. Promotion came again when he was moved back to Rowsley Sidings to take over Number 1 Signal Box, and the family went to live at Number 1 Whitworth Avenue, Broadwalk, with the children now attending Darley Council School.

Both of them began night school education, with Peter learning shorthand. He went to work in Leeds as a traveller for P.G. Tips, just before war started. He had a strong desire to join the R.A.F. and volunteered whilst in Leeds.

Joining at 18 years of age, he trained as a rear air gunner and just before his death was to be trained in wireless operations as well. Peter was a good marksman who, whilst at Darley, had owned an air rifle and often went out hunting with his father, who owned a gun licence and kept a dog for retrieving.

Peter joined No. 9 Squadron at R.A.F. Honington, near Thetford in Suffolk. Flying Wellington bombers, a fine two engined aircraft, he went on many missions over Germany with Bomber Command. On one of these hazardous missions the plane was badly damaged by anti-aircraft fire and they limped home, with a number of the crew injured. They had to recuperate over a lengthy period, with an extended leave.

Bomber Command's night blows against Germany grew heavier. On the night of May 30th/31st 1942, the first 1000-plane night assault by Bomber Command against the important railroad marshalling yards at Cologne caused heavy damage.

On the night of his last mission, (31st July/1st August 1942), Peter's plane was involved in another 1000-plane bombing raid, this time on the steelworks and industries of Dusseldorf, on the River Rhine. His plane was one of 40 planes brought down that night, with the loss of nearly 300 air-crew.

Peter's parents received a letter from his Wing Commander, J. Southwell, stating that nothing was heard of the air craft after the take off. "Your son was a very keen and efficient air gunner and his loss is a great blow to us all".

Peter Donelan is commemorated in the Reichswald Forest War Cemetery at Kleve, Germany, in grave 9. G. 5. Many airmen in the cemetery are those who died in the intensive air attacks over Germany

Early training. Peter Donelan is the middle man in the second row.

Peter Donelan, second from the left, with members of his air crew.

and their graves were brought in from other cemeteries.

Six days after Peter's death, the squadron moved base to R.A.F. Waddington, near Lincoln, where they began to fly the splendid four engined bomber, the Avro-Lancaster.

Peter's parents and his sister Sidone at his graveside at Kleve, in the 1950's.

PILOT OFFICER JOHN ALWYNE WAIN,
No. 114644, 151 Squadron,
Royal Air Force Volunteer Reserve.
(*Died on Monday 10th August 1942, aged 21 years.*)

Alwyne's father, John Wain, originated from Rowsley (22 Midland Cottages) and was a railway engine driver based at Rowsley Sidings. After marriage, he and his wife, Florence Annie, moved to "Ivy Dene" at Northwood Lane, where they brought up three children, Alwyne (b. 1921), Doreen and Audrey.

Sergeant Pilot John Alwyne Wain, 1941,
in his Defiant plane.

In 1931, after winning a free place from Chuchtown School, Alwyne went to Lady Manners School, Bakewell, till he was 18 and applied to join the Royal Air Force as war started. For a short time he took a temporary office job in Chesterfield, until he could be accepted for war service. His cousin, Bert Ricketts, was already flying in the R.A.F., and it was he who first introduced him to a love of flying when they discussed the matter on Bert's periods of leave.

After joining up, he trained as a pilot and became a sergeant pilot, flying Defiants first of all. On a number of occasions whilst training he would pass close over the family home at Northwood and roll his wings, causing his mother's face to turn white.

Pilot Officer John Alwyne
Wain in 1942.

Eventually he became a pilot officer and by 1942 he was serving with 151 Squadron on Mosquitoes. Based at R.A.F. Wittering, near Peterborough, he was a night-time fighter pilot, whose job it was to intercept German raiders during the Blitz on British cities and towns during 1941/1942. (It is worth noting that major components in the construction of the fuselage and control panel of Alwyne's Mosquito were constructed of Bakelite plastics, made at the Darley Dale based Bakelite factory, sited next to Gregory's Timber Yard, in Old Road.)

His younger sister, Doreen, recounts how he thoroughly loved flying and was always great fun when he came home on leave. However, in his serious moments, he realised it was unlikely that he would survive.

Shortly before his final mission he told his family that he was expecting to be sent abroad to be based on the Mediterranean island of Malta, in defence of the beleaguered islanders and garrison. However, on the wild and stormy night of Sunday 9th August 1942, the Squadron found themselves relocated from Wittering to R.A.F. Coltishall for an interceptor mission. Radar had picked up signals of enemy raiders and the Mosquitoes took off to patrol the eastern approaches. The following is a copy of a letter sent by the Wing Commander of his Squadron to Alwyne's father, two days after he was killed.

"Dear Mr. Wain, It is with the deepest regret that I have to inform you that your son, Pilot Officer Alwyne Wain, is missing from an operational patrol during the early hours of Monday morning.

The circumstances are not fully known, but as far as we can tell, he was shot down in combat with an enemy air craft off the East Coast of England.

Just before midnight on Sunday, your son took off on an operational patrol and at 1-30a.m. sighted an enemy raider heading out to sea. He immediately gave chase and from then on no further messages were received from him.

At the first light on Monday morning, a flying boat and other aircraft of the Air Sea Rescue Services carried out a search and some time later the wreckage of your son's plane was found. The weather by that time had greatly deteriorated, and although the flying boat made a number of attempts to land alongside, owing to the heavy swell running, it was unable to do so. Fast rescue launches were summoned and immediately put off and they were later joined by heavier launches, but in spite of all efforts the wreckage eventually sank. Although the pilot's body was not actually seen, no hope should be entertained of his survival.

Pilot Officer Wain was one of my most capable and experienced pilots. He was always ready and willing to undertake any job of work and could be relied upon to do his work well. He loved flying and was regarded as an exceptionally good pilot. He served his Squadron and his Country faithfully and his keenness was an inspiration to us all.

Although normally of a reticent manner, in action he was a cool and determined fighter pilot, eager to engage the enemy and showing great courage in combat.

Amongst his colleagues in the Mess, Alwyne was immensely popular and his quiet and shy manner endeared him to all who knew him.

May I on behalf of myself and all the officers and airmen of the Squadron, express the very deep sympathy we all feel with you in your bereavement."

Alwyne Wain's name is inscribed on Panel 72 of the R.A.F. Memorial at Runnymede in Surrey. The Memorial commemorates over 20,000 airmen who were lost in the Second World War and have no known graves.

We have seen how his uncle, Herbert Wain, had been killed in action on Flanders Fields in 1918 and now the Second World War was claiming another member of the family.

ABLE SEAMAN TERENCE ALLSOP, No. C/SSX18142, H.M.S. Nigeria, Royal Navy.
(Died on Wednesday 12th August 1942, aged 24 years.)

Terence was the youngest child of Tant and Winifred Allsop, with siblings Tony, Sylvia, Nancy, Joyce, Patricia and Dinah. They lived at 15 South Park Avenue, Broadwalk, close to Tant's place of work in Stancliffe Quarry Yard.

Left, Edward Stephenson, right, Able Seaman Terence Allsop,

Terence went to Darley Dale Council School and in 1922 joined 'Fox' patrol of Darley Scouts, based in Stancliffe Quarry Yard. He began work at Paton and Baldwins factory, Matlock, in 1933, but in November 1934 he began an apprenticeship as an electrician at Mill Close Lead Mine.

Joining the Royal Navy as a volunteer in the mid 1930's, Terence

H.M.S. "Dainty" in Hong Kong Harbour c.1937.

trained at Chatham Naval Base in the Torpedo Division and in 1936 found himself in the Mediterranean Sea taking part in the blockade of Spain during the early stages of the Spanish Civil War. By 1937, however, he was stationed out in the Far East, near Hong Kong, at Wei-Hai-Wei Naval Base, where his ship, H.M.S. "Dainty", formed part of the 8th Destroyer Flotilla. It was an exotic peacetime location but times were tense in this theatre of operations because of the Japanese invasion of the Chinese mainland and the crisis in Manchuria.

By 1939 Terence was back in Britain and operating on torpedoes on the Royal Navy 6-inch gun cruiser, H.M.S. "Ajax". As war was declared, "Ajax" was the flag ship of the naval force that intercepted the German pocket battleship "Graf Spee" at the Battle of the River Plate, in the South Atlantic, on December 13th 1939, and was in "at the kill" when the "Graf Spee" was scuttled in Montevideo harbour. During the action, the two after turrets of "Ajax" were knocked out. At 8-54p.m. on 17th December the Ajax's aircraft reported "Graf Spee" has blown herself up".

When the "Ajax" returned for repairs, Terence became part of the crew of the cruiser H.M.S. "Nigeria". By 1942 the besieged Mediterranean island of Malta was in desperate straits, and the Admiralty organised Operation "Pedestal" to force through a convoy to the island.

The Admiralty drew heavily upon the Home Fleet. H.M.S. "Nelson", with the "Rodney", three large carriers, seven cruisers (including Terence on board "Nigeria") and thirty two destroyers entered the Mediterranean on August 9th. The enemy had meanwhile strengthened his air forces in Sicily and Sardinia.

On August 11th this fleet, escorting fourteen fast merchant ships, was off Algiers. The carrier "Eagle" was sunk by a U-boat but the "Furious" successfully flew off her Spitfires to Malta. The next day the expected air attacks began. One merchant ship and a destroyer were sunk and the cruiser "Indomitable" damaged. Thirty nine enemy aircraft and an Italian U-boat were destroyed.

On approaching the "Narrows" on the evening of the 12th August the night brought a crescendo of attacks by U-boats and E-boats and by the morning of the 13th August, seven merchant ships had been lost, as well as the cruisers "Manchester" and "Cairo". Two other cruisers, including H.M.S. "Nigeria" and three of the merchant ships were damaged by torpedoes.

Undaunted, the survivors held on for Malta and after further enemy action, five gallant merchant ships got through with their precious cargoes. The loss of 350 officers and men and so many of the finest ships was grievous. The reward justified the price exacted. The strength of Malta revived, British submarines returned to the island, and, with the striking forces of the Royal Air Force, regained their dominating position in the Central Mediterranean.

It is both sad and ironic that Terence Allsop, a seaman trained in the operational activities of torpedoes, was killed in the explosion caused by an enemy torpedo during the earlier desperate action on the 12th August. This was the second time during the war that a ship he was serving on was torpedoed. On this occasion he was not so fortunate. His body was never recovered and his name is etched onto the facade of the Chatham Naval Memorial in Kent, on Panel 52, 3.

The last Darley man to be killed during 1942 was:

ABLE SEAMAN JACK FIELDING,
P/JX 275041, H.M.S. "BLEAN", ROYAL NAVY.
(*Died Friday 11th December 1942.*)

Jack Fielding.

Jack was the eldest child and only son of William and Agnes Fielding, living at 2 Laburnum Cottages, Hackney. William worked as a quarryman at Farley Quarry, but when Jack left All Saints School he went to work in the weighing office at the Gas Works on Bakewell Road, Matlock.

He volunteered for the navy in the summer of 1940 and trained as a gunner at H.M.S. Collingwood, Portsmouth. Whilst training at Portsmouth his ship came under attack and Jack was fortunate to survive. Later, whilst on board H.M.S. "Tynwald", the ship was attacked and sunk off the Northern Ireland coast. He arrived back home shell shocked and extremely poorly.

On the last leave before his death, he walked with his young sister Barbara to All Saints School, on his way to Matlock Station. Putting his hand into his pocket he produced a handful of small coins as a parting gift to his sister. Sadly, it was the last time Barbara or any member of the family would see Jack.

His ship was destined for North Africa in November 1942 as part of the American/British invasion of Algeria and Tunisia (Operation "Torch"), forming part of a large convoy of ships entering the

Mediterranean Sea. The convoy was attacked and Jack's ship was one of sixteen lost in the action. Although injured and spending several hours in the water, Jack was rescued and brought ashore.

He was unable to return to Britain with the rest of the surviving crew members but eventually he was placed on board the hospital ship H.M.S. "Blean", homeward bound. Unfortunately, on Friday 11th December 1942, a torpedo from a marauding U-boat found its target and H.M.S. "Blean" was sent to the bottom of the sea. A telegram arrived at Laburnum Cottages announcing that Jack was missing but it was not until Good Friday 1943 that his family were told that he was officially reported as having died. After surviving three sinkings his luck ran out on the fourth occasion.

Jack Fielding is commemorated on Panel 63, column 3 on the Portsmouth Naval Memorial.

During the remainder of 1942, British forces, including men from Darley Dale, were mainly concerned with preparations for the forthcoming decisive battle of the North African campaign, El Alamein (October 23rd to November 4th) and the planned invasion of North Africa by British, American and Free French forces from the eastern approaches in Operation "Torch", on November 8th. The plan was to crush the German and Italian forces in the Western Desert, under Field Marshal Rommel, and the German and Vichy French forces in Algeria and Tunisia under the command of General Von Arnim, before the two groups could link up.

We see the repercussions from these events when two Darley soldiers died in March/April 1943 on the North African mainland in the latter stages of the defeat of Rommel's Afrika Korps, and a Darley submariner died in the dangerous waters close to the Mediterranean island fortress of Malta.

After the defeat of the Afrika Korps in North Africa, May 1943, attention was then turned to the Allied invasion of the Italian mainland, but the first stage in this process was to be the capture of the Italian island of Sicily. During this successful operation, between July 9th and August 17th, a Darley crewman in the Royal Navy was killed in action, whilst in the following invasion of the Italian mainland, in early

September, another Darley soldier succumbed. The final toll for the year 1943 came to six when, in August, a Darley serviceman, training in England, died in hospital from natural causes.

WARRANT OFFICER CLASS 11, BATTALION SERGEANT MAJOR HAROLD WOOSNAM, No. 1059298, 111 Field Regiment Royal Artillery.
(Died on Monday March 22nd 1943, aged 36 years.)

Battery Sergeant Major Harold Woosnam 1942.

Harold was born in 1905 at Frizington, Cumbria, the son of John Woosnam and his wife Jane. John was working at Whitehaven Colliery, but was sent out to a mining area in Canada by the company who owned the Cumbrian colliery.

Jane followed him to Canada, leaving young Harold to be brought up by their friends, the Wilsons, in Carlisle. Moving to British Colombia, the Woosnams had another child, Enid, born in Vancouver 1909, before John was sent to South Africa to work on the Gold Coast, whilst Jane stayed in Durban with young Enid. Evelyne was born in South Africa, but in 1922 John was sent back to England to help in finding new veins of lead at Mill Close Lead Mine, South Darley. After first lodging at the Three Stags Head Inn, Darley Bridge, the family moved to South Park Avenue, Broadwalk, where only two rows of houses had been constructed at this point.

During all this time Harold had stayed with the Wilsons in Carlisle, hardly ever seeing his family. In 1921, at 16 years of age, the six feet three inch youth joined the Royal Horse Artillery with the son of the

Harold, Audrey (nee Hayto) and Carl Woosnam c.1941 at Hayto's shop, Broadwalk.

Wilson family. After receiving an injury from a horse he then joined the Royal Artillery, and, for the next few years he saw Empire service in China, India and Egypt.

However, in his mid twenties he took his leave of the army because he wished to come home and get to know his family better. In 1929, his father John was sent out to Siberia, in the Soviet Union, by the Consolidated Gold Company, owners of Mill Close Mine. After his return to Mill Close he was diagnosed with silicosis and had to retire.

Harold had by now met Audrey Hayto, a daughter of the family who owned one of the newly constructed shops at Broadwalk. Audrey ran the sweet shop downstairs, whilst her sister Rita ran a hairdressing business above.

Harold began working on the surface at Mill Close Mine but, as a born soldier, he missed the army life dreadfully and disliked the work at Mill Close. He married Audrey Hayto and in 1935 a son, John, was born but at five weeks of age he died, quickly followed by the baby's grandfather, John, senior. They were buried together on the same day. Another son, Carl, was eventually born whilst the family were living on Northwood Avenue, Broadwalk.

As a reservist, Harold couldn't wait to get back into the army as war was about to be declared. He kept telephoning to see if he would be required. Eventually he arrived in France with the British Expeditionary Force but was evacuated in June 1940 from Dunkirk. His unit of the Royal Artillery was one of the last to get away from the beaches, because they were still using their artillery pieces to protect the perimeter defences. At the last moment, they destroyed their guns and waded out to one of the last transports to escape.

Eventually, in late May 1942, Harold sailed for North Africa via the Cape of Good Hope and arrived at Alexandria, in Egypt, where his Battery became part of the newly formed Eighth Army, under the command of General Montgomery.

From September to October 1942, preparations were made by Montgomery for the assault upon Rommel's forces that would decide the outcome of the North African campaign, the Battle of El Alamein.

At 9-40p.m. on October 23rd, 1000 British guns, including those in Harold Woosnam's Battery, opened fire along a six mile front. By the 4th November the entire Axis front crumbled, initiating the Axis decline in this desert theatre of war. The victory saved the Suez Canal and was a curtain raiser for the Anglo-American invasion of North Africa four days later.

Between November 5th and December 31st the Eighth Army pursued Rommel's forces over the vast stretches of the Western Desert, though the Field Marshal skilfully evaded entrapment. By February/March 1943 Harold was on the borders of Tunisia, with the Axis Forces squeezed between the Eighth Army and the Anglo-American force. It was here, in February, that Harold received a letter from home telling him of the birth of his son Maxwell.

At the Battle of Mareth (Tunisia), between the 20th and 26th March 1943, Montgomery, with greatly superior forces, assaulted the Italo-German positions. Despite heavy bombardment from the artillery, the 15th Panzer Division counter-attacked in the moonlight, checking the British, but the Allies now held the initiative.

Sadly, during the German counter-attack, Harold had received a shot in the back on Monday 22nd March, and died from his wounds. His wife, Audrey, received a letter from the Reverend F.H. Buck, Senior Chaplain to the New Zealand Forces, stating that Harold was brought into a dressing station seriously wounded and unconscious and died shortly afterwards.

Harold Woosnam was buried in Gabes War Cemetery, but at a later date he was moved to Sfax War Cemetery, Tunisia, and was buried in Grave XIII. A. 18.

ABLE SEAMAN VICTOR RANDOLPH HARRIS, No. D/SSX17882, H.M. Submarine "Thunderbolt".
(*Died on Sunday 28th March 1943.*)

As a very young child Victor Harris lived with his mother Annie and step father at Bakewell. For most of his life, however, he lived with his grandmother Harriet at Number 1 Limetree Avenue, together with his brother Roland.

Vic joined the Royal Navy in 1936, training at H.M.S. Pembroke before serving abroad on various surface ships. At the outbreak of war he was faced with the choice of serving in the submarine branch or becoming a crew member on a destroyer. He decided to train to become a submariner and his relations, especially his Uncle Arthur, were unhappy with his choice, especially when he joined H.M. Submarine "Thunderbolt", as a torpedo handler.

Uncle Arthur, who had fought with the Tank Corps during the Great War, thought the vessel was dogged by bad luck, for the

Able Seaman
Victor Randolph Harris.

"Thunderbolt" was actually the former submarine "Thetis", which, in 1939 had sunk with the loss of many lives. Arthur Harris was to be proved correct.

At 1-40p.m. on June 1st 1939 the newly launched "Thetis" had submerged whilst undergoing acceptance trials in Liverpool Bay. When it was located, 130 feet below the surface, off Llanndudno, only four men had escaped, and, with the death of 99 seamen, it proved to be the greatest submarine disaster since the Great War.

On August 28th 1939 the salvage vessel "Zelo" lifted the craft and on October 3rd it was beached on the coast of Anglesey, where all the bodies were removed. By the middle of 1940 the submarine was being repaired for further service and had been renamed "Thunderbolt" by the time Vic Harris became a crew member.

By early 1943 "Thunderbolt" was operating in the dangerous waters of the Mediterranean Sea, during the latter days of Operation "Torch". At the end of March, Vic's grandmother received a letter informing her that it had put to sea to patrol the waters off the island of Malta, but no further word had been received from the vessel and it was thought that it may have hit a mine or suffered from a depth charge attack on the 28th March. No bodies were ever recovered.

Victor Harris is commemorated on the Plymouth Naval Memorial, Devon.

His younger brother Roland also joined the Royal Navy later in the war, after spending some time at the firm of Lammon, Archer and Lane, which had taken over the Matlock firm of Paton and Baldwins to make munitions for the wartime economy. Happily he was to survive his wartime service.

However, Victor's uncle, Edward Harris, was not so fortunate. Having left Darley Dale to work at Wirksworth and settle there in married life, he joined the army and was captured by the Japanese at Singapore. It was whilst he was working on the notorious Burma Railway that Ted Harris died. Uncle and nephew had therefore died in the same war.

PRIVATE HENRY (HARRY) HARLOW,
No. 5892230, 5th Battalion Northamptonshire Regiment.
(Died on Thursday 8th April 1943, aged 19 years.)

Harry's father, Fred Harlow, was a stonemason at Stancliffe Stone Quarry Yard, and, with his wife Edith and family, came to live at Holt

Top Cottages, near Ladygrove. Harry and his older brother Fred went to Darley Council School, and though the family moved to Number 5 Church Road in the mid 1930's, they still attended the Greenaway Lane School. Harry was a good athlete and won the cup for running in three consecutive years, winning it outright. When Harry was killed in the war his father returned it to the School and it was renamed the Harlow Cup.

After leaving school, Harry was employed as an accounts clerk in the

Private Harry Harlow.

offices at Johnson's Flour Mill, Ladygrove. He became a sides man at St. Helen's Church and was a member of the Matlock Liberal Club.

Soon after war was declared, Fred Harlow joined the R.A.F. and spent most of his service in the Middle East, whilst Fred, senior, was in Darley Home Guard. In April 1942 Harry was called up at the age of 18 and travelled from Matlock Station on the 16th, with Tansley man Leonard Cantrill, son of William and Annie Cantrill of 2, Nottingham Road, and South Darley's Colin Hadfield. They all became members of the Northamptonshire Regiment, although Colin later became separated from his two colleagues.

In October 1942, the 5th Battalion, including Colin Hadfield, sailed from Scotland to take part with the Americans and Free French in occupying the whole of French North Africa from Morocco to Tunisia and link up with Montgomery's Eighth Army, who were attacking Rommel's

Leonard Cantrill, in earlier times, in his schooldays at Tansley.

Afrika Korps from the west, through Libya.

Shortly after the landings near Algiers in November 1942, Colin was captured and in further operations, the Battalion suffered other casualties (see "A Derbyshire Parish at Peace and War – South Darley" for the action involving Colin Hadfield). Harry Harlow and Len Cantrill were amongst the reserves in England who travelled to Tunisia to make up the numbers in the 5th Battalion.

A few days before Christmas 1942 they played their part in one last attempt to break through enemy lines and reach Tunis by Christmas. Up in the mountains, wireless silence was maintained, and when the attack was cancelled due to atrocious weather conditions, the 5th Battalion knew nothing of this and carried on (the mule carrying the wireless set had fallen over a precipice). A bloody battle at close quarters ensued on Christmas Eve and Christmas Day, but the 5th Battalion managed to withdraw.

By January 6th 1943 the Battalion moved to the Goubellat plain and went into defensive positions. On February 26th the Germans launched a three pronged attack and fierce fighting raged for several days on the Northamptons front and casualties occurred. One of these was 19 year old Len Cantrill from Tansley, who was killed on the 26th February. (Len had last been seen severely wounded. He was reported as missing and sadly it was not until a year later that his parents were told that he was presumed killled on the 26th.)

The Battalion played a crucial role in the "Battle of the Peaks" in early April 1943, aiming to clear the mountains of German troops, to enable the road running through the area to become a line of communication for any advance on Tunis.

By 3-50a.m. on 7th April the Battalion was creeping forward at the same time as British artillery opened up a great barrage. At 4-10a.m. the forward companies rushed the few remaining yards and most objectives were taken, but "B" Company was held up. They withdrew a short distance and for the rest of the day all gains were consolidated and they settled down for the night, during which heavy mortar fire continued at intervals.

At 9a.m. on the 8th April, "A" Company attacked and captured Point 343, taking more than 50 prisoners of a German Mountain regiment, with the loss of "A" Company's officer. The Germans withdrew from the peaks, abandoning much equipment.

In the hard, bitter fighting of these two days, the Battalion received just over 80 casualties, including two officers and 19 other ranks killed. Amongst the dead was Harry Harlow, who died as "A" Company fought the Mountain troops.

Harry is buried in Grave 2. D. 8 at Medjez-El-Bab War Cemetery, 60 kilometres west of Tunis, whilst the name of his Derbyshire colleague, Len Cantrill, is commemorated on Panel face 25.

Shortly after the war, Fred Harlow, senior, travelled on a Dakota plane

Mr. and Mrs. Fred Harlow visit their son, Harry's, grave in Tunisia.

from Croyden aerodrome, on a British Legion pilgrimage, to visit his son's grave. Due to serious flooding in Tunisia at the time, the plans had to be aborted, but some time later Mr. and Mrs. Harlow were able to attend the grave.

LEADING TELEGRAPHIST T. AUBREY BOWLER, No. P/SSX31071, H.M.S. "Dundonald II", Royal Navy.
(*Died on Thursday 15th July 1943, aged 21 years.*)

Aubrey was the only child of Thomas Edwin Bowler, engine driver at Rowsley Marshalling Yard, and his wife Bertha Eva Bowler, living at Number 6 Torrfield Cottages, Green Lane.

After leaving Darley Churchtown School, Aubrey worked in the offices of Stancliffe Stone, but joined the Royal Navy a few months before war was declared. He trained as a wireless telegraphist at H.M.S. Victory, Portsmouth, and was posted to join the aircraft carrier H.M.S. "Eagle".

He was involved in numerous operations on "Eagle", including sailing to the Cape of Good Hope, but by 1943 Aubrey was a crewman on H.M.S. "Dundonald II". Following the successful conclusion of the North African campaign in mid May 1943, plans were prepared for a combined allied force of 160,000 Empire and American troops to invade Sicily as a prelude to the assault on mainland Italy.

In preparation for such a combined operation, Aubrey found himself stationed in the west of Scotland, in the Ben Nevis area, taking part in commando style operations in the

*Leading Telegraphist
T. Aubrey Bowler.*

mountains. During this period he would return home on leave wearing army trousers and jacket and naval hat, with the insignia of "Combined Operations" worn on his shoulder.

On the 10th July 1943 the invasion of Sicily began, with H.M.S. "Dundonald" supporting the landings. The Italians, who would shortly make peace with the Allies and re-enter the war on their side, offered little determined resistance but German opposition was vigorous and stubborn.

British forces made their landings on the S.E. corner of the island, between Pachina and Syracuse. As on all the other days of the landings, H.M.S. "Dundonald" was attacked vigorously by enemy planes on Thursday 15th July, St. Swithins Day. A group of sailors, including Aubrey Bowler, was caught out in the open on the deck of the ship. Ironically, if he had stayed there he might have escaped unscathed, but the party ran for the shelter of the metal covers, and Aubrey was hit in the back by bullets from the attacking plane. He died hours later from his wounds.

Aubrey Bowler is buried in Grave III. A. 10 Syracuse War Cemetery, Sicily, Italy, with the majority of the other burials being servicemen who died during these landings, or in the early stages of the campaign.

PRIVATE JOHN BRIDDON,
No. 14334106, 310 Company Pioneer Corps.
(Died on Tuesday 10th August 1943, aged 19 years.)

John was the son of James and Edith Mary Briddon. The family had lived at Middleton-by-Youlgreave, where James was a farmer, but eventually they came to live at Number 15 Whitworth Avenue, Broadwalk.

Private John Briddon and twin sister Midge, who served in the W.A.A.F.

John Briddon volunteered and was posted to 310 Company Pioneer Corps, whose base was at Edwinstowe, near Mansfield, Nottinghamshire. He had not been in the army very long before he developed acute appendicitis and was rushed into Kilton Hill Hospital at Worksop.

Unfortunately, John died under the anaesthetic, whilst the operation was being performed. His body was brought home and he was buried in the graveyard at Youlgreave Parish Church, in August 1943.

His twin sister Midge served in the Women's Auxiliary Air Force from 1943 to the end of the war.

PRIVATE IVAN PLANT,
No. 2379247, 2/4th Battalion
King's Own Yorkshire Light Infantry.
(Died on Wednesday 8th September 1943, aged 20 years.)

Ivan was the son of Harold Gregory Plant and Amy Plant of Orchard Road, Grove Lane, Darley Dale. He and his brother Noel had been born in the Bonsall area but the family came to live on Darley House Estate in

Left: Ivan Plant.
Right: Ivan Plant and the 'shoe shine' boy, in North Africa.

1930. His father, Harold, formerly the landlord of The King's Head at Bonsall, worked in the signal box at Darley Station and Ivan worked on the Midland Railway at Millers Dale. In 1939 the family moved into a new house on Orchard Road. Two years later Ivan volunteered for service and joined the Yorkshire Light Infantry.

In May 1943 the Axis forces under Rommel had been defeated in North Africa and by the middle of August the invasion of the island of Sicily had resulted in the evacuation of both German and Italian forces. With the capture of Sicily, the Mediterranean was again opened as an Allied sea route.

The war-weary Italian nation toppled Mussolini from power on July 24th, during the Sicilian operation and an Armistice was signed secretly with Italy on September 3rd 1943, to be effective from September 8th.

It was on September 3rd that the 5th British and 1st Canadian Divisions of the Eighth Army crossed the Straits of Messina to land in Calabria (the toe of Italy). The German Commander in Italy, Kesselring, correctly guessed that the main invasion would be further north on the mainland, at Salerno. He initiated delaying action in the south, while still watching the Salerno area.

In Calabria, practically no opposition was encountered. Reggio was speedily taken, and the advance began along the narrow and hilly roads of the region. The Germans were fighting their rear-guard action more by demolitions than by outright battle.

In a few days the divisions of the Eighth Army had reached Locri and Rosarno, while an infantry brigade, containing Ivan Plant, landed by sea at Pizzo, but found only the tail of the retreating Germans. There was little fighting, and yet the advance was severely delayed by the physical difficulties of the country, demolition carried out by the enemy, and his small but skilfully handled rearguard actions.

It was during such an action that Ivan Plant was killed. However, his parents were to suffer the pain of not knowing whether he was dead or not when Ivan was simply posted as being missing. It was not until November 1944, a year later, that they were informed that he was now officially presumed to have died of wounds. An official letter received by his parents stated :

"A report has been received from the military authorities overseas that your son when last seen was very seriously wounded. We now believe he must have succumbed to his wounds, shortly after September 8th 1943".

No body was ever recovered, and although he was killed in the south of Italy, his name is commemorated on Panel 9 of the Cassino Memorial, far to the north. His name can also be seen in Hackney Methodist Chapel.

The year 1944 opened with the Axis Powers on the defensive in the West. Hitler's Russian gamble was lost, the eastern front crumbling. Italy was eliminated, North Africa cleared, and the Mediterranean sea lanes opened. In the United Kingdom, American strength was accumulating in astounding abundance.

However, the U-boats still menaced the Atlantic, Arctic and Mediterranean sea lanes and the embattled German economy was producing war materials at ever increasing rates, despite the ravages of Allied bombers. The war was still far from a decision.

From their bridgehead in the British Isles, the Allies held the priceless advantage of strategic interior lines and could, in principle, attack Germany at any point. But where, when and how? We now know of course that the invasion, code named Operation "Overlord", would come in Normandy on D-Day, June 6th 1944. Meanwhile, the difficult assault on the mainland of Italy continued, against highly motivated soldiers, in sound defensive positions and well led by the German Commander, Field Marshal Kesselring.

During 1944, four Darley servicemen were killed in action during the Italian campaign, one fell during the advance through Belgium, after the successful invasion of "Fortress Europe," and a Darley sailor died in a British hospital from natural causes.

PRIVATE FRANCIS PERCY WILSON, No. 5888540, 1st Battalion The Loyal Regiment (North Lancashire).

(Died on Wednesday 16th February 1944, aged 28 years.)

Left: Percy Wilson.
Right: Wedding of Percy Wilson and Ethel Atkin.

360

Percy's father, Francis Charles Wilson, had lived for a time in Pennsylvania, America, before arriving at Rowsley from Bournemouth. Working on the railway, he settled down to married life with his wife Edith and son Percy, on Chatsworth Road.

After leaving school, Percy was apprenticed to shoe repairer Duncan Elliot of Rowsley, but when Mr. Elliot retired, Percy set up in business on his own in a shed along Chatsworth Road, often collecting and delivering on his bicycle. By this time he was courting Ethel Atkin from Starkholmes Road, Matlock, and the pair were often to be seen riding the district on their tandem.

Just before Percy was called up, in 1940, he and Ethel were married, but soon afterwards he began training with the North Lancashire Regiment. At the end of January 1943 he embarked for North Africa and arrived during the closing stages of the defeat of Rommel's Afrika Korps in April and May 1943.

During 1943 the Allies invaded Sicily and landed on the Italian mainland. September 9th saw the assault at Salerno, where the beachhead was secured and by October Naples was seized. However, by December, the Germans had established their formidable defensive zone, the Gustav Line, with Monte Cassino the key obstacle.

In early 1944 the British commander, Alexander, planned a frontal attack on the Gustav Line, assisted by an amphibious landing at Anzio (Operation "Shingle"). The Anzio force was intended to advance inland to cut the German communications line and force evacuation of the Gustav Line.

On January 22nd the landings took place unopposed, with 50,000 troops and 5200 vehicles establishing a beachhead, some seven miles deep. The Germans' quick reactions brought reinforcements from the north and pinned the Allies to their beachhead.

During these actions Percy was hit in the stomach by a sniper's bullet and died on the 16th February from his wounds, the very day on which the Germans counter-attacked with a series of brutal blows that drove back the outlying Allied units.

Percy was the first Rowsley man to be killed in the war and he is buried at Anzio War Cemetery in Grave III. J. 7.

Within the space of two days in early September 1944, Darley was to hear of the death of three of its parishioners, two being killed in Italy and one in Belgium.

PRIVATE LAWRENCE TROY BARDILL,
No. 6298932, 2/7th Battalion,
The Queen's Royal Regiment (West Surrey).
(Died on Saturday 2nd September 1944, aged 32 years.)

Lawrence was born at Stapleford, Nottinghamshire, and came seeking work in the Matlock district. He lodged on Darley Avenue, Broadwalk, and met Mary Bennett, whose family lived on the same avenue. The Bennetts moved to Wychbury House, 10 Peakland View, and Lawrence lodged with them. They married in May 1936 and continued to live with Mary's parents. A daughter, Pauline, was born in 1941.

Lawrence Troy Bardill and fiance Mary Bennett, near Four Lane Ends, Darley, just before the war.

Lawrence was "called up" in January 1942. For the previous two years he had been employed by Lehane, Mackenzie and Shand, contractors, on the third instalment of the Bamford to Ambergate Aqueduct (by the Derwent Valley Water Board). The contract consisted of laying 47 inch diameter steel pipes with bitumen lining. Lawrence was involved as an inside jointer, responsible for making good the continuity of the bitumen lining at the joints and repairing defective places.

By November/December 1942 Lawrence was involved in the combined American, British and French landings in Algeria and Tunisia,

Private Lawrence Bardill, second from the right, back row, in North Africa.

which, by mid May 1943 had successfully linked up with the Eighth Army's advance from the west. The German and Italian forces in North Africa had finally been defeated.

The Battalion was eventually to take part in the invasion of the Italian mainland, but on 21st January 1944, Lawrence was wounded and out of action for some time. After recovering, he returned to his Battalion and in August 1944 the West Surrey Regiment formed part of the Eighth Army as it attempted to break the German defensive position known as the Gothic Line.

The advance was from Ancona to Rimini, on the Adriatic coast, with Rimini captured on the 21st September. However, in the earlier stages of the advance, Lawrence Troy Bardill was killed on Saturday 2nd September, leaving a widow and young daughter of three years.

Lawrence is buried in Grave II. C. 59 Gradara War Cemetery, Italy, midway between Pesaro and Riccione, together with other colleagues who gave their lives in attempting to break the last major German fortified positions, the Gothic Line.

PRIVATE HENRY (HARRY) RILEY MADDOCKS, No. 13049630, Signaller, 5th Battalion Sherwood Foresters.
(*Died on Monday 4th September 1944, aged 28 years.*)

Harry was born in the Lumb Lane area of Northwood, his father being John Maddocks. He joined the Sherwood Foresters in the latter part of

363

1942 and at St. Helen's Church, Darley, on August 4th 1943, at the age of 26, he married Phyllis Ena Wain, a 27 year old widow and daughter of Hillside joiner and nurseryman, Hugh Gregory.

Shortly after his marriage he went with his Battalion to North Africa, to take part in the invasion of Europe through Italy. By this stage Harry had trained as a signaller in wireless communications in his platoon.

By August 1944 the Battalion had fought their way through to the Adriatic sector of the campaign and were ready to attempt in helping to storm the Coriano Ridge, the last important ridge in the way of

Marriage of Private Harry Maddocks and Phyllis Ena Wain (Gregory) at St. Helen's August 4th 1943.

the Allied advance. Its capture was the key to Rimini and eventually to the River Po.

On the 30th August 1944, five days before the attack began, Harry wrote a few scribbled lines home to his wife. He writes that his feet feel like two lumps of raw meat and that he is "dog tired". The last week had been tramp, tramp, tramp, with six hours sleep in four and a half days, but he writes that one consolation is that every mile he marched these days was one nearer home.

In an earlier letter on the 4th August, one year to the day of his wedding at St. Helen's Church, Harry writes movingly and lovingly about the most wonderful day of his life, their wedding day. He muses eloquently about his great love of cycling in the Peak and in Snowdonia before the war descended upon them to blight their lives.

Harry looks forward to returning so that they can go on their honeymoon and writes that he hopes the Russians keep advancing at their present phenomenal rate so that he can get back home. Later, he turns to thoughts about after the war and earning a living, so that he can support her.

"I shall not go back to the old slipshod days of Stancliffe, with its dirt, dust and noise". He writes that he would like to get into the post office, as a linesman, using his newly acquired skills as a signaller. He finally looks forward to having a home of their own and the prospects of maybe starting a family.

One month later he was dead.

German parachute and Panzer troops, aided by bad weather, resisted

Private (Signalman) Harry Maddocks.

all attacks on their positions on the Ridge between the 4th and 12th September. In ferocious fighting on the first day of the attack, Harry was killed.

On the night of 12th September, the Eighth Army re-opened its attack with the 1st British Armoured Division and the 5th Canadian Armoured Division. This attack was successful in taking the Ridge, but marked the beginning of a week of the heaviest fighting experienced since Monte Cassino.

A letter arrived for Harry's wife on the 22nd September, written by Captain Jack Carson of the 5th Sherwood Foresters.

"How very sorry the boys of the platoon and myself are. Harry was killed in the afternoon of the 4th September by a mortar shell which exploded just above his slit trench and was killed outright. He did not suffer pain.

As you know he joined us about nine months ago and during that time we have got to know each other pretty well. He was a first class signaller. He was very popular with the other lads and we feel his loss."

On the 13th October a letter arrived from Harry's pal, Private Keith Naylor.

"It was a shock to me at the time to learn he was gone because a few minutes before he was speaking to me. He was in a trench at the time and received a direct hit by a mortar bomb. I was in the same rifle company as him, for signallers are attached to them in battle.

At the time we were in a general melee. By the time we organised again we discovered Harry was missing. Harry was as brave as they come and never shirked his duty. He died as so many others have died – for England".

A final letter, from Captain Joseph Newell, arrived on October 20th, expressing deepest sympathy.

"Harry was employed as a signaller in this Battalion and this work demands great courage and skill. He never failed to show these qualities. His death was instantaneous, suffering no pain".

Harry Maddocks is buried in Grave V. E. 4, Coriano Ridge War Cemetery, just west of Riccioni, a seaside resort on the Adriatic coast.

PRIVATE KENNETH STANLEY TOFT,
No. 14670212, 1st Battalion Dorsetshire Regiment.
(Died on Thursday 7th September, aged 19 years.)

Kenneth and his younger brother Maurice were born at Hackney, their parents being Victor and Edith Toft. When Darley House Estate was built in the 1930's, they moved to Number 16, where their sister, Joy, was born in 1934.

Victor drove the bread van for the Derwent Co-operative Society, before later selling hardware and crockery on market stalls at Matlock, Chesterfield and Worksop, whilst Edith had been a tailoress at Marsdens in Matlock in her younger days. Sadly, after a long illness, she died in 1943, aged 42 years.

Before joining the army, Kenneth had served in the 6th platoon of "B" Company, Darley Home Guard, together with his father and brother Maurice. In November 1943 Kenneth was called up and joined the Royal Norfolk Regiment. He then transferred to the Dorsetshire Regiment, before embarking for France, shortly after the Normandy landings of June 6th 1944, as part of the British Second Army.

The Toft Family.
Victor (Home Guard), Kenneth (Home Guard), Maurice (Home Guard), Joy.

Between August 27th and September 4th the advance across the Low Countries towards the German "Westwall" began. Possession of the Belgian port of Antwerp was needed to provide supplies, for the 300 mile long logistical line from the Normandy beaches was stretched almost to breaking point. Montgomery therefore advanced into the Low Countries, with Brussels being entered on September 3rd and Antwerp captured the next day.

However, Hitler ordered that the Albert Canal be held to block further advance and that the Scheldt estuary and water systems around Antwerp must be defended. Until these were cleared, Antwerp was of no use as an Allied port, and therefore clearing Antwerp became the main mission of the Second Army between the 4th and 14th of September.

The advance to Antwerp had been swift – over 200 miles in under four days – but the pace could not be maintained. The enemy managed to destroy the crossings over the Albert Canal between Antwerp and Hasselt and it was defended by ten battalions, some of them quite fresh. The army forced a crossing west of Hasselt on September 6th but there was hard fighting and it was not till four days later that they reached the Meuse – Scheldt Canal and took a bridge which was still intact.

367

It was during these actions around Antwerp that Kenneth Toft lost his life, reported missing whilst crossing one of the numerous waterways in the area. They were fired upon by the Germans and a number of soldiers who could not swim, including Kenneth, died in the waters.

Joy Evans, sister of Kenneth Toft, attending the grave of her brother in Schoonselhof Cemetary, Antwerp, Belgium.

A letter to Victor Toft from the Commanding Officer of the company reads; "He was out on patrol when he was killed and was buried by the padre. He is a great loss to us. His courage and never failing cheerfulness were a great example to the rest of the company".

His body was buried later in Grave II. C. 24 at the Schoonselhof Cemetery, Antwerp, Belgium.

Meanwhile, from Italy, certain Bomber Command aircrews flew on missions in support of the Balkan and Polish resistance fighters. It was in one such operation that another Darley man lost his life.

FLIGHT SERGEANT JOHN THOMPSON,
No. 642357, 148 Squadron, R.A.F.
(*Died on Sunday 29th October 1944, aged 23 years.*)

The Thompson family moved from Two Dales to live at No. 5 Limetree Avenue in 1928. James (Jimmy) Thompson had married Lizzie Charlesworth and they raised a family of eleven children. Lizzie had been brought up at The Laundry, Painters Nook., and during the First World War we saw how she became a nurse at the Whitworth Institute Red Cross Hospital. James was a goods guard on the L.M.S. at Rowsley

Marshalling Yard.

John attended Darley Churchtown School and was a member of the Church Club organised by Eric Griffiths, the vicar's son, at the Rectory. Eric was a keen cine-film maker and it is poignant to see shots of John on film, taken during the 1930's.

Joining the Royal Air Force just before war was declared, John became a navigator and took part in raids across Europe. Eventually, with training, he was promoted to Flight Sergeant and was posted abroad as a crew member with No. 148 Squadron.

Flight Sergeant John Thompson at Derna airfield on the Libyan coast 1943.

It was very noticeable to his family that over the years in the R.A.F. his Derbyshire accent was lost. Just before entering the air force he had met a young girl from London who was attending St. Elphins Girls School, in Darley. He kept in touch with her and just before being posted to North Africa, he married Joyce in London.

At Derna airfield, Libya, North Africa, 1943. Flight Sergeant John Thompson is on the left.

On the 14th March 1943 John's squadron, stationed at Derna, near the Libyan coast, became a Special Liberator Flight, with special duties. Its Liberators and Halifaxes were engaged in dropping arms and supplies to resistance forces in Greece, Albania and Yugoslavia and in January 1944 it moved to Brindisi, in Italy, and added a Lysander flight for pick-up missions to the resistance fighters.

Halifaxes completely replaced Liberators at the same time and Poland and northern Italy became the main area of operations for the squadron. As the Russians overran

Poland, missions over the Balkans again formed the bulk of the Squadron's work, the final effort over Poland being an attempt to supply the Polish resistance forces in Warsaw by long-range sorties from Southern Italy.

Between August and the end of October 1944, a full scale rising against the German occupiers took place, whilst the Russian forces nearby, simply held back for political reasons and allowed the proud Poles to be annihilated. It was whilst John Thompson was on a long-range mission to drop supplies in the Warsaw area that his plane was shot down.

His body was never recovered and his name is commemorated on Panel 3, column 2 of the Malta Memorial, which stands outside the main entrance to Valletta Harbour.

The last Darley serviceman to die in 1944 was serving in the Royal Navy.

TELEGRAPHIST DONALD STANDISH SOPPITT, No. P/JX454881, H.M.S. "Hunter", Royal Navy.
(*Died on Thursday 23rd November 1944, aged 19 years.*)

Born in 1925, Donald was the youngest of George and Minnie Soppitt's nine children. The Soppitts originated from the Bradford area of Yorkshire but arrived in Darley Dale around 1925 and resided at No. 1 Peakland View, Broadwalk. George Soppitt had served in the Great War and had suffered considerably. It changed his personality and view on life and he died in 1928. Times became difficult for the family. To make ends meet, Minnie Soppitt kept a haberdashery shop in the front room of her house, selling buttons, cottons etc.

After leaving Darley Churchtown School, Donald went to work at Bemrose, the printers, at Derby. He was a good artist and was encouraged by the head of the firm to attend Derby Art College.

During the earlier years of the war, brothers Jack and Dennis served in the British Army, whilst sister Marjorie joined the Royal Air Force. Another brother, Cyril, was in a reserved occupation as a lorry driver and amongst other tasks, found himself looking after Italian prisoners of war in the Hartington area.

Donald was called up on March 26th and joined the Royal Navy, training to be a telegraphist, on the south coast. He eventually joined H.M.S. "Hunter", based at Plymouth, and began training exercises off the south coast.

On August 15th 1944, H.M.S "Hunter" supported the invasion of Southern France, in Operation "Anvil-Dragoon", with the objective of freeing the port of Marseilles for supply and protecting the southern flank of the Normandy landings.

In September 1944 the Germans began evacuating the majority of its garrison troops from the Greek Aegean and Ionian Islands and Donald was again involved in supporting the recovery of these islands.

*Telegraphist
Donald S. Soppitt.*

Unfortunately, whilst the ship was returning to England, in November, he was taken ill with peritonitis and had to be removed by breechers-buoy. The family was informed and his mother had an extremely difficult job in travelling to the hospital in Plymouth, due to wartime transportation restrictions. Donald died in hospital.

His body was returned to Derbyshire and he was buried in Grave 83 in St. Helen's Churchyard, with British Legion standard bearers in attendance. Minnie Soppitt was devastated by her loss and died soon afterwards.

The year 1945 would see seven more Darley families receiving news of the death of their loved ones, with the first casualty occurring on board a Royal Navy ship patrolling in home waters. Shortly afterwards, a second victim would be claimed by the Italian campaign. Throughout the autumn and winter of 1944, the breakout from the Normandy landings had seen British forces advancing through Belgium and Holland and in the winter and spring of 1945 they continued this advance towards the Rhine and across the mighty river defences into the heart of Germany. Two Darley soldiers would die during these operations. Meanwhile, the fighting in Italy continued and contributed to the death of another soldier.

At the end of March a Darley airman lost his life over the Norwegian mountains and news arrived in June of the final death, when a P.O.W. of the Japanese lost his life in the terrible conditions of one of their camps.

ABLE SEAMAN WILFRED JAMES BOWLER, No. P/JX161662, H.M.S. "Thane", Royal Navy.
(*Died on Monday 15th January 1945, aged 22 years.*)

Wilfred Bowler was born at Starkholmes, Matlock, in 1922. In the late 1930's his mother and father, with their younger son, Lesley, went to Hull to find work and settle down. Wilfred remained with his grandparents, Mr. and Mrs. Bowler, in the Darley area, residing in the newly built Hooleys Estate, at No. 115 Bakewell Road. A few years later, a sister, Margaret, was born in Hull.

Wilfred Bowler and his wife Daphne.

When war was declared it was not long before Wilfred enlisted and joined the Royal Navy as an Able Seaman. During his training he met Daphne, a girl from Romford, Essex, whom he married.

In August 1943 Wilfred was a crew member of H.M.S, "King George V" when it escorted Winston Churchill, on board the "Queen Mary", across the Atlantic to his meeting with President Roosevelt, at Halifax, Canada. Unfortunately, Wilfred was struck down by appendicitis whilst in America and could not return to Britain on his ship.

When he had recovered in the Canadian hospital he became a crew member of an 11,420 ton American built assault air craft carrier, H.M.S. "Thane", that was handed over to the Royal Navy on the 19th November 1943. It was sailed back to Britain and was used mainly for ferry and transport duties, carrying Numbers 831, 834 and 851 Squadrons of the Fleet Air Arm.

On the 15th January 1945 H.M.S. "Thane" was lying at anchor at the mouth of the Firth of Clyde, Scotland. Out in the North Channel, German U-boat U. 482 had been operating since the 1st December 1944 with seeming immunity from counter-attack. Based at Bergen, Norway, and part of the 11th U-boat Flotilla, its captain was 30 year old Hartmut Graf von Mattuschka, an experienced submariner who had been awarded the German Cross in Gold on the 12th September 1944, for sinking four vessels in the space of a week.

The 7429 ton Norwegian motor vessel "Spinanger" was torpedoed and badly damaged by U-482 on Monday 15th January and later that day she spied H.M.S. "Thane" lying at anchor. She attacked the aircraft carrier and scored hits with two torpedoes. Wilfred Bowler had been on the "Fore Noon Watch" duty and had retired to the mess. The Royal Navy ship was badly damaged, with the loss of 10 sailors, including Wilfred.

It was whilst withdrawing from this patrol in the North Channel, that U-482 was intercepted by the 22nd Escort Group of five ships, including H.M.S. "Amethyst" (of future Yangtze River fame). A pattern of depth charges was laid and U-482 was sunk on the 16th January 1945, with the loss of all 48 crew men.

Wilfred Bowler's body was brought home by rail in a coffin to Matlock and was given a military funeral, before being buried in St Giles Churchyard, Matlock, the grave being marked by a military tombstone.

Though living in Darley Dale when he went off to war, his name was not inscribed on the Darley Dale war memorial. This omission was only rectified in 2002 due to the efforts of Doug Goodall of Hooleys Estate and Wilfred's sister Margaret and cousin Joan Whetton. His name will now be honoured in its rightful place.

DRIVER HUBERT REGINALD MACLEAN,
No. T/199573, Royal Army Service Corps.
(Died on 17th March 1945, aged 29 years.)

Hubert (Bert) was born near Leomster, Herefordshire, in 1915, the son of John and Caroline Maclean. His elder sister Mabel and younger brother Donald completed the family.

In 1926 Toft and Tomlinson, hauliers and motor engineers, had transferred their works from Youlgreave to a newly constructed complex on the A6 at Northwood, called Unity Garage, and Unity Villas were built for the Toft and Tomlinson families.

Caroline Maclean was the sister-in-law of Jim Tomlinson, and in 1929 John and Caroline moved to Darley Dale, to take up residence on the recently built Broadwalk development, on Darley Avenue. John became the book keeper and accountant for the haulage company.

Driver Hubert Maclean, R.A.S.C., and his wife Gwyneth (nee Humphries).

Bert became a lorry driver for Toft and Tomlinsons, and on the 31st July 1937, he married Gwyneth Humphries from 2 Peakland View, Broadwalk. They began married life at Holt Drive, Hooleys Estate, where a daughter, Jill, was born on the 16th March 1939. Eventually, they went to live at Northwood Lane.

When war broke out, Bert was in a reserved occupation. However, he was determined to play his part in helping his country and volunteered. He trained at Aldershot and joined the Royal Army Service Corps, serving in the Sevenoaks area of Kent, where his main role was as a motor-cycle dispatch rider and driver.

Another child was expected but in the late Autumn of 1942 Bert embarked for North Africa to take part in the invasion of Algeria and Tunisia, code named Operation "Torch". Veronica Marilyn was born on 21st January 1943 and was never to see her father.

By May 1943 the fighting in North Africa came to an end. During this period as a dispatch rider, Bert came one day upon a driver having difficulty in replacing the twin tyres of a large lorry. He smiled when he saw the problems they were creating and offered advice. When questioned by an officer, standing nearby, it was discovered that he had been a fitter in his civilian life. Within a week he became a fitter in the R.A.S.C.

Bert was involved in the invasion of Italy in 1943 and in the long campaign against the German defenders, after the capitulation of the Italians. By March 1945, he was in Northern Italy, near the Adriatic coast, taking part in preparations to break through the Argenta Gap and funnel out into the expanses of the Po Valley. He wrote back home to Gwyneth that there was only one more major river to cross. The stretch of water referred to was the River Po, but sadly, he was never to cross it.

On the 17th March Bert was the pillion passenger on a motor cycle and was carrying a spare engine part for a broken down lorry. A donkey cart pulled out suddenly ahead of them, causing the motor bike to crash. The driver survived his injuries but Bert died ten hours later from his head injuries, having never regained consciousness.

Sadly, he had just written a letter to his eldest daughter, Jill, for her sixth birthday on the 16th March. A few days later the family received news that Bert was dead.

He is buried in a cemetery at Cesena, inland from the Adriatic coast, between Rimini and Bologna. After the war Bert's parents were able to visit his resting place, and later still his widow Gwyneth and daughter Marilyn travelled to the graveside.

Later still, Gwyneth married another Second World War soldier, Coldstream Guardsman George Coleman, and they had two sons, but George also proved to be a wonderful father for Jill and Marilyn.

LIEUTENANT HENRY WHARTON DERBYSHIRE,
No. 198615, of the Staffordshire Yeomenry
Royal Armoured Corps.

(Died on Saturday 24th March 1945, aged 33 years.)

Henry, Donald and Eric were the sons of nurseryman Henry Derbyshire and his wife Eleonor, living at "Springfield", Darley Hillside.

The Derbyshires had started their nursery business at Whitesprings in around 1870 but moved to "Springfield" on Foggs Hill just before 1914, specialising in heathers and rhododendrons. All three boys went to the Ernest Bailey Grammar School, where Henry was keen on rugby and sport in general.

On leaving school, he went into the Westminster Bank at Bakewell, was then transferred to Chesterfield and was at the Hathersage branch at the time

Lieutenant Henry Wharton Derbyshire and his wife Edith.

he enlisted. He joined up early in 1940 and went to the Middle East with the Royal Armoured Corps the following year, 1941.

Whilst on embarkation leave, Henry was married to a Northern Ireland girl, Edith Jean Hurst, of Lisburn.

Henry was one of the "Desert Rats" with the original Eighth Army, and he followed Field Marshal Montgomery from El Alamein right through the North African campaign. With others of the famous "Eighth" he was brought back to this country to form the spearhead of the attack on Normandy.

He again went overseas on D-Day plus 6, but was wounded by

shrapnel, and was home again shortly afterwards. He made a good recovery and returned to active service.

Despite gallant action by the British 1st Airborne Division at Arnhem in September 1944, Montgomery's bold plan failed in its attempt to turn the northern flank of the German defences, the Siegfried Line. The Rhine barrier still faced the Allies and the German defence was still intact.

During February and early March 1945, Montgomery launched a pincer movement to clear the Rhineland on the western side of the German Rhine, with the Staffordshire Yeomenry well to the fore. By March 3rd the pincers met at Geldern and German resistance began collapsing. The last German bridgehead, opposite Wesel, was wiped out and Montgomery's armies stood on the Rhine.

He launched his Rhine crossing north of the Ruhr, at Wesel. The British 2nd Army led off, behind the support of some 3000 guns on a twenty mile front, and a heavy air attack. A daylight drop of two airborne divisions by parachute and glider landed north of Wesel, with Darley and Rowsley airman, Bert Ricketts, involved in towing one of the gliders during the airborne assault.

German resistance was fierce but relatively ineffective. Montgomery's army group was soon pouring over 12 bridges by the 26th March and two days later had broken through a final German stand at Haltern on the Lippe River.

Sadly, during severe fighting on the second day of the crossing of the Rhine, Lieutenant Henry Derbyshire was killed in his tank, by a shot to the head. His body lies buried in Grave 60. A. 19. in the Reichswald Forest War Cemetery, Kleve, Germany.

Fourteen months later, after the end of the war, the Derbyshire family was further shattered by news of the death of another son :

SERGEANT DONALD DERBYSHIRE,
No. 548179, Royal Air Force.
(*Died on Monday 27th May 1946, aged 29 years.*)

Donald, his mother's favourite, had reluctantly joined the family firm. He was desperate to fly and travelled to Nottingham Aero Club for lessons. During the war he joined the R.A.F., hoping to become a pilot officer, but during his medical, it was found that he possessed a spare rib, which could have caused extra pressure to be exerted on internal organs during flying at a high altitude.

Sergeant Donald Derbyshire.

He was therefore devastated when he was not accepted for a flying role in the R.A.F., but nevertheless continued in the service and became a sergeant on the ground staff. In the later stages of the war he was posted to India and was involved in the war against Japan.

Remaining in the R.A.F. after the war, Donald was in Karachi in May 1946 when he was involved in an accident in the lorry he was driving, resulting in him receiving a broken neck. He died in the British General Hospital, Karachi, and is buried in Grave I. D. 7. At Karachi War Cemetery, Pakistan.

FLYING OFFICER HERBERT WAIN RICKETTS, No. 54692, Navigator 299 Squadron, Royal Air Force Volunteer Reserve.
(Died on Saturday 31st March 1945, aged 26 years.)

Bert Ricketts was born in 1919, the son of William Henry and Bertha Ricketts of Midland Cottages, Chatsworth Road, Rowsley. His father was a guard on the railway, based at Rowsley, and his mother was the sister of Herbert Wain who had been killed in Flanders in 1918. Bert was named after his uncle.

Bert's mother died when relatively young and he and his younger brother Selwyn were brought up by their grandmother, living at Northwood Lane. As a result of this, he and Selwyn attended

Churchtown School and Bert won a free place at the Ernest Bailey Grammar School.

When war began, he had volunteered for the R.A.F., becoming a sergeant/observer by June 1940 in 235 Squadron, flying Blenheim aircraft based at Thorney Island, near Portsmouth. Although the Blenhim was later justifiably credited as a successful night fighter, it was not suited to the cut and thrust of action over the skies of France during the German invasion of the Low Countries or during the Battle of Britain, and many air crew were shot down. It was reported that in June 1940, Bert's aircraft was hit by flak over Dunkirk and the crew only just man-aged to return safely with their plane. On

*Flying Officer
Herbert Wain Ricketts.*

Saturday August 17th 1940 his plane overshot the runway and crashed on landing after a night patrol. The aircraft was a "write-off" but fortunately the three man crew escaped without injury.

During the Battle of Britain, in August/September 1940, the Squadron was involved in the life and death struggle against the German Luftwaffe in the skies of Southern England. Bert came out of that conflict unscathed but not long afterwards, whilst on patrol, the crew had to escape from their plane by parachute and Bert landed in neutral Eire, where he was interned. After making a nuisance of himself, he was repatriated and returned to duty.

When the crisis of 1940 was over, he began training as a navigator, in Bomber Command and took part in many missions over Europe. On the 21st March 1944 he was commissioned as a Pilot Officer and on the 17th May 1944 he arrived at the Operational Training Unit at Ashbourne Airfield, in Derbyshire, where air crews came together to train before being sent as a full crew to fly on operations from other bases. It was here that he became a member of a Stirling bomber crew, comprising Flight Lieutenant Trevor-Roper and pilot-officers Brinkworth, Elliot, Peat and Hayward. On 21st September 1944 Bert was promoted to Flying Officer.

Pictured by their Stirling bomber, left to right:
Pilot officers Brinkworth, Elliott, Flight Lieutenant Trevor-Roper, Peat and Bert
Ricketts. One member, Kenneth Hayward was absent.

The crew took part in many hazardous missions and began training in towing Horsa gliders, carrying soldiers. Their training was put to the test, when, on the 24th March 1945, they towed one of the many Horsa gliders to be released during the start of the operation to cross the River Rhine at Wesel and then drive on into Germany.

Only a few days later, at 9p.m. on the night of Friday 30th March, they took off from Shepherds Grove airfield on their last mission, a supply drop over Norway. The purpose was to drop urgently needed supplies to the Norwegian Resistance Freedom Fighters, known as MILORG. The missions were not without incident as they had to cross a considerable part of the North Sea at a very low altitude to avoid radar detection.

On reaching Norway, the pilot was required to fly the aircraft over the mountainous terrain and rely greatly on the skill of his navigator, Bert Ricketts. On occasions they had to fly below the mountain's height, experiencing excessive turbulence. The long flight durations were often the result of difficulty in locating the target (dropping zone) and continually changing course in order to avoid anti-aircraft gun fire.

Unfortunately, in the early hours of Saturday March 31st Bert Rickett's plane was shot down close to Vierli in Norway and all six crewmen perished. They are buried in Sondeled (Indre) Churchyard, Norway, in a collective grave. It is to be found at Indre Sondeled, on the south east coast road between Arendal and Brevik. His name was also to be found at Rowsley chapel, carved on a plaque on a chapel table, specially made by Mr. Tom Ambrey.

It is an interesting, though sad fact, that Bert's cousin, Alwyne Wain, was also killed during the Second World War, serving in the Royal Air Force as a pilot officer.

LANCE CORPORAL ARTHUR LESLIE WHEATCROFT, No. S/57762, 3rd Petrol Depot, Royal Army Service Corps.
(*Died on Sunday 15th April 1945, aged 25 years.*)

Leslie Wheatcroft had been born in Matlock in 1919, the only child of Arthur and Millicent Wheatcroft. Arthur served in the First World War and when he returned to France in 1918, his wife was expecting their first child. He was never to see his son Leslie, because he contracted pneumonia in the early stages of the worldwide epidemic and died in France on Armistice Day, November 11th 1918.

Leslie Wheatcroft.

Millicent never remarried and struggled to bring up her son. In 1936 they moved to live next door to her sister, Maud Goodhead, on Chatsworth Avenue, Hooleys Estate. Les had worked at Drabbles Mill, Lumsdale, after leaving school, but by the late 1930's he was working at Smedleys Hydro. Les Wheatcroft enlisted in the army in 1939, one of the first from Hooleys Estate to do so, and after initial training he joined the Royal Army Service Corps. By early 1940 he found himself in France with the

British Expeditionary Force, at the 3rd Petrol Depot of the R.A.S.C.

It was their task to drive the fuel tankers to the supply dumps and so allow the mechanised army to run smoothly and efficiently. On May 10th the German Army launched its attack through Holland and Belgium and the British forces moved into Belgium to help stop the onslaught.

During the fighting, Les was captured. Eventually, he was taken as a P.O.W. to Poland, where he was made to work on a farm. It could have been worse, for many prisoners in Poland were made to work in the coalmines. Les survived five long years of captivity and privation, but as the Soviet armies surged inexorably towards the German borders in 1944/45, Les Wheatcroft found himself with large numbers of other P.O.W.'s on a forced march into Germany, to escape the clutches of the Russians.

In April 1945, the long straggle of prisoners and their guards were attacked on the open road by American war planes, mistaking them for the enemy. After the war, a soldier arrived at Hooleys Estate to tell Leslie's mother that he had been present at the time of the tragic accident, and that he had seen Les in a German hospital shortly before his death.

Strangely, Leslie Wheatcroft has no known grave, and instead his name is commemorated on Column 134 of the Dunkirk Memorial, a memorial usually reserved for those who died in the German Blitzkrieg of 1940, or at Dunkirk. It is my belief that his soldier colleague was trying to save Millicent Wheatcroft a little pain and that in fact Leslie had been killed in an explosion from one of the bombs released by the Americans and his body was simply never recovered.

TROOPER JOHN WILLIAM LOMAS,
No. 4985394, "C" Squadron, 27th Lancers, Royal Armoured Corps.
(Died on Sunday 22nd April 1945, aged 34 years.)

John William Lomas, or Jack as he was commonly called, was born in December 1910 at Youlgreave, the son of Walter and Jane Elizabeth Lomas. He was the eldest of four children (Reynold, Harry and Annie) and their father Walter started a painters and decorators business.

They moved to "Saxonholme", on Limetree Avenue, Broadwalk, in 1926/27, where the three brothers helped their father in the business.

On the 7th April 1930, Jack Lomas married Annie Spencer, from Ashover parish, at Chesterfield. She had worked as a domestic servant at Stancliffe Hall School. They lived first at Two Dales and then Hackney, but with five children, more space was required and so in 1939 they moved to 109 Bakewell Road, on the recently completed Hooleys Estate.

By the time that war started, Jack was head of the decorating firm and so was in a reserved occupation. However, on the 12th December 1940, he was called up and enlisted in the Sherwood Foresters. On the 1st November 1941 he transferred to the Royal Armoured Corps, and ten months later was posted to the 27th Lancers, where he became the driver of an armoured car.

On one occasion, whilst driving between camps, he parked the vehicle on the A6, by his house on Bakewell Road. Many of the

Driver Jack Lomas and his wife Annie.

children from Hooleys Estate gathered round and swarmed over the armoured vehicle.

On the 14th January 1944 Jack embarked from England and landed in the Middle East sixteen days later. For the following 12 months he was involved with a delivery squadron in North Africa, delivering tanks and other armoured vehicles to the regiments, but by the 25th January 1945 he was in No. 199 Transit Camp in Italy, before being posted again to the 27th Lancers at the end of February. For the next two months he was to take part in the final stages of the 8th Army's war in Northern Italy.

Across the whole 50 mile front there was only one dry gap, where the road north to Argenta ran between Lake Comacchio and the floods created by the breaching of the dykes along the rivers.

The tanks and armoured cars of the British 8th Army were specially equipped for these amphibious operations. On the 9th April the enemy artillery positions were blasted by the Allied air forces and by 1000 guns, whilst the infantry and armoured forces surged forward. By the 16th April the German forces were still fighting doggedly, but the armoured forces, including the 27th Lancers performing their scouting duties, had fanned out north of the Argenta Gap, into the Po Valley and were inching forward. The German line was near breaking point.

On 22nd April the British armoured divisions met the advancing American forces behind the retreating Germans, who were now trapped and in complete disorder. The cease fire was declared on May 2nd and the bitter, forgotten war in Italy was over.

At 12a.m. on the 22nd April, "A" and "C" Squadrons made for a bridge that was reported open. By 4p.m. they were across the bridge and pushing north. "C" Squadron received a civilian report that the enemy were using the church steeple in Formignano as an observation post and shells were fired at it, scoring three direct hits.

The village of Sabbioncello Vittore was held in strength by the enemy. 3 Troop "C" Squadron, passed through the village at speed without being fired on. A bridge was covered by two 7.5 cm. anti-tank guns, but their crews did not have time to man their guns before No. 3 Troop had passed over. However, the leading scout car of No. 6 Troop, driven by Jack Lomas, received a direct hit, and both he and his gunner were killed outright.

Ten days later the war in Italy was over. Jack's family was expecting to receive these glad tidings at any moment but instead the dreadful news of his death arrived at Hooleys Estate.

Jack Lomas is buried in Grave II. E.5. at the Argenta Gap War Cemetery, between Ravenna and Ferrara.

The war ended in Europe with the defeat of Germany and Victory in Europe (VE Day) was celebrated on Tuesday May 8th. Matlock folk strung out bunting on Monday evening, flags of the big Four Powers flew from the Town Hall and coloured lights were fixed on the Hall Leys entrance, the Promenade and the Fishpond at Matlock Bath. It was wonderful to see the lights displayed after years of "blackout" conditions.

Rain fell on Tuesday morning, but the skies cleared later and the streets of Matlock filled with crowds. Bands played in the park and in the evening there was a dance in the Town Hall. Short services had been held in the churches, soon after Winston Churchill's announcement over the "wireless", and the bells rang out. Some 200 people gathered in Crown Square at midnight to sing community songs.

Schools were closed for two days holiday and in various parts of Darley Dale, VE Day was celebrated with street parties for school children in the different localities. Bunting and flags were hung from the houses and trestle tables were brought out into the open air and a tea provided for the children.

At Hooleys Estate, funds were raised for the occasion when the women organised a ladies football match in the fields across the road from the Estate. The plan was for a large street party, but because of the forecast for inclement weather, the organisers accepted the offer by the owner of Grey Friars (next to Valley Lodge Residential Home) for the people to use his field and outbuildings for the event. "A good time was had by all", especially as a bar had been set up in one of the barns.

The residents of Limetree Avenue and Peakland View, led by Mr. Walter Smith, the manager of Ormes Shop (now Paul Plumbing), organised a street tea party, together with games and may pole dancing, whilst other avenues on Broadwalk, such as Darley Avenue, held their own parties.

The war was not yet over, however, for in the Far East, the British Army, the "Forgotten Army" of the Burma campaign was still locked in deadly conflict with the Japanese Imperial forces. As the Allies successfully fought their way through the Burmese jungle terrain and on into Malaya, it was to be in this main theatre of war that Darley's last victim was to die, not in the heat of battle, but after enduring three years in the atrocious conditions of a Japanese Prisoner of War camp.

Raising money for Victory in Europe celebrations, Hooleys Estate, May 1945.
Back row: Mrs. Taylor, Mrs. Grant, Mrs. Barwick, Mrs. Camp, Mrs. Stringer,
Mrs. Byard, Mrs. Gill, X, Pat Esplin, X, Mrs. Ankers, X, Mrs. Goodall.
Front row: Mrs. Harrison, Mrs. Gilbert, Mrs. Baker, Mrs. Birkett, Mrs. Needham, X,
Mrs. Jepson, Mrs. Fletcher.

V.E. Day celebrations for Limetree Avenue/Peakland View residents, 8th May 1945.
Back row: Charlie Mackie, Cedric Smalley, Geoffrey Sellors.
Next row: B. Hill, Mark Thompson, John Hill, X, Rodney Hill, X, Eric Mayall,
John Humphries, Peter Eaton, Jackie Tindall, Ann Thompson, X, Jane Tindall,
Peter Fearn, Henry Thompson, ? Petit, S. Bickley, Shiela Ball.
Next row: Brian Webster, X, Michael Curzon, X, S. Smith, X, X, X, M. Smith,
Lillian Saunders, Irene Mackie, David Pope, John Saunders, X.
Front row: X, Pauline Hallows. A. Mackie.

GUNNER HARRY SHELDON,
No. 1777933, 78 Battery,
35th Light Anti-Aircraft Regiment, Royal Artillery.
(Died on Tuesday 22nd May 1945, aged 35 years.)

Harry was born in 1910, in a cottage opposite the Druid Inn, at Birchover. His father worked at Birchover Quarry, but died of silicosis at an early age, leaving his wife Hannah to raise the family, consisting of Cyril, Jack, Hilda, Annie, Harry and Vera.

Eventually, Harry began work at Mill Close Lead Mine at South Darley and drove the underground electric battery powered locomotive on the 70 fathom level. Planks and steel loops supported the roof, leaving room for the locomotive to run. Riding on the loco was forbidden, although some drivers allowed men to ride in the tubs. Wagoners on the 62 level pushed their small wagon loads of lead and stone to a chute and tipped it

Gunner Harry Sheldon and his wife Anne (nee Holland) on their wedding day in 1941.

down to the 70 fathom level, where it was taken by the locomotive, driven by Harry, to the main up shaft. Two of Harry's brothers, Cyril and Jack, were engine drivers employed at the L.M.S. Marshalling yard at Rowsley.

In 1933 he went from Birchover to live with his mother at Darley House Estate. After Mill Close was closed due to the flooding in 1938, Harry went to work for International Combustion at Derby.

In his spare time Harry was a keen sportsman and played cricket and football for Birchover at a time when the village was renowned for its local footballers. He also played for Darley Dale Cricket Club. When Harry was eventually called up he could easily have obtained the doctor's help in postponing this action, for he was suffering from a serious knock he had received during a football match, but he declined the opportunity since he wished to participate in the action.

Joining the Royal Artillery, he married Matlock girl Annie Holland in October 1941, whilst on leave from training, and by November 1941 had embarked for service overseas. After a few weeks of marriage, he was never to see his wife Annie again.

The Theatre of operations was the Far East and the ship's destination, the fortress island of Singapore, at the southern tip of the Malayan peninsula. Harry's battery of anti-aircraft guns were unloaded and positioned in readiness for the defence against likely aggression from Japanese forces.

The 7th December 1941 had seen the United States of America and Japan enter the war as a result of the fateful Japanese attack on Pearl Harbour. What had previously been a European conflict now became a global one.

On the 8th December 1941 General Yamashita's 25th Army landed in Northern Malaya. The British command in the area was in turmoil and the troops at the front poorly trained. Thus, after the small R.A.F. forces had been overwhelmed by superior Japanese air power, Yamashita's 100,000 men were able to move smoothly inland towards the ultimate object of any invasion of Malaya, the great island fortress of Singapore.

Soon after the shock of the first landings, the British were further discomforted by the loss of their only two capital ships in the area. The battleship "Prince of Wales" and battle cruiser "Repulse" had raced north from Singapore to engage the Japanese supporting forces but with no air support the Japanese air strikes found them, and after a furious battle, the two ships succumbed to large numbers of bombs and torpedo hits.

By the 31st January 1942, only the island of Singapore was left. Moreover, the fortress had been designed solely against attack from the sea, whereas the Japanese were now attacking from the landward side, where there were no fixed defences or heavy artillery. On February 8th the Japanese landed on the island, and after desperate fighting captured the water reservoirs. This sealed the fate of the population and garrison, which, together with Harry's 78 Battery, Royal Artillery, surrendered unconditionally on the 15th February, some 70,000 British troops being taken prisoner.

In the short term, it put the Japanese in a fine position for their planned invasion of the rich Dutch East Indies. In far away England, Harry's mother never forgave Chuchill for putting her son in such danger.

Amongst the captured British troops was Harry Sheldon, who became a prisoner of war of the Japanese. Eventually he was removed to a P.O.W. camp in Sarawak, North Borneo, where he was to spend the next three years in hellish conditions, abused by his captors and suffering from hunger and disease.

Shortly before the P.O.W. camp was liberated, it was believed by his family that his guards took him out to be shot. He died on Tuesday 22nd May 1945, aged 35 years, and was later laid to rest in the Labuan War Cemetery, on the small island of Labuan in Brunei Bay, off the coast of N.W. Borneo.

Years later, Annie Sheldon remarried, but always treasured the memories of her times with Harry, keeping all his letters that were sent during his time as a prisoner of war. When friends later went out to that part of the world they called at the cemetery and were able to provide Annie with photographs of Harry's final resting place.

Gunner Harry Sheldon's grave
in Lebuan War Cemetary, on Labuan Island,
off the coast of N.W. Borneo.

As I come to the end of the account of those Darley Servicemen who did not survive the war years, mention must now be made of two names on the war memorial for whom no details have been found. Both **HARRY HARRIS** and **FRANK OSBORNE** have proved elusive, but their names are honoured in this book alongside those of their colleagues. Nothing would give me greater pleasure than for a reader to be able to provide me with information about their lives, and the lives of Harry Grey, William A. Owen and Leonard Houghton from the Great War.

Victory over Japan Day (V.J. Day), held in early September 1945 by Churchtown Triangle residents.

Back row: X, Nora Monkhouse, Mrs. Walters, Mrs. Waller, Mrs. Howes, Mrs. Muir, Bette White, Mrs. Webber, Tom Bowler, Mrs. Fentem, Mona Andrews, Billy Goodwin, X, Cyril Howes, Norman Hotchin, John Smedley, Mrs. Corfield.

Next row: Charlie Muir, Tommy Walters, Mrs. Riley, Mrs. Bowler, Eric Willers, Dick White, X, Gwen Sayles, Horace Sayles, Goe Pinkney, Mrs. Wardman, Mrs. Bland, Mrs. Witcher, Jack Witcher.

Next Row: Ray Howes, X, Keith Andrews, Billy Wass.

Next row: Philip Hickman, Derek Fenten, Roy Walters, X, Nelly Bramhall, Eunice Willers, Olwyn Morton, Margaret Paterson, Bernice White, Julie Lane, Pat Lane, ? Briddon, John Wass, Terry Andrews, X, X.

Next row: Florence Marsh, X, X, Flo Pickford, Barbara Morton, Michael Poulson, Elizabeth Riley, Brenda Morton, Doreen Morton, X, X, Marion White, Ian Bland, Roy Walters, X, X.

Front row: Geoff Marsh, Jeffrey Pinkney, Janette Pinkney, Jeanette Waterfall, X, Joan Howsley, X, John Riley, Sheila Stringer, Howard Walters, Norma Bland, Enid Willers, Sheila Bland, Brindley Morton, Margaret Lane, Donald Willers, Graham Bland.

Victory over Japan Day (V.J.) for Darley House Estate residents, August 1945, at Darley House.

Back row: X, X, Mrs Cooke, Brian Wildgoose, Raymond Phillips, Mrs. Woolley, Mrs. Kenworthy, Derek Marsden, Mrs. Robinson, X, Jean Wood, Miss Williamson, Charles Wildgoose, Mrs. Wildgoose, Mrs. Clarke, X, X, Enid Wildgoose, Billy Wildgoose, Mrs. Smith, Mrs. Marsden, Mrs. Wildgoose, Faye Wildgoose, Sidney Wildgoose, Mrs. Ellis, Mrs. Wood, Mrs. Maddocks, Mrs. Cowley, Margaret Jolly.

Next row: Vic Beresford, Vernon Moore, Rita Marsden, Joy Toft, Queenie Wheeldon, Pat Smedley, Joy Rouse, X, Margaret Woolley, Peter Marsden, Owen Moore.

Next row: Mick Jolley, X, David Robinson, Sheila Clough, X, Bob Rouse, John Cooke, Alan Robinson, Margaret Smith, Joan Smith, X, Joyce Jackson, Margaret Kenworthy, X, Peter Wood, Brian Ellis, Rosemary Maddocks.

Front row: Kathleen Blair and Geoffrey, Edward Windle, Celia Allen, Barbara Robinson, X, ? Wragg, Paddy Thompson, David Thompson, Deana Andrews, Maureen Wragg, Wendy Walker, George Robinson, Eunice Woodhouse, Janet Woolley, X, Shirley Robinson, David Ellis, Michael Marsden, Mary Randall, Cynthia Wragg, Ann Woodhouse, Pat Jolley.

391

On August 6th 1945, an atomic bomb was dropped over the Japanese city of Hiroshima, killing 78,000 and injuring 70,000, whilst on the 9th August a second atomic bomb was exploded over Nagasaki, killing 40,000 and injuring 25,000. The Japanese offered to surrender and on September 2nd 1945 the official surrender took place on board the battleship U.S.S. "Missouri", anchored in Tokyo Bay.

In Darley Dale, the news was received with relief and happiness, but the celebrations were more muted than on the occasion of Victory in Europe. However, the Churchtown/Green Lane Triangle "did themselves proud" when they organised a VJ Day celebration for themselves. A tea was provided in the British Legion Hut (nowadays where the Cubs/Brownies meet) and games were held in the adjacent field. Darley House Estate residents also gathered in the grounds of Darley House, a fitting venue at which to celebrate the occasion. On VE Day, Northwood Lane children had been entertained at the Firth Derihon Shadow Factory, but on VJ Day their celebrations took place in the Bull Acre Field (at the side of the newly constructed Lowe's Garage). The tea, set out on trestle tables, was held inside the wooden garage building, recently constructed out of second hand packing cases. Games were organised and the nearby telegraph pole was used in a "greasy pole" competition.

At long last the Second World War had come to an end and with it, Darley Dale's participation in the global conflict. The people of Darley had experienced the closeness of war with the arrival of evacuees from the threatened urban areas, the distant views of the "Blitz" on Sheffield and Derby and the activities of locals in the Darley Home Guard and ARP during the anxious days of 1940/41, when there was a real threat of German invasion and a perilously fine line between victory and defeat in the Battle of Britain.

It was, however, the involvement of family and friends in combat in the different theatres of war, that brought home to Darley folk the dangers and perils of the wartime situation. For those who returned home safely to Darley Dale, there was relief and joy, but for thirty families and their relations and friends there was only sadness.

EPILOGUE

THEIR ACHIEVEMENT—
PEACE FOR A NEW GENERATION

By November 1949 the names of 29 Darley Dale men who had died during the Second World War were etched in stone on the war memorial in the grounds of the Whitworth Institute. On Sunday 5th November 1949 the Remembrance Service was held at the Cenotaph, combined with a special service of dedication of the plaque bearing their names. The Reverend R.J. Stanford conducted the service and flag bearers of the British Legion were in attendance.

The men being honoured on that Sunday morning joined the list of combatants who had sacrificed their lives during the Great War of 1914-1918, bringing the total who had died to 93.

Each death bore testimony to the sacrifice made by both the individual and his family. Sadness and heartache would be shared in each of the said households and arguments could be made as to whether different policies and actions by democratic governments could have prevented the two world conflicts, and therefore the deaths of the men from Darley Dale.

I believe, however, that by 1939 the Second World War became a "Just War", fought against an evil tyranny that wished to impose its policies on other nations and peoples against their will. The pre-war actions of the Nazi regime in Germany and especially the terrible deeds that came to light during the course of the war, help us to see that those who fought against such oppression were justifiably fighting with honour for a finer, higher cause.

Although the argument for calling the First World War a "Just War" from the Allies point of view is less clear and sharply defined, I believe that such a case can be made.

The first great catastrophe of the 20th century was chiefly the result of Germany's international ambitions. German unification had created a nation that combined the most dynamic economy in Europe with a regime that in many respects had hardly emerged from feudalism. The Kaiser sought for his nation the status not only of a Great Power, but of a World Power.

If it remains impossible to consider the First World War as a struggle between good and evil as unequivocal as the Second World War, the moral case for the Allies against Germany is still strong.

Some 5000 civilians were killed by the German military in their advance through neutral Belgium and the medieval library at Louvain was burned to demonstrate that they meant business. German troops on the Eastern Front burned and massacred systematically, a foretaste of their behaviour in Russia a generation later.

When the German Army retreated 25 miles to the Hindenburg Line in 1917, they slaughtered the cattle, laid waste the villages and poisoned the wells. For some historians, the belief is held that if the Kaiser and the militaristic class had prevailed in the First World War, the consequences for the freedom of Europe would have been dire.

The treaties of Brest-Litovsk and Bucharest, which Germany imposed on revolutionary Russia and her ally Rumania, illustrate all too clearly what those consequences might have been.

The Bolsheviks, under Lenin, were desperate to buy time for their own agenda inside Russia and agreed to cede sovereignty of Russian Poland, Finland, Ukraine, Georgia and the Baltic states, altogether losing 34% of her population, 32% of her agricultural land, 54% of her industrial capacity and 89% of her coal mines. In addition, she agreed to pay six million marks in reparations.

Rumania was treated even harsher, if possible. The draconian measures imposed on her reduced Rumania's sovereignty to a farce and her people to economic servitude. When a Rumanian diplomat protested, a German staff officer replied, "You call it a harsh peace? Just wait till you see what we are preparing for France and England".

The action of a victorious Germany over her enemies in the East stiffened resistance in the West and strengthened the resolve to fight on to the end and destroy the militarist power in Germany. This renewal of resistance helped calm fears in the spring of 1918 when the great German offensive threatened disaster, and was retained through to the final counter-offensive in the summer and on the road to victory.

When people look at the history of Britain and the world after the Second World War, with all its imperfections and lost chances, some may wonder whether the fallen combatants lay down their lives in vain. However, without the sacrifice made by these men of Darley, and countless other men and women from numerous parishes across the United Kingdom, the country would nowadays be a sadder, poorer and more inhospitable place in which to live. Their fight for freedom against tyranny resulted eventually in the victory of democracy and free will over repression and totalitarian instincts, however frail and tenuous the hold on liberty remains.

During the first fifty years of the 20th century the people of Darley Dale were twice called upon to defend their country and democratic way of life, in long term bloody struggles. Since the ending of the Second World War, another fifty years have passed without the necessity of other generations of Darley folk having to be called to the defence of their nation and democratic principles. For this, we have to thank such men as those whose names are inscribed on the Darley war memorial.

The highest honour and debt of gratitude that can be bestowed upon these men within the pages of the Epilogue is to illustrate by means of photographs the immediate post-war generation who benefited from their sacrifices. Not for the new generation the slippery road to war but instead the security of long term peace. As one of that generation who did not have to bear arms I give thanks to the 93 men of Darley who gave their lives, and to those who also fought alongside them, and survived.

The Armistice Service in the Whitworth Park on November 5th, 1949, combined with a special service of dedication of the plaque bearing the names of the Fallen 1939-1945. The Reverend R. J. Stanford conducted the service.

February 1949, re-opening of the Whitworth Institute after being in the hands of the War Department during the Second World War. Members of the British Legion after the opening of the wing that became known as the British Legion Hall. (Now the Terrace Room and formerly the Naafi in the war years.)

Left to right: Caroline Smith, Trevor Smith, Cairo Smith, Mrs. Edna Smith.
Mrs. Edna Smith is shown driving the shooting brake at the Red House in 1946, shortly after the house had been returned to them by the army. In that year, her husband William started the Darley School of Equitation at the Red House (the forerunner of the Red House Stables Working Carriage Museum). Over the next few years William Smith built up a stable of 100 horses, with a large proportion of the business connected to the private schools in Darley, Matlock and Bakewell districts, when horse riding was part of the school curriculum.

1946 Christmas party for Northwood Avenue (Broadwalk) families, in Churchtown School.

Back row: Mr. Allwood, Mrs, Davies, Bob Allsop, Marjorie Parks, Gerald Robinson, Dennis Allsop, Arthur Parks, X, X, X, X, X, X, Arthur Fletcher, Dennis Allwood, X, Danny Corfield, Mr. Corfield.

Next row: Mrs. Haynes, X, Mrs. Adkins, Vera Bark, X, Elsie Parks, X, X, Gwen Ayre, Dorothy Corfield, X, Mrs. Corfield, Mabel Thraves, X, X, Father Christmas (Mr. Albert Davies).

Next row: George Parks, Dorothy Briddon, Marjorie Briddon, Harriett Briddon, Mrs. Jackson, Carol Taylor, Pam Bark, X, X, Mrs. Parks, Elsie Neal.

Next row: X, X, X, Sylvia Taylor, X, Maureen Taylor, Arthur Fletcher.

Front row: Mrs. Allsop, Ian Allsop, Elsie Stephenson, Roy Stephenson, X, X, Alan Stephenson, Ken Parks, Ann Bark, Brenda Fletcher, Muriel Taylor, Betty Winthrope.

May pole dancing by Darley House Estate girls on 1st May 1948.
Organised by 'Queenie' Wheeldon, the girls performed on Darley House Estate, on
Woolliscroft's field (behind the Silver Service garage) and at the Whitworth Hospital.
Joyce Jackson, Pauline Cowley, Maureen Wragg, Shirley Robinson, Deana Andrews,
(Queen), Ann Woodhouse, Celia Allen, Cynthia Wragg, Eunice Woodhouse,
Sheila Clough, Wendy Walker.

The First Darley Dale 'Darby and Joan' Club c.1951, in the recently opened Whitworth Park.
Back row: X, X, Mrs. Wilson, Mrs. Allsop, X, Mrs. Martin.
Next row: X, Mrs. Smalley, Mr. Young, X, X, X, X, X, X, X, X, X, Mrs. Bark, X, X, X/
Next row: Mr. Allsop, X, Mrs. Gregory, X, X, X, Mrs. Young, Mrs. White, Mrs. Taylor, Mr. Taylor, Mr. White.
Front row: X, X, X, Mr. Mellor, Mr. Thomas, Mr. Taylor, X, X, X, X.

Loscoe Row c.1949/1950, showing Brian Wood.

In the late 1950's, the houses were condemned as unfit for habitation and in 1959 Ken Knowles bought seven of the fourteen cottages from the Charlesworths. For the next eighteen months he and his wife Joan demolished them by hand, using only pick and hammer. Their intention was to build a bungalow on the site, using the gritstone blocks from the cottages. Thirteen of the cottages had been made of gritstone which was rendered, but the fourteenth, previously used as a shop in the first two decades of the 20th century, and later in the 30's and 40's, was made of dressed sandstone, without any render. The other seven cottages were demolished by the Charlesworths shortly afterwards.

St. Helen's Church Choir at the Patronal Festival (Festival of patron saint – St. Helen) in August 1950.
Back row: Jack Asbury, Peter Brown, Gerald West, John Wass, John Norman, John Humphries, John Gregory, Richard Atkinson, Walter Wall, Frank Convery, Harry Daniels, Reverend R.J. Stanford, Arthur Smith, Philip Wigfall, Ronald Wall, Cedric Smalley, George Potter.
Front row: Michael Paulson, X, Eric Mayall, Gordon Bateman Bacon, Brindley Martin, Phillip Taylor, Roy Walters, Peter Eaton.

Darley Churchtown School football team 1947/48 season. In the same season they were winners of the South Peak Football Shield.
Back row: Mr. Bartram, Ray Armitt, Donald Willers, Alf Bowler, Ray Tuffin, John Brownlee, Brian Lane, Mr. Dick Wragg (sports master).
Front row: Graham Bland, Freddy Rogers, Harold Smedley, Roy Webster, Ray Slack, Ron Roskelly.

Darley Dale County Primary School children who competed in the Matlock Bath Music Festival in 1949.

The choir was conducted by their teacher, Leslie Fearn and are shown in the Pavilion car park.

Back row: Joan Littlewood, Jean Stringer, Roy Webster, Iris Fleay, Ann Woodhouse, Diane Soppitt, Kathleen Wheeldon, Barry Toft, Betty Pearson, Lucy Seymour.

Middle row: Mavis Webster, Eunice Charlesworth, Marjorie Hodgkinson, Alan Watts, Beryl Marsden, Joan Bennett, Ann Davies, Alan Smedley, Billy Cass, Mavis Privett, Carol Barker.

Front row: Marion Wall, Sylvia Fearn, Ann Cellard, ? Wilson, Jean Askew, Malcom Wilson, Errol Roose, Angela Smith, Harold Birkett.

Prize giving at Darley Council School 1950.

Back row: Mr. Moore, Mr. Bailey, Mrs. Clarke, Mr. Sellors, Miss Kirkham, Mr. Henderson, Mrs. Bond, Miss Kirkland, Mrs. Wild, Harold Lomas, Mr. Rhodes.

Middle row: Mrs. Hancock, Mr. Hibbs, Mrs. Hibbs, Joe Hancock, Mrs. Broome, Mr. Walters, Mrs. Rhodes, Roy Webster.

Front row: Neville Allwood, Betty Sparks, Janet Taylor, Richard George Hodgkinson, X, Joy Rouse, Roy Askew, Janet Harrison, Rita Newborough.

Cookery lesson in the new pre-fabricated classroom at Darley Council School 1949.
Background row: X, X, Angela Smith, Jackie Toplis, Freda Birkett, Pauline Thornhill, Joy Rouse, Rita Newborough, Ann Woodhouse.
Foreground row: Ann Mallett, Mavis Charlesworth, Patricia Stephenson, Barbara Bowers, X, Margaret Woolley, ? Allsop, Miss Gee.

Christmas Nativity scene at Darley Council School c.1950/1951, held in the dining room.

Back row: X, Pam Allen, X, Ann Woodhouse, Paul Bennett, Tom Woodley, X, ? Jones, David Champion, Roy Askew, Mavis Bond, Rita Newborough, ? Bailey.

Middle row: X, X, X.

Front row: Shirley Redfern, Pat Morton, Barry Barker, Jean Stringer, X, Errol Roose, Maureen Wragg, Pauline Askew, Alan Watts, Deana Andrews.

Inter-school quiz at Matlock All Saints School 1954.

All Saints School, with 116 points, defeated Darley Primary School (scoring 85 points) in an inter-school quiz on spelling, reading, history, geography, nature study and general knowledge.

All Saints School team (left) include (standing): S. Turner, P. Espig, D. Wright, J. Kersey. (Seated, left): R. Hallows, S. Wright, B. Lewis, W. Peck.

Darley Primary School team (right) include (standing): G. Jepson, A. Wright, M. Taylor, D. Taylor. (Seated, right): P. Jolley, J. Bowler, P. Lomas, E. Briddon.

At the back are the headmaster Mr. W.J. Hunt (All Saints), question master, Miss A. Knight and headmaster (Darley Dale) Mr. W.B. Williams.

Darley Primary School Prize Day 1956.

Prize winners left to right: John Mackay (Head boys' cup), Roy Stephenson (Athletics cup boys), Roger Saunders (Lions team captain),
Jennifer Dight (Athletics cup girls), Faye Wildgoose (Lions team captain), Geoffrey Cass (the Jenkins swimming medal).
The house championship cup was won by the Lions, beating the Eagle team. In this year, 1956, the school uniform was introduced to the
school.

Choir and recorder group from Darley Dale Secondary Modern School, Greenaway Lane. The school opened in January 1953 under headmaster Joseph Hancock.

Back row: Doreen McNevin, Pamela Stephenson Sylvia Wilson, Josephine Porter, Susan Harrison, Eileen Holland, Margaret Thraves, Joyce Smith, Enid Williams, Pat Goodwin, Barbara Morton, June Brewell, Ann Smedley, John Smith, Janet Vallance. X. X. Margaret Daniels, Sheila Smith.

Third row: Mark Thompson, Isaac Wilson, Jennifer Byard, Ken Walker, Eunice Charlesworth, Harold Birkett, Eve Cochrane, Joan Littlewood, Irene Newton, Mavis Webster, X, Sylvia Fearn, X, Joyce Rogers, X, Mavis Privett, Brenda Ollerenshaw, Malcolm Sellors, Joyce Allsop.

Second row: Pat Morton, Alan Watts, Keith Stanbrook, Peter Dunn. X, Hilary Gregory, Denise Lane, Joan Partridge, Paddy Thompson, Mary Barratt, Kathleen Millwood, Betty Coleman, Eileen Dunn, Betty Pearson.

Front row: Errol Roose, Roy Webster, Shirley Redfern, Margaret Seal, Joan Bennett, Jean Stringer, Maureen Wragg, Hazel Kinder, Pauline Askew, Deana Andrews.

*Teaching staff at Darley Dale Secondary Modern School, when it opened in 1953.
Left to right, back row: Bill Bowler, Duncan Sellors, Mr. Murdock, Mr. Boden,
Mr. Henderson.
Front row: Jean Scrivens, Mrs. Essie Clarke, Joe Hancock, 'Digger' Moore,
Jean Crowder.*

Darley Churchtown School 1947/48.

Back row: Phyllis Chatbourne, Jean Allison, Nellie Bramhall, Mavis Slater, Eileen Needham, Noreen Gadsby, Eileen Briddon, Eileen Bishton, Margaret Moorby, Ron Whitehead.

Next row: Alwyn Griffiths, Roy Webster, Trevor Welbourne, Harold Smedley, Henry Thompson, Orlando Wilson, Ronnie Duggins, Tony Welbourne.

Next row: Audrey Andrews, Beryl Smith, Pat Lane, Joan Cleal, Eileen Gilbert, Alice Hopkinson, Olwyn Morton.
Front row: John Wass, Hedley Wilson, Michael Boam, Eric Mayall, Donald Willers, John Holland, Geoffrey Porter.

Darley Churchtown School 1948/49.

Back row: John Brownlee, Gordon Marsden, Donald Willers, Eileen Needham, Mr. Ronald Whitehead, Noreen Gadsby, Michael Boam, George Blackham, Raymond Tuffin.

Next row: Barbara Marsden, Jean Wood, Ann Foxlaw, Marie Brassington, Dorothy Petts, June Smedley, Noreen Bark, Nellie Bramhall, Plwyn Morton, Jean Dakin, Diane Wain, Dorothy Broomhead, Sheila Slater.

Next row: John Humphrey, Audrey Knowles, Marina Needham, Cicely Wood, Alice Hopkinson, Lily Waterfall, Jean Heathcote, Norma Holmes, Joan Cleal, Marie Ball, Winifred Fearn, Orlando Wilson.

Front row: Norman Glossop, Gordon Johnson, Anthony Welbourne, Malcolm White, Ronald Roskilly, Robert Evans, Raymond Armitt, Graham Bland, David Carson, Eric Mayall, Dennis Elliott.

Darley Churchtown football team, winners of the Bunting Cup in 1952, on Causeway Lane, Matlock.
Back row: John Charles Bartram, Ray Armitt, Richard Brown, John Riley, Howard Walters, Alan Flitter, Eric McNevin, Roy Bradshaw, Kerry Hill, Mr. Clay.
Front row: Graham Hobson, Geoff Norman, Malcolm Johnson, Malcolm Plant, Ady Duggins.

Darley Primary School 1953.

Back row: X, John Macale, X, Timothy Bower, X, Roger Jackson, Martin Briddon, John Heathcote, Keith Taylor, Martin Burton, Freddy Gill, Robert Maddox.

Middle row: Rachel Wood, Susan Evans, Peter Daffern, X, Joan Crowter, X, Miss Woodhead, James Hayto, Jacqui Hibbs, Sandra Hodgkinson, Annette Wagstaffe, Cynthia Allsop.

Front row: Nicky Czok, X, Pam Maddocks, Peter Dalton, Trevor Bolton, Wendy Wheatcroft, Monica Bond, X, Margaret Overton.

Darley Dale Primary School 1953.

Back row: Janice Blair, Stuart Shimwell, Jane Walters, Robin Farmer, Christine Allsop, Richard Pope, Brioni Hudson, Wendy Swift, John Hipkin, Maureen Wills, John Cafferty, Ethne Windle, Tony Beresford, Susan Merrett.

Middle row: Alwyn Soppitt, Janice Privett, Anthony Smith, Ann Knowles, Mrs. Ivy Bond, Kathleen Antcliffe, Hilda Brightmore, Sheila Morton, Kay Patilla.

Front row: Nigel Antcliffe, Tony Richardson, Keith Blair, James Hendry, Brian Bond, Roland Harris, Adrian Webster, X, Peter Soppitt.

Darley Primary School class photograph 1953.

Back row: Pat Davies, Muriel Taylor, Pam Soppitt, Edward Windle, Anita Jenkins, Gordon Clifford, Susan Lee, Barbara Tolliday, David Horrobin, Sheila Redfern, Judith Wardman, Ivan Redfern, Barbara Robinson, Veronica Knighton.
Next row: X, Shirley Fearn, Barbara Webster, Rosemary Coleman, Pam Holmes, Barbara Woolliscroft, Edgar Bailey, Janet Bridge, Jennifer Seal, Carol Taylor, Pat Jolley, Shirley Holmstrom, Pauline Saunders.
Front row: Ronnie Byard, David Ellis, Richard Eaton, Geoff Gill, Barry Richardson, Duncan Bailey, Keith Previtt, David Lownds, John Maddox, Graham Jepson.

Darley Dale Primary School 1953.

Back row: Malcolm Taylor, Alan McHale, Eric Gascoigne, Brian Wood, Brian Richards, Alan Stringer, Selwyn Woolliscroft, Raymond Phillips, Alan Wagstaffe, Jack Carter, Dougie Bamford, Ian Slatter.

Middle row: Christine Fletcher, Dorothy Bond, Margaret Cass, Patricia Lomas, Beryl Allen, Margaret Woolley, Mrs. Hancock, Kathleen Robinson, Eileen Briddon, Valery Pearson, Judith Trew, Jacqueline Bowler, June Fletcher.

Front row: Adrian Charlesworth, Alan Wright, Bruce Harrison, David Wragg, John Hallom, John Dalton, Roy Turkington, Peter Patilla, Roger Yarwood, Max Woosnam.

Darley Council School Christmas Play c.1955/56.
Back row: Peter Toft, John Cafferty, Timothy Bower, Lesley Kirkham, Ann Knowles, X,
Keith Blair, Peter Daffern, Wilfred Hughes.
Next row: Kay Patilla, Janice Previtt, John Hipkin, Adrian Webster, Susan Merrett,
Brian Bond, Stuart Hardy, Janice Blair, June Raynor, Kathleen Anthony.
Next row: X, Irene Stone, Sandra Baker, Lorna Taylor, Brioni Hudson.
Front row: Richard Pope, Martin Burton, Keith Taylor, Anthony Smith, Robin Farmer,
Richard Carline, Colin Winder, Tony Berresford.

Darley Dale County Primary School Choir at Ripley and District Schools' Musical Festival on May 14th 1958 at Ripley County School.
Back row: X, X, X, Stuart Hardy, Monica Bond, Brioni Hudson, X, Janice Prevett, Pam Hallows, Joy King, X, Diane Bower.
Next row: X, X, X, Ann Logan, X, Wendy Wheatcroft, Barbara Hibbs, Pam Maddocks, X, X, Ian Jepson, James Hayto, X, X.
Next row: X, X, David Lang, John Woolliscroft, Keith Taylor, X, Rachel Wood, Annette Wagstaffe, Joan Crowter, X, Lorna Taylor, X, Jacqui Hibbs, Patricia Williams.
Front row: Peter Lomas, X, X, Sandra Hodgkinson, ? Bond, X, X, X, X, X, Margaret Jepson, Daphne Flude.

Prize winners at Darley Dale Primary School, 1956/1957.
Back row: Ann Wright, Maureen Wills, David Milton, John Hipkin, Jacqui Taylor, Keith Taylor, Jane Walters.
Front row: Ethne Windle, Joan Crowter.

Firth Derihon workers in holiday mood after the war's end.

Phyllis Twigdon, Bette White, Edith Prime, Felicia Cropper, Jean Bane, Mary Ellis (Flint), Ann Corfield.

Operating one of the 40cwt. drop stamps at Firth Derihon c.1953.
Horace Sayles, George Grant, Ivan Wright.

*1967– Firth Derihon employees who had worked at Mill Close Lead Mine in the 1930's.
Mr. Green, Ivan Wright, George Waller, Ernie Redfern, X, X, Mr. Gill, X, Cyril Taylor.*

Crowning of Darley Dale Carnival Queen in July 1952.
This was the first revival of the pre-war Darley Carnival, on the initiative of the Darley
Public Band, who wished to equip themselves with new instruments.
Back row: George Gilberthorpe, John Turner, Alf Hanson, Harry Gill, Billy Webster,
Dyson Charlesworth, Mrs. Wain, Mrs. Boden, Jim Garrity, John Samson Wain,
Jock Boden.
Front row: Fred Allison, Hilary Bowler, Marion White, Mavis Fearn,
Adrian Charlesworth, Caroline Smith.

*Darley House Estate children on a float during Matlock Carnival c.1949/1950.
Betty Wheeldon, Deana Andrews, X, Ramon Phillips, Barbara Robinson, Pauline
Cowley, Wendy Walker, Eric Gascoigne, X, 'Queenie' Wheeldon.*

Darley House Estate boys on their float at Matlock Carnival c.1950.

Graham Moore, Eric Gascoigne, Michael Marsden, Brian Ellis, David Wragg, George Robinson, Les Cowley, Alan Robinson.

Darley 'Queenies' football team, during the 1952 Darley Carnival.
They lost 4-1 to 'Northwood Swifts'. The referee was Eddie Shimwell, landlord of the
Plough Inn, and the Blackpool full back, who went on to win the F.A. Cup during the
'Stanley Matthews final'.
Back row: Etty Briddon, Olwyn Morton, Mary Greatorex (Mary Bill), Linda Slack,
June Woodhouse, Rosie Horribin.
Front row: Milly Littlewood, Mary Rogers, Ursula Brookhouse, Carol Taylor,
Nancy Woodhouse.

Firth Derihon (Spanish Seranade), winning second prize at Darley Dale Carnival 1952.
Miss Bark, Ettie Briddon, Cynthia Parks, Ann Thompson, Marie White, Kathleen Wilson, ? Fearn, ? Gilbert.

Firth Derihon float at Matlock Carnival c.1949.
Evelyn Allen, Pam Bark, Jean Evans, Rosie Kirkham, Barbara Oldfield, Midge Briddon,
Florrie Moore, Harry Oldfield.

The Nag's Head Pub darts team (Two Dales) 1952/1953 season.

Back row: George Draper, Lew Barker, Charlie Stevens, Bill Robinson, Laura Barker, Clem Simpson, Norah Barker, Harry Coleman,

Bessie Pilkington, Joe Barker,

Phoebe Barker, Cyril Maddocks, Bill Horrobin, Bob Pilkington, Ernie Redfern,

Jack Mills.

Front row: Ursula Brookhouse, Jack Brookhouse.

Sunday School scholars and teachers at the newly built hall, 1954, at Dale Road Methodist Chapel.

Back row: Edith Taylor, Cissie Witcher, Iris Crooks, Humphrey Boam, John Mackay, X, Malcolm Taylor, Stuart Toft, Edward Milner, Robert Maddocks, Peter Toft, Barry Boam, Wendy Hobson, Enid Gadsby, Rhoda Bowler, Angela Smith, Audrey Taylor.

Next row: Geoffrey Marsh, Marion Peak, Marlene Waller, Rosemary Maddox, Joan Partridge, Michael Boam, Maureen Taylor, Trevor Boam, David Taylor, Valerie Evans, Joan Maddocks.

Next row: Joan Crowter, Timothy Briggs, Keith Taylor, Rosemary Moore, Muriel Taylor, David Monkhouse, Beryl Kirby, Nancy Partridge, Barbara Tolliday, Stuart Sack, Sylvia Taylor, John Allsop, X, Elizabeth Ball, Val Pearson.

Next row: ? Crowder, Dennis Hickman, Martin Berton, Aubrey Evans, Robert Maddox, Peter Crowder, Pam Maddocks, Christine White, Reggie Wood, Sandra Hodgkinson, Richard Harris, Lorna Taylor, Michael White, Wendy Swift, June Pearson.

Front row: Janice Blair, Annette Wagstaffe, Roger Brindley, Nancy Wood, Angela Billingham, Susan White, Linda White, X, Marion Marsden, Gillian Talbot, David Milton, Ann Milton, Trevor Hobson.

Laying a brick for the new Darley Road Methodist Sunday School, October 1953.
Edward Milner.
Malcolm Taylor, Maureen Taylor, Keith Taylor, Muriel Taylor, Harry Woodhouse,
Sylvia Taylor.

Dale Road Methodist Sunday School c.1954.

Back row: Valerie Evans, Iris Crooks, Margaret Brimble, Cissie Witcher, Edith Taylor, Edward Milner.
Next row: Stuart Slack, John Smith, Trevor Boam, David Taylor, Valery Pearson,
Joan Partridge, Nancy Partridge, Rosemary Maddox, Marlene Walker, Muriel Taylor, Sylvia Taylor, Barbara Tolliday, Joan Maddocks,
Maureen Taylor.
Next row: X, Rosemary Moore, Beryl Kirby, June Pearson, X, Janice Blair, Humphrey Boam, Martin Burton.
Front row: Keith Taylor, Roger Brindley, Aubrey Evans, Annette Wagstaffe, Joan Crowter, Peter Crowder, Angela Billingham, David
Monkhouse, Reggie Wood, Roland Harris.

Dale Road Methodist Chapel Fete at Crichton Porteous's house, Two Dales, c.1954.

Back row: Angela Smith, Nancy Partridge, Joan Partridge, Val Evans, Malcolm Taylor, Iris Crooks, Beryl Kirby, Mr. Moore.
Middle row: Pam Maddocks, Ann Milton, Sandra Hodgkinson, Val Pearson, Muriel Taylor, Rosemary Moore, X, X, Janice Blair.
Front row: X, Lorna Taylor, Annette Wagstaffe, Jane Wagstaffe, Aubrey Evans, X, X, X, X, X.

Hackney Methodist Chapel anniversary c.1951.
Back row: X, X, X, X, X, Graham Winder, Errol Roose, X, Brian Ellis, Michael Marsden.
Next row: Shirley Croft, Betty Street, Rose Winder, Margaret Robinson, Pam Wild,
Cicily Price, Maisy Medcalf, Millie Smith.
Next Row: Mavis Goodwin, Kathleen Wheeldon, Janet Hudson, Joyce Smith, Ann Davies,
Diana Soppit, Pauline Cowley, Cynthia Wragg, Maureen Wragg.
Next row: Charlie Croft, Reverend Swarbrick, Brenda Soppitt, Lilian Robinson,
Ann Winder.
Next row: Leslie Kirkham, Ramon Phillips, Brian Durose, Douglas White, Peter Wild,
David Ellis, Leslie Cowley, Mrs. Oldfield, Edna Price, Mr. Allen.
Next row: Ted Hawley, Brenda Frith, Pam Allen, May Winder, Margie Smith,
Bruce Harrison, Eric Gascoigne, Alan Wright, Beryl Allen, Margaret Champion,
Mr. Farnsworth (organist).
Front row: Barbara Robinson, Janet Robinson, Pam Soppitt, Jane Walters,
Christopher John Goodwin, Pat Davies, Ethne Windle, Brenda Wragg, Jacqui Davies.

Raising money for Hooley's Estate Coronation Day celebrations.
Back row: Mr. Ankers, H. Ballington, B. Housley, B. Goodwin, D. Knowles, ? Bond,
Sam Morton, ? Newton.
Third row: Mr. Livey, B. Gregory, G. Page, Mrs. Stevenson, J. Housley, Mrs. Gregory,
Mr. Ankers.
Second row: Reg Middleton, J. Vearnals, B. Barwick, Mrs. Holmstrom.
Front row: Ann Harrison, Elsie Coleman, Hazel Gaunt, Esme Byard.

Raising money for Coronation Fund, Hooley's Estate 1953.

Sam Morton, X, Mr. House, X, Esme Byard, X, Mr. Middleton, Mrs. Stevens, Hazel Gaunt, Mrs. House, Mrs. Toft, Brenda Barwick, Mrs. Gregory, J. Vearnals.

Darley House Estate Coronation Committee 1953.

Cyril Cooke, Nancy Woolliscroft, Jimmy Woolliscroft, Mrs. Moore, Mrs. Windle, George Moore, Mrs. Crooks, Connie Smith, Sam Crooks, Mrs Roose, Judith Windle, Frank Windle, George Andrews, Harry Knowles, May Knowles.

1953 Coronation Day celebrations for Darley House Estate residents, held at St. Elphins School.
Second row of Children: Edward Windle, David Wragg, George Robinson, X, Eric Gascoigne, X, Brian Ellis, Tony Beresford, Selwyne Woolliscroft, David Ellis, Godfrey Blair, Barbara Woolliscroft, Pat Jolly, X, Janet Woodley.
Front row of children: Ehne Windle, Susan Merrett, Keith Blair, David Jordon, Clifford Robinson, Brioni Hudson, Peter Woolliscroft, Barbara Robinson, Anthony Lawton, John Woolliscroft, Alan Kinder, Brenda Wragg, X, Janet Robinson, Christine Robinson, Nigel Wheeldon.

* Meanwhile, the Two Dales and Broadwalk residents met in the Whitworth Institute grounds for an afternoon of sports on the football pitch, next to the railway line. Committee members had to clean out the former Tea Room in the park and make preparations for a Coronation Tea of ham and tongue salad, jelly and trifle. Cutlery was collected from many households and coloured cotton tied round the handles to avoid mistaken identity, with resulting loss of property.

*Friday night old time and sequence dances for children at the Whitworth Institute,
organised by Tom Goodwin and Herbert Hardy in the early 1950's.*
*Back row: Marie Wilson, Derek Grimshaw, Tony Keane, Derek Ashworth,
Harold Burkett, Herbert Hardy, Tommy Goodwin, X, Billy Winthrope, Barry Riley,
John Saunders.*
*Next Row: Evelyne Smith, X, Eileen Holland, Jennifer Jepson, Janet Taylor,
Peter Stephenson, John Smith, Barbara Twigg, Elizabeth Riley, Harry Meakin,
Sheila Bland, Peter Lomas, Alan Stevenson, Margaret Lane, Janet Keane, Paul Barratt,
Cynthia Stone, Barbara Morton, Enid Willers, Jackie Davies, X, June Ballington,
Jean Kaye, Jackie Morris, Mike Hayward, Margaret Wilson, Betty Coleman.*
*Next row: Brenda Barwick, Joan Bennett, Margaret Seal, Maureen Saunders, Ann Bark,
Pat Stephenson, Angela Smith, Brenda Fletcher.*
*Next row: Margaret Marsden, Beryl Marsden, X, Marion White, X, Lilian Kemp,
Carol Birds, Annette Fletcher, Dorothy Briddon, Joan Gilbert, Joyce Mellor,
Sylvia Wilson, Jeanette Waterfall, Mavis Gregory, Peter Chandler, Margaret Thraves,
Val Wall, Shirley Stevenson, Faye Dodds.*
*Next row: Barbara Griffin, Sylvia Taylor, ? Barker, Carol Barker, Barbara Webster,
Joan Littlewood, Mavis Webster, Roy Gill, Derek Holland, Ian Garrity, John Hickman,
Barry Barker, Susie Harrison, Keith Talbot, Roy Webster, Alan Marsden.*
*Next row: Duncan McDowell, Johnny Hill, Shirley Rogers, Olwyn Morton,
Joan Housley, Faye Wildgoose.*
*Front row: Barbara Watts, Roger Talbot, Roy Turkington, Ivan Redfern, Barry Green, X,
Doreen Morton, X, Doreen Chandler, Jill Lane, Carol Hayward, Muriel Taylor,
Betty Tomlinson.*

441

For a number of years after the Second World War ended, the people of Darley Dale had still to endure a degree of hardship, similar to that faced during the wartime period, for rationing had certainly become more restrictive.

But for the residents of a number of the top avenues on Broadwalk, an eagerly awaited annual social event was the trip to the seaside organised by George Parks of Northwood Avenue, during the early and mid 1950's. Money raised from a football club competition, together with contributions of 6d a week collected from each household by young helpers, allowed five or six buses to be hired from Dimbleby's Bus Company of Ashover. The avenues' residents, relatives and friends were thus provided with an excursion to Blackpool, Southport, Cleethorpes or Skegness.

The photograph shows the author and his elder brother, Malcolm Taylor, in 1953, beside one of the Dimbleby buses during a 'break' on the journey. This was usually taken at a roadside public house, before the coming of the motorways and their attendent service stations. At the time of writing, many long standing residents from those Broadwalk days still remember with affection these trips to the seaside.

On this happier and more optimistic note, as the new 'Elizabethan Age' began its course, it is time to bring to a conclusion this remembrance of life in Darley Dale during the first half of the 20th century.

442

INDEX